D0152336

Wilbur's Poetry

WILBUR'S POETRY

Music in a Scattering Time

BRUCE MICHELSON

The University of Massachusetts Press   Amherst

MIDDLEBURY COLLEGE LIBRARY

Copyright © 1991 by
The University of Massachusetts Press
All rights reserved
Printed in the United States of America

LC 90–20353
ISBN 0-87023-741-1
Designed by Susan Bishop
Set in Linotron Bembo by Keystone Typesetting, Inc.
Printed and bound by Thomson-Shore, Inc.

Library of Congress Cataloging-in-Publication Data
Michelson, Bruce, 1948– .
Wilbur's poetry : music in a scattering time / Bruce Michelson.
p.   cm.
Includes bibliographical references and index.
ISBN 0-87023-741-1 (alk. paper)
1. Wilbur, Richard, 1921–   —Criticism and interpretation.   I. Title.
PS3545.I32165Z78   1991
811'.52—dc20   90–20353

British Library Cataloguing in Publication data are available.

Chapter 2, "Words," is a revised and expanded version of "Wilbur's Words,"
originally published in *The Massachusetts Review* 23, no. 1 (1982), © 1982 by The
Massachusetts Review, Inc.

Acknowledgment is made to publishers, journals, and individuals for permission to
reprint selections from material by Richard Wilbur under copyright.
    Harcourt Brace Jovanovich. From *The Beautiful Changes and Other Poems,* © 1947
and renewed 1975 by Richard Wilbur: "Attention Makes Infinity" and "The Regatta";
excerpts from "Water Walker," "Superiorities," "A Simplification," "Caserta Garden,"
and "The Beautiful Changes." From *Ceremony and Other Poems*: excerpts from "Year's
End," © 1949 and renewed 1977, and "Beowulf," © 1950 and renewed 1978 by
Richard Wilbur. From *Things of This World*: "The Mill"; excerpts from "Love Calls Us
to the Things of This World," "John Chrysostom," "Marginalia," "The Beacon," "For
the New Railway Station in Rome," "Charles Baudelaire: L'Invitation au Voyage,"
and "Beasts," © 1956 and renewed 1984, and from "Merlin Enthralled," © 1981 by
Richard Wilbur. Excerpts from the following translations: *The School for Wives,* ©
1971 by Richard Wilbur; *Jean Racine: Andromache,* © 1982 by Richard Wilbur; *Jean
Racine: Phaedra,* © 1986 by Richard P. Wilbur; *Molière's Tartuffe,* © 1961 and renewed
1989 by Richard Wilbur; "Introduction" to *The Misanthrope,* © 1955 and renewed 1983
by Richard Wilbur.
    Harcourt Brace Jovanovich, Inc., and Faber and Faber. From *Advice to a Prophet
and Other Poems,* © 1961 and renewed 1989 by Richard Wilbur: "Ballade for the Duke
of Orleans" and "Stop"; excerpts from "The Undead," "Eight Riddles from
Symphosius," "A Christmas Hymn," and "Junk." From *The Mind-Reader: New Poems*:
"In Limbo," © 1975; excerpts from "The Fourth of July," © 1974, "Rillons, Rillettes,"
© 1966, and from "Cottage Street, 1953," "Teresa," "Children of Darkness,"
"Flippancies," and "The Prisoner of Zenda," © 1976 by Richard Wilbur. From *New*

(Permissions to reprint copyrighted material continue on page 258)

For Theresa, Hope, and Sarah

Contents

Acknowledgments   ix

1. Homelessly at Home   3

2. Words   36

3. Quarreling with Poe   61

4. Longer Poems   82

5. Chances   121

6. Wilbur as Translator   162

7. The Figure a Poet Makes   197

Notes   225

Bibliography   243

Index   253

Acknowledgments

PORTIONS of this book were completed with support from the University of Illinois Research Board and the Illinois Department of English. Here in Urbana, Robert Dale Parker, James Hurt, Zohreh T. Sullivan, and Joel Super have read all or part of the manuscript and have offered generous and wise suggestions, as has Robert B. Shaw of Mount Holyoke College. I have had important help as well from Melanie Wisner and the staff of the Houghton Library at Harvard, from John Lancaster of the Amherst College Library, and from J. W. C. Hagstrom, an independent and learned Wilbur enthusiast. While Richard and Charlotte Ward Wilbur have treated me to exhilarating, gracious, and candid conversation, failures in my reading of Wilbur's work or my commentary on his personae are my own mischief, not theirs. Earlier and shorter versions of chapters 2 and 3 have appeared, respectively, in *The Massachusetts Review* and *The Southern Review*, and I am grateful for permission to redevelop them here.

Wilbur's Poetry

1. Homelessly at Home

PEOPLE who rove in the papers of American writers must occasionally reckon with the peculiar etiquette of the modern mind, small rituals in the West's formal and informal definition—and circumscription—of the self. In libraries we can examine the notebooks of fine postwar poets, who as young men and women hammered out verse which astonished reviewers, altered the directions American poetry would take, and assured their eminence as prophets for this age, and sometimes as its martyrs. On those same notebook pages, where individual lines may change and build like storm clouds, one sometimes sees grocery lists in the poet's ink and hand, little errand reminders, memos to buy milk or drop off the car for an oil change. By consensus, and for many sound reasons, none of that "counts": we postulate, or take it for granted, that dramas enacted on the page proper of a self struggling to voice cosmic-scale intuitions and terrors, reveal somehow a different entity from other sides and moods of the same creature—other, marginal selves who stubbornly wonder, all the while perhaps, what their children, lovers, or editors are up to, what the new shocks will cost, what is in the icebox for lunch, where the clean clothes are for tonight's reception. This reflexive culture of ours endorses such compartmentalizations of self, and this wonderful or terrible capacity for being ordinary and sublime, manic-visionary and flat-footed sane, in the same half hour. And as a culture we seem to lack the vocabulary or the will to address that many-sidedness or discuss what it might signify about our real and continuing relationship to our own most powerful experiences and ideas. We do, however, know how to be ironic about this condition and keep such paradoxes at bay with jokes: this anarchist-nihilist craves tenure and a big raise; that dismantler of the bourgeois identity is a loving, bourgeois wife and mother; the science-hating, world-chagrined poet, now on a state payroll, chairs the policy committee of the faculty senate and worries

3

over spreadsheets stored in his hard-drive computer, along with micro-processed drafts for one more sutra.

In such drab comedies of alienation, what can slip away unheeded is something conceivably true, or even profound, about the bargains we regularly must strike with experience and with our own thinking, and with the literary art which this culture produces and values. When the evening poetry reading has ended, everybody, even the fervent admirer, must rise and return to the mingled thing called—contemptu-ously or otherwise—everyday life: from the abyss the way somehow leads onward to tables of cappuccino and white wine, or home to warm, private places in this chilly postmodern universe; if one would write verse tonight, or words about poetry, one must also unpack the dishwasher, negotiate with the cat, and tomorrow go about the civil business of living with others and operating in this illusory world. Does it do us credit to dismiss so much of the self as merely unsteady in its profoundest recognitions? Perhaps. But one might also ask where the art is which ventures, with neither banality nor sanctioned ironies, into this fullness of being, this consummately human capacity to carry so much within at once—anguish, hope, epistemological wonder—and this stubborn, or wise, or darkly amazing engagement with the world as found and lived.

In the following pages I make a case for reading Richard Wilbur as a rare kind of American artist, a poet who, even in an age of bold verse, forces a widening of our sense of what it is to be, to think, to believe, and to dread, and who can meld much of the pain and the light of human experience into one rich utterance. Wilbur's unique voice and his refusal of certain contemporary fashions have made some readers either uneasy or downright suspicious of his art, and while I hope to reconsider him without grinding hatchets or getting lost in disposable debate about what "true" experimentation might be in complex times, the published commentary to date on Wilbur suggests that I should seek, in these opening chapters, to complete or set right some common impressions. My thesis is simple: that Richard Wilbur is a "darker," more complex, passionate, and original poet than reviewers and sum-up essays about postwar poetry usually make him out to be,[1] a serious artist for an anxious century. That, for the sake of setting discussions in balance; the more important and pleasant task is to demonstrate that Richard Wilbur's poetry is many-faceted, personal, and intense in ways that have not been recognized. Such work can be done without vio-lence, for darkness, deep feeling, and long thought overshadow many of his poems, even some of his ostensibly breezy and cheerful ones. In published summaries of American verse and its history over the past forty years, Wilbur has sometimes been made to seem out of step, a poet of sunshine and comfort, or a lone Christian in an age which has foregone faith. Much better to think of him as a poet of sunlit intervals, of many brief afternoon moments bordered always by shades. One way or another, it seems a mistake to think of him as a poet of safe creeds and certainties. Wilbur's vision now seems to me quite as troubled as, for example, that of Robert Lowell, Randall Jarrell, and others of the "Middle Generation" which claims him, and of which so many are now gone. But Richard Wilbur writes verse that sounds and patterns itself in ways that are importantly his own, and one has to be patient to read him well.

"The Mill" does nicely for a beginning. Not discussed carefully heretofore,[2] and rarely anthologized, this poem offers several points of entry into Wilbur's art. "The Mill" is an elegy—not simply for a friend, but for the ultimate loss of every mind's accumulated lore, its perceptions, its special intuitions, its own strange, perishable, and perhaps wonderful connections:

> The spoiling daylight inched along the bar-top,
> Orange and cloudy, slowly igniting lint,
> And then that glow was gone, and still your voice,
> Serene with failure and with the ease of dying,
> Rose from the shades that more and more became you.
> Turning among its images, your mind
> Produced the names of streets, the exact look
> Of lilacs, 1903, in Cincinnati,
> —Random, as if your testament were made,
> The round sums all bestowed, and now you spent
> Your pocket change, so as to be rid of it.
> Or was it that you half-hoped to surprise
> Your dead life's sound and sovereign anecdote?
> What I remember best is the wrecked mill
> You stumbled on in Tennessee; or was it
> Somewhere down in Brazil? It slips my mind
> Already. But there it was in a still valley
> Far from the towns. No road or path came near it.
> If there had been a clearing now it was gone,
> And all you found amidst the choke of green
> Was three walls standing, hurdled by great vines
> And thatched by height on height of hushing leaves.
> But still the mill-wheel turned! its crazy buckets
> Creaking and lumbering out of the clogged race

And sounding, as you said, as if you'd found
Time all alone and talking to himself
In his eternal rattle.
                        How should I guess
Where they are gone to, now that you are gone,
Those fading streets and those most fragile lilacs,
Those fragmentary views, those times of day?
All that I can be sure of is the mill-wheel.
It turns and turns in my mind, over and over.[3]

One may hear Robert Frost here, especially in the lines about vine-choked ruins, lines which in their plainness, relentless syntax, and thumping meter recall the description of a "town that is no more a town" in Frost's "Directive," and perhaps the concealed and enigmatic forest ruin of "The Woodpile." Frost was Wilbur's mentor at Harvard and for a dozen years after, and much will be said later about the complexities of a Frost presence in Wilbur's poetry. But one can see readily that in its identifying qualities, "The Mill" is not a Frost poem reupholstered. The opening five lines make that clear—in their lack of clarity. Wherever we are, whoever this dying "you" might be, this is a place and a human situation with no analogue in Frost. More important, the key mystery of these opening lines, just how this dying friend has "failed," finds no answer in the poem, though what follows encourages a guess that it has to do with something both subtle and urgent, some enterprise all must take part in, always perhaps in vain. This is an aseptic, empty locale where minds must grope for something to look at—the play of a meager sunset upon lint particles floating in the air seems a last recourse for an imagination that yearns for some external world to engage with, and finds none.

Two minds turn inward, therefore, sharing the ambiguous "pocket change" of memory, reminiscence which might mean much or nothing. The mythology of death hangs over the scene: the idea of a whole life passing in review, and the shape and meaning of it finally coming clear. But such moments may hold no revelations at all, only a final breathing-out of consciousness in small, leftover recollections, the buzzing of Emily Dickinson's terrible fly. A faltering consciousness empties itself, and what a companion gathers in is only, perhaps, misunderstood or meaningless fragments of disappearing life.

But these verses explore more than the pathos of one unique self, one body of experiences passing from the world, more even than the waste of all hard-won memory as we die. It is not extravagant to suppose that this small story is partially about the poetic act, the poetic

6

predicament as Wilbur conceives it. In one's private pathways one comes upon powerful intuitions, epiphanies which cannot finally be sounded, tested, or satisfactorily explained. Yet they seem to mean something, and if one tries to pass them along, they go forth robbed of their glow, spoiled. The dying friend has evidently failed in private ways, but he has also failed as human beings do, failed to get it all said somehow to enrich others and make experience understandable to the self. This friend is ending life without ever knowing what it meant: hardly an unusual plight. But the recollected mill has been conserved by the old magic of poetry. Possessed by the experience, the listener in that room has found a way to pass it on again, through the poem. No loss is complete in Wilbur. And no victory.

What does this mill signify? And what does the listener mean when he says he is "sure" of it? The mill vexes because it persists in several realms at once—spinning, if you will, with possibilities. First, the poem emphasizes the culminating image as an image received *second hand*. The denial of immediate, personal impression, the frustration of a subject-object spark-jump such as one might have in Wordsworth, or in Frost's "For Once, Then, Something," or in a wealth of pastoral poems since 1800, confers importance on the mill, undercuts its wonder at the same time, and shifts the center of its symbolic gravity. The mill matters because of how someone else has described it: the friend's words about the ruin move the speaker as much as the vision which the hearer's own imagination builds out of them—and so this half-imagined, half-known place has epistemological motions to match the turning wheel and swinging buckets. It does and it does not exist, full of the dignity and the spuriousness of legend. The vertigo here is not fun-house mechanistic, but rather the dizziness of watching moving water: the Romantic moment of seeing (perhaps) into the life of things, recollected long after, with appropriate tranquillity—then recollected again, with turmoil, by somebody else.

Other qualities of the remembered vision contribute to its disorienting effect: a darker side of the mill is that its motion is almost a set-piece symbol for the futility of thinking, of remembrance itself, of struggling with the world through poetry. Poetry and ruins have had much in common for at least two centuries. Round and round the old wheel goes, doing no good, going nowhere, with no one bearing witness—that too is an underside of the recollection, going round with brighter possibilities that the surprise encounter might suggest: the revelation come upon by chance, the god or the hidden spirit surprised in the deep woods, the sudden, mystical apprehension of the way things really are. The dynamics of this closing seem richer still when

7

one compares it to the end of "For Once, Then, Something," a Frost
poem which is discussed more often for its importance as a lesson in
Frost's conception of the poetic act than for its technical qualities as
verse:

> *Once,* when trying with chin against a well-curb,
> I discerned, as I thought, beyond the picture,
> Through the picture, a something white, uncertain,
> Something more of the depths—and then I lost it.
> Water came to rebuke the too clear water.
> One drop fell from a fern, and lo, a ripple
> Shook whatever it was lay there at bottom,
> Blurred it, blotted it out. What was that whiteness?
> Truth? A pebble of quartz? For once, then, something.[4]

Wilbur's ending is in some ways more mannered, more a flourish
worked up to meticulously in the main body of the poem—yet Frost's
final lines seem, in comparison, oddly conclusive, as a comment about
problems on which thinking can never be finished. Frost seems to be
through worrying with his quartz pebbles; Wilbur's mill, suspending
this elegy rather than wrapping it up, represents not merely a phenomenological trap we have to live in, but also a lingering unease that
comes of feeling that condition acutely. The poet is "sure" of the mill
wheel: there is strong irony in such a choice of words, for this wheel is
unsureness incarnate. But what is "sure" is the place such an image
makes for itself in the mind. And the mind, for Wilbur, works in ways
that set it apart from the mind Frost reveals at the center of his best
poems. The mind, in Wilbur's poems, can seem to stay haunted longer,
after conscious, deliberate thinking is done.

This glimpse of Wilbur's complex response to Robert Frost, an
affectionate and sometimes aggressive dialogue which warrants longer
study in the following chapters, offers a look into other characteristics
of Wilbur's verse. "The Mill" does several things at once, is several
poems in one: a pastoral elegy for a single human being; an elegy for the
loss or waste, in this world of words, logic, and mortality, of the best
intuitive knowledge; a poem about the precarious life and unsure
consequences of visionary poems. More, "The Mill" is classic Wilbur
in that the poem is a green forest of transformed and personalized
literary echoes. With Bloomian anxiety or otherwise, Wilbur's imagination is uncommonly enriched by the many other voices it knows;
consciously or not, it brings to bear so much that it has taken in, as it
reckons with new perceptions, new experiences. A line like "If there
had been a clearing now it was gone," seems to reverberate with Frost:

the unassignable "now," the syntax resisting and slowing the eye, seems to come from the Frost contortions that begin a poem like "Directive": "Back out of all this now too much for us." But two lines later in "The Mill," a burst of alliterative excess recalls, say, Poe's "The City in the Sea" as much as it does moments in Frost: ". . . three walls standing, hurdled by great vines / And thatched by height on height of hushing leaves."

Other writers have established that a reading of Wilbur must deal carefully with his notorious and deceptive connections to Poe,[5] and a chapter in this study treats that matter; but there are other resonances here, suggestive of how complete is Wilbur's fluency in the Western poetic tradition, and how he puts into practice his faith that dialogues with the world are in vital ways conversations or quarrels with its poetry. The tighter, repeating measures in the closing lines of "The Mill"—

> How should I guess
> Where they are gone to, now that you are gone,
> Those fading streets and those most fragile lilacs,
> Those fragmentary views, those times of day?

—may have roots running back to François Villon, whose mannered laments for lost times Wilbur has translated ably. There may be other voices echoing here as well: Dickinson perhaps, and Stevens, who both show up more audibly elsewhere in Wilbur's poems. It does not make much difference which other poets one can tease out of Wilbur's lines. What matters, for a beginning, is the manifold character of this discourse, at once with immediate experience and with a wide heritage of poetry; and the fact that this voice is nonetheless unlike any other we have now or have had before.

If the age demands a share of ferocious seriousness from its poets, then "The Mill" may qualify as an ambitious and somber poem, announcing its skepticism and high sobriety in its very first lines and keeping up the mood to the end. But what bold dialogue with the times—if we want that—turns up in something so light, so suspiciously comfortable, as this?

A LATE AUBADE

> You could be sitting now in a carrel
> Turning some liver-spotted page,
> Or rising in an elevator-cage
> Toward Ladies' Apparel.

9

You could be planting a raucous bed
Of salvia, in rubber gloves,
Or lunching through a screed of someone's loves
With pitying head,

Or making some unhappy setter
Heel, or listening to a bleak
Lecture on Schoenberg's serial technique.
Isn't this better?

Think of all the time you are not
Wasting, and would not care to waste,
Such things, thank God, not being to your taste.
Think what a lot

Of time, by woman's reckoning,
You've saved, and so may spend on this,
You who had rather lie in bed and kiss
Than anything.

It's almost noon, you say? If so,
Time flies, and I need not rehearse
The rosebuds-theme of centuries of verse.
If you *must* go,

Wait for a while, then slip downstairs
And bring us up some chilled white wine,
And some blue cheese, and crackers, and some fine
Ruddy-skinned pears.

One might as well start with the touchiest line, about "woman's reckoning." Gender politics notwithstanding, this is self-evidently love talk, between people who do not have to strike political poses for each other in bed. The poem is the love song of the Lazy Chauvinist, who will in another instant be rousted to join the rest of men when his bespoken blue cheese is brought upstairs and thrown at his head. Because even ardent lovers can take a dim view of being wakened by somebody's amorous verse or delivered a monologue when thinking about the business of the coming day, the aubade has always been a light, self-satirizing form, and the one at hand shows resemblances to what Sirs Toby Belch and Andrew Aguecheck manage for Olivia. The comedy here seems comparably full, because the poem playfully retrospects on "centuries of verse," and because it is also about time itself, in a serious if not a sober way—about time's reckoning, by woman, by man and poet, by old and new worlds. For at least two reasons this aubade is "late": the time for its singing is "almost noon"; and the poem has come along late in the aged and possibly exhausted tradition of occasional love verse. Love itself may not have worn out, either in this long morning or the endless succession of poems; but what threatens its expression is the fate of time itself, over those centuries. The joke and the problem are that we may have lost, somehow, sufficient sense of what time is, how it passes, what we should do with it. John Donne and his beloved are bothered by the natural cadence of the sun rising; but what troubles this latter-day bedroom bard is civilization's conspiracies since then, to work havoc on the day, befuddle men and women into fugue states, and frustrate their own wiser rhythms. All of these things we could be "doing," reviewed so briskly in the first three stanzas, are instances of taking too long to do too little, or about locking a real or complete self away to accomplish almost nothing. The most dreadful and perfectly expressive possibilities are those that close the list in the third stanza. No dog could be unhappier on a leash than a setter; and no experience of art could be worse than experience on a leash, tediously explained by academics who will not take their hands off your sleeve; and trebly awful is the art itself if it serves only as pretext for clever explications. Whether this lazy-morning swipe is fair to Schoenberg is not an issue; the broad, basic point seems right—that in our own late morning, art can have an imitation life, as a coal tender for critical steam engines.

And so, as the first small crisis in this poem, the question "Isn't this better?" suggests several meanings. Isn't this better than another lecture? Isn't this ever-elaborating tetrameter, this showboat rhyming, better than some of what passes elsewhere for words and music? Isn't this Renaissance/vaudeville poem, composed of one-liners, better than high seriousness in some other poems—even, perhaps, other poems in this same collection? "A Late Aubade" is not a hymn to foolishness, to superficiality: it is, at least to this point, an affirmation that no human being operates at highest pitch all the time; that whatever its grounding, angst is something that comes and goes; that pious reasoning can also lead to the squandering of precious life; and that sometimes it might indeed be "better" to let the doings, high and low, of everyday existence do for a while on their own. The latter half of the poem follows the oldest ways of Western poetry in celebrating love, leisure, wine, good food—sacraments which go on as they always have, as delights of life, even for tormented, high-serious poets off duty. And Wilbur's quest, here and in more ambitious poems throughout his career, is evident in this poem. The effect is not to lighten contemporary verse, but to stretch it a little, to bring within its reach sides of existence for which the etiquette of anxiety has made little accommodation, to redefine poets and consciousness more broadly than poems commonly do.

Richard Wilbur has seen his share of the dark side of existence in this century; without intruding into his private life, one can observe that his credentials as a veteran of the abyss are convincing. In his early poems, the dead soldiers, war-weary GIs, and SS officers are memories of war seen close up and firsthand. In the late forties, however, when Randall Jarrell was working on "A Camp in the Prussian Forest," his harrowing up-close account of concentration camps he had never seen, and Robert Lowell (who for various reasons had also stayed home) was reworking some of his own carnage poems for *Lord Weary's Castle,* Wilbur, just back from three years in the combat infantry, was putting together his first and most brashly beaux arts collection, *The Beautiful Changes*—replete with Stevensesque meditations, Frostian pastoralism, and certain unclassifiable hybrids which signaled Wilbur's finding of his own voice. The collection might now seem perversely wrong time, wrong place. Reviewers were calling for the next major poet to speak as a survivor of the apocalypse, appropriately traveled, disconsolate, and battle scarred;[6] instead Sergeant Wilbur presented himself as a metaphysical-minded tourist who somehow had missed the crisis. "Attention Makes Infinity," from this first collection, reads like a Stevens excursion into pregnant voids and tumbling abstractions— except that the poem's closing is suspiciously cheerful compared to the shady places where Stevens often winds up; and Wilbur's abstractions seem somewhat less rigorous:

> The kingdom of air, of lightly looming air
> That crowns us all king spinners, let it swing
> Wide of the earth and any foundering
> In the sea's reflection, the forest's manifold snare.
>
> Air is refreshment's treasury; earth seems
> Our history's faulted sink, and spring of love;
> And we between these dreamt-of empires move
> To coop infinity away from dreams.
>
> See, every yard, alive with laundry white,
> Billowing wives and leaves, gives way to air:
> A blown pedestrian upon the square
> Tosses a clanging trolley out of sight.
>
> Then air relents to skyward with a sigh,
> Earth's adamant variety is remade;

The hanging dust above the streets is staid
And solid as the walls of Central High.

Contagions of the solid make this day
An infiniteness any eye may prove.
Let asphalt bear us up to walk in love,
Electric towers shore the clouds away.

Stevens's rhetorical flourishes seem evident here, in all this about king spinners, billowing wives, relenting air. There is an abundance of illuminated, empty "air" in early Wilbur, and to read through these first poems again is to look through a lens that seems trained a dozen degrees above the landscape, above anything one could look at hard instead. This is not simply a case of a young poet borrowing overmuch from Stevens's ethereality and trusting his own voice and imagination as yet too little; this is a refusal of any particular except the general particular, the generalized pedestrian, the laundry of "every yard." Wilbur already knew how to be concrete, having learned much from Frost. In this same volume, the opening three quatrains of "Caserta Garden," in their focus and their style, seem from a different imagination:

Their garden has a silent tall stone-wall
So overburst with drowsing trees and vines,
None but a stranger would remark at all
The barrier within the fractured lines.

I doubt they know it's there, or what it's for—
To keep the sun-impasted road apart,
The beggar, soldier, renegade, and whore,
The dust, the sweating ox, the screeching cart.

They'd say, "But this is how a garden's made":
To fall through days in silence dark and cool,
And hear the fountain falling in the shade
Tell changeless time upon the garden pool.

Frost may again be a partial creditor for lines like these, these cadences, and most notably the skeptical musing on what others—other people in the village, visitors, city people—might not understand about such a landscape. Forty years later, what matters in rereading *The Beautiful Changes* is not that Wilbur played ventriloquist in his first book, for there are enough poems here that are confidently in his own voice. The point is rather that these are two poles around which poems of *The Beautiful Changes* seem gathered: the controlled, qualified pastoral celebrations which recall Frost; the Stevens sojourn to the place made abstract, characterized by the vegetable, the fountain, the weather, the air. Wilbur will not take one directly to those battlefields near that Caserta garden, fields which he himself saw not as a tourist but as a soldier; for one reason or another, *The Beautiful Changes* refuses to engage with what others were writing passionately about in 1947, whether they knew the facts firsthand or not. War-weariness might have had something to do with this, or perhaps the unmanageability, at that time, of material so personal. But a pattern is established which continues throughout Wilbur's career: the personal adventure, the private catastrophe, is an oblique presence in the verse, something seen out of the corner of an eye fixed intently upon something else. One cannot piece together a biography of the man out of the poems; and through the times of the Beats, the confessional poets, the privatists, one movement after another, Wilbur has refused an abject dive into his personal life.[7] Questions which arise from this remarkable stance need to be faced in later chapters: whether or not this is an archaic mannerism casting doubt on his artistic honesty, whether this is some failure of nerve, or whether this is a contemporary species of courage we are not used to seeing.

And then there is the "problem"—from a current perspective—of Wilbur's perfection, his unmatched virtuosity in rhyme, in complex meter, in the classic art of making poems.

Perfection, in our time, seems to need good excuses, even sometimes a kind of apology. There is little to be gained by lamenting or celebrating such assumptions in contemporary poetic taste; it may indeed be a tribute to the age's cultural maturity that wary critics no longer confound supreme craft with high art; or, as those who bemoan the state of things suggest, collective distrust of the sublime may amount to an aesthetic nervous tic, an affected unaffectedness which sooner or later could embarrass some of the postwar American conversation about the arts. Anyhow, the conventional wisdom seems to be that language is supposed to break down, and Wilbur's usually does not; poems are expected to fail, at some crucial moment, to reach perfect imaginative dominion over a subject—and overtly at least, Wilbur's do not usually make that kind of gesture. When they are *about* imaginative failure, they decline to exemplify failure themselves. And this finish, this polish—Donald Hall among others has called Wilbur the best technician in the English language since Herrick[8]—can seem wayward. For the last seventy years much of the discussion in and about British, Irish, and American poetry has stressed the breakdown of the form, failures of the word, the poet's self-validating sigh of

giving up, stoic defeat in battles with conventional forms, and insurrections against previous poems—sometimes chief among them the
poet's own. The struggling end to "The Waste Land" helps set it, in
common evaluations, above Eliot's poems of consolation; the unfinish-
able lines of "Ash Wednesday" have evidently meant more to generations than the highly finished ones of "Four Quartets"; commentaries
seem to cheer when Stevens gives up on a florid conceit and meekly
wishes himself a "thinking stone," or when Berryman slams against
the glass in sonnet after bruising sonnet, or Bishop veers between
urbanity and troubled, spontaneous exclamation in poetry which dramatizes emotional bad timing, or Merwin, in a rhetorical despondency,
freeze-dries his once-opulent verse down to unreconstitutable dust.[9] In
all of this is seen, again and again, the poet in his or her political and
epistemological place. To "see into the life of things," in this time, is to
see that one cannot see into external life, but only into that confusion,
inchoate rage, and inadequacy which supposedly defines the contemporary self.

While such a summary unfairly reduces a great deal of twentieth-
century poetry, my intent is to catch, with unavoidable rough-handed-
ness, persistent, commonplace ideas about what a poem can aspire to in
addressing and representing experience. Conversely, the adjectives
people grope for when trying to describe Wilbur as a minority voice in
such a time sometimes have an uneasy, even condescending sound to
them: there is mention of polish, cleverness, craftsmanship, melo-
diousness, trickery, precision, elegance, and so on. To read through the
Yeats volumes after *The Tower,* or the sequence of Robert Lowell's
books of verse after *The Mills of the Kavanaughs,* with each one rising in
insurrection against the one preceding, is to see melodramatized versions of one classic gesture which goes back really to the end of the First
World War—a self-legitimizing gesture which we do not see Richard
Wilbur making. Why not? Is it some die-hard archaism, some reactionary or naive idea about the poetic act, some unexamined country-
wordsmith idea adapted in part from Frost? Or does Wilbur know
what strange, untimely thinking his shapely poems seem to affirm?

An answer takes time, because Wilbur's idea of poetry is complex,
representing unusual ideas about what words are, what imagination is,
what it means to take risks in making a poem, what place poems can
hold in consciousness itself, and what they can do in engaging consciousness with world. Subsequent chapters in this book will take on
these questions individually, probing details of Wilbur's idea of poetry.
But this perfection, as unorthodox, provocative gesture, has been so
much in the foreground of Wilbur's poetry that one needs to face it, at

least in a general way, right off. In *Advice to a Prophet* one can find suitably outlandish, perfect works. Though one was first published in a genteel *New Yorker* issue of April 1961, the dapper wave that this poem seems to make to crowds of poetry and other poets of those years is to me astounding:

BALLADE FOR THE DUKE OF ORLÉANS

who offered a prize at Blois, circa 1457, for the best ballade employing the line "Je meurs de soif auprès de la fontaine."

Flailed from the heart of water in a bow,
He took the falling fly; my line went taut;
Foam was in uproar where he drove below;
In spangling air I fought him and was fought.
Then, wearied to the shallows, he was caught;
Gasped in the net, lay still and stony-eyed.
It was no fading iris I had sought.
I die of thirst, here at the fountain-side.

Down in the harbor's flow and counter-flow
I left my ships with hopes and heroes fraught.
Ten times more golden than the sun could show,
Calypso gave the darkness I besought.
Oh, but her fleecy touch was dearly bought:
All spent, I wakened by my only bride,
Beside whom every vision is but nought,
And die of thirst, here at the fountain-side.

Where does that Plenty dwell, I'd like to know,
Which fathered poor Desire, as Plato taught?
Out on the real and endless waters go
Conquistador and stubborn Argonaut.
Where Buddha bathed, the golden bowl he brought
Gilded the stream, but stalled its living tide.
The sunlight withers as the verse is wrought.
I die of thirst, here at the fountain-side.

Envoi

Duke, keep your coin. All men are born distraught,
And will not for the world be satisfied.
Whether we live in fact, or but in thought,
We die of thirst, here at the fountain-side.

One recalls of the early sixties that the enterprise of poetry, having been thoroughly Ezra Pounded, had learned to prefer its statues broken. So here is something out of the commonplace: a late entry—about five centuries late—in a verse-for-money contest requiring use of what seems a stock courtly-love paradox. Could anything be more out of step with ruthless sincerity than resuscitated court poetry, poetry to please patrons, poetry dedicated to furbishing someone else's idea? Wilbur does not stop at half-measures: locking himself in the tormentingly narrow rhyme schemes of Ronsard and du Bellay (and of course Ezra Pound)—three rhymes for one thirty-line poem—Wilbur puts on a show of his mastery of the craft, his ability to keep his grace under all sorts of technical, intellectual, and cultural pressure. But what does this come to? An empty, reactionary return to poetry-as-show? An answer lies in the process by which the Duke's required conceit is transformed, stanza by stanza, into something larger and more unsettled than a Renaissance duke might have thought possible—into, in other words, an observation on the place and the point of poetry itself.

For taken alone, the Duke's line suggests either a conventional groan from the repertoire of courtly love, or an equally conventional lament from that age, that no coveted loveliness seems so fine when it is actually won. Wilbur's opening stanza obligingly plays ball in the Duke's court; aside from the ingenious word weaving that goes on here, having to do with rainbows and rainbow trout ("bow" in the first line, then wet "spangling air" in the fourth, and "fading iris" in the seventh, suggesting both the iris in the trout's eye and that other transient "iris," the Greek rainbow), the stanza and its sentiments are Renaissance standards: they read like an apt translation of the sort of poem a fifteenth-century duke could expect in such a competition. Even the fishing metaphor, upon which the stanza runs, is timeless, familiar, and within reach of a Renaissance poet. So far this seems only a mannered exercise. But the stanza following takes a long step in another direction. Both in its allusions and in what it intends, it seems hazier. Out of a classical myth bin Wilbur reaches for Ulysses, as a French poet might have done centuries before; yet the Ulysses-Calypso story in *The Odyssey* does not resemble Wilbur's version. Strictly speaking, there is justification for that variance. Homer was largely lost to the high Middle Ages, and even Dante, who brings Odysseus into the *Inferno*, had not read *The Odyssey* himself. Nonetheless it seems that here Wilbur's "Ballade" begins to blur, that its allusions begin to interfere with one another. Ulysses the lone, shipwrecked, middle-aged amnesiac, who keeps happy company for years with Calypso, melds with some nameless modern sailor looking for shore-leave thrills. The meaning of the stanza is comparably tangled: love and lust are mixed thoroughly enough to prevent readings of this as an easy allusion to or safe variation on Homer. Ulysses, after all, was apparently happy on Calypso's island, while this speaker's troubles seem, at least in part, to be those of a sexually insatiable adolescent, waking up starved every morning.

This is an important moment in the development of the "Ballade": the poem draws uncertainly away not just from classical and Anglo-French Renaissance traditions, away from other poems in the Duke's inventory, but away also from simpler, overworked ironies about the human condition. Animal desire and courtly love are neither glibly reconciled here nor artificially separated. This dying of thirst is suffering that cannot be reduced, cannot be made out as aesthetic or visceral, noble or base. The Duke's required metaphor makes better sense now than it did when the subject was fish and Platonic yearnings for the ideal: to die of thirst by a fountain-side is, or ought to be, to die in confusion, not to concede defeat in some bounded, comprehensible game of desire. But the interesting point is that the speaker's trouble—our trouble—has grown broader and deeper, moving beyond aesthetics and other idealisms to encompass more of human nature. Further, the poem, in some of its subtler qualities, is beginning to wobble. There is a breakdown of sorts underway here, yet it is not mechanical: the lines still scan, the rhymes still seem effortless. The trouble lies in the seeing and in the implicit self-knowledge. The controlled meditations about trout and rainbows, the stanza in which the world seems ironic yet harmonious and imaginatively open, give way to paradoxes that do not harmonize at all and cast doubt instead upon the seer himself—who he is, and what, ultimately, he wants. It matters that the second stanza makes less sense than the first, for to break the bounds of the contest and the conventions of a bygone time, the poem must come to that other, more dubious thirst, that wider disorientation which could plausibly kill human beings at the brink of succor. The problem the poem is approaching is whether any real sense can be made of us, of poetry, or of the visible world.

Dropping love and sex, the third stanza opens with an epicene Platonic question. Here, if one wants it, is a technical wobble in the poem to match its rising uncertainties: Wilbur has set out from a pedigreed classical question only to abandon classicism as a source for the wisdom he now needs and to discard as well the Duke's inadequate conceit. The safe game of writing in and for the French Renaissance is left in the dust by what follows. These conquistadors, for example, will not be along in history for at least another fifty years, and The Buddha is someone whom few people in the Duke's time and place would know about, much less the mythology of The Buddha's life. Breaking the imaginative rules of the game he has been playing, the poem escapes into contests more urgent than this duke has sponsored. The Buddha reference is subversive, for not only does it suggest a failure of artifice to capture beauty rightly, but also it refuses the Midas myth, which stands ready as the same kind of allusion, the sort which this Duke or most Westerners would understand. Verse can kill: that is the last stanza's culminating theme before the refrain, and the idea is expressed so bluntly as to be unmistakable for an archpoet's coyness about his own art. The scene is set now for the *envoi* which closes the poem, for there is little chance that this can be taken as a conventional self-deprecating tip of the hat. The crucial line of the *envoi* is the third one: as we shall see later on, it is one of Wilbur's hallmarks that poems end in wordplay that is anything but merely playful. The line is about both metaphysics and temperament: it sums up meanings that underlie the blurring in the second stanza. To live "in fact" is to have a true existence or to live a life made up of "facts" rather than fancies, abstractions, speculations; to live "in thought" is either to be such a meditative creature or to live "in thought" in some dimly apprehended yet more *complete* way. Perhaps only our thoughts and dreams are true, or perhaps we ourselves are really only "thought" of, as Wilbur suggests in another place, by "the God who dreams us, breathing out and in"— another idea he has gathered from non-Western sources. Sublimely, pathetically, absurdly, we die of thirst because we cannot decide who or where or what we are, nor find the right words even to express the confusion and the want. Wilbur's perfect little contest poem has to do with the failure of poems and the much larger imaginative failures which poets, even the best of them, must bear well in mind.

Then it all makes sense; it works wonderfully—which, perhaps, is what is wrong with this poem. Mechanically, it does everything which to some scholastic tastes reeks with insincerity and empty graces. And there is an element of the preposterous in the basic idea of this poem, an idiocy either nicely or accidentally caught in "Duke, keep your coin." Such high-handed refusal might be an appropriate gesture, or a hackneyed one, in a courtly poem; but given that this Duke and his contest have been gone for ages, Wilbur seems to be drawing attention to himself as coming late again for the party and refusing a prize which is not for the taking anymore. So how does Wilbur come off here? As the last courtier, the tattered aristocrat-practitioner of an obsolete art?

In a time which, perhaps by rights, is suspicious of elaborate explanations, one wonders how much leeway one can grant such a poem, allowing its boggling civility to be explained away. In poems of the English language, high formality and high anxiety have kept good company at least since Donne—but what satisfactory apology can be made for grace which seems so defiant of the contemporary scene? In addressing the bygone Duke, Wilbur converses with the tradition of formal verse; while his own poem contends for honors and elegance, it speaks recognitions that all such art, polished or otherwise, must falter. For Richard Wilbur, that is a predicament of poets in any age: because language and poetry are inherently artifice, what varies is how that artifice tries to pass itself off as truth. The "Ballade" is a poem about formality in art, formality as a preposterous imprisonment, but nonetheless a power we have—and to let it go is to die even farther from the fountain-side, to give up on coming closer to expression. For Wilbur, this condition is not bourgeois resignation—it is part and parcel of being alive, and of striking what bargain one can with words and one's own desire. Even so, this poem might seem mordant: the understated and therefore devastating rudeness of the accomplished aristocrat, speaking his mind quietly among crowds of passionate, inarticulate hicks.

To hear such a voice better, and feel its intent, rather than accept dry rationalizations about it, one should hear it speak at other times and provocations—to know Wilbur's range one must read many more poems. So Wilbur can hold the field with the Renaissance at its own game; what can he do as a "deep image" poet, talking in a sense to his actual peers in the poet's craft? I say deep image by design, because Robert Bly and some of his colleagues occasionally have given Wilbur a drubbing, cataloguing him as a stodgy leftover modern, still plying trades learned of Frost and Stevens and Auden after the time for such verse was done.[10] Bly has gone this way and that in what he has insisted that poems should be and do, but this deep image idea that poetry should be charged with images rising unmitigated from the unconsciousness is a favorite of his. Wilbur, having translated Baudelaire, Mallarmé, and other French symbolists, knows his way around in the poets who made possible the deep image as an American undertaking—but when he tries the trick himself, does bitter love for high formality get in the way, disguise some inability to leap into the mind's darker waters and paddle out again? The imagery of "Ballade" seems classic, made interesting chiefly by the blendings and the experimentation with focus. Here is what can happen when this poet dreams:

> What rattles in the dark? The blinds at Brewster?
> I am a boy then, sleeping by the sea,
> Unless that clank and chittering proceed
> From a bent fan-blade somewhere in the room,
> The air-conditioner of some hotel

To which I came too dead-beat to remember.
Let me, in any case, forget and sleep.
But listen: under my billet window, grinding
Through the shocked night of France, I surely hear
A convoy moving up, whose treads and wheels
Trouble the planking of a wooden bridge.

For a half-kindled mind that flares and sinks,
Damped by a slumber which may be a child's,
How to know when one is, or where? Just now
The hinged roof of the Cinema Vascello
Smokily opens, beaming to the stars
Crashed majors of a final panorama,
Or else that spume of music, wafted back
Like a girl's scarf or laughter, reaches me
In adolescence and the Jersey night,
Where a late car, tuned in to wild casinos,
Guns past the quiet house towards my desire.

Now I could dream that all my selves and ages,
Pretenders to the shadowed face I wear,
Might, in this clearing of the wits, forgetting
Deaths and successions, parley and atone.
It is my voice which prays it; mine replies
With stammered passion or the speaker's pause,
Rough banter, slogans, timid questionings—
Oh, all my broken dialects together;
And that slow tongue which mumbles to invent
The language of the mended soul is breathless,
Hearing an infant howl demand the world.

Someone is breathing. Is it I? Or is it
Darkness conspiring in the nursery corner?
Is there another lying here beside me?
Have I a cherished wife of thirty years?
Far overhead, a long susurrus, twisting
Clockwise or counterclockwise, plunges east,
Twin floods of air in which our flagellate cries,
Rising from love-bed, childbed, bed of death,
Swim toward recurrent day. And farther still,
Couched in the void, I hear what I have heard of,
The god who dreams us, breathing out and in.

Out of all that I fumble for the lamp-chain.
A room condenses and at once is true—
Curtains, a clock, a mirror which will frame
This blinking mask the light has clapped upon me.
How quickly, when we choose to live again,
As Er once told, the cloudier knowledge passes!
I am a truant portion of the all
Misshaped by time, incorrigible desire
And dear attachment to a sleeping hand,
Who lie here on a certain day and listen
To the first birdsong, homelessly at home.

The bursts of language here—the poem is called "In Limbo"—tend to steal one's response to it; there are lines which I find hard to get out of mind as sheer assemblages of English sound. And so the poem's mystery might earn only secondary notice, when in fact the poem lives on it and takes chances within it. "In Limbo" is about a mind drifting in and out of the hypnagogic state where, as Wilbur says in several essays, Poe makes his most fruitful excursions. Characteristic of Wilbur rather than of Poe, this poem ultimately "wakes up," comes back to the daylight world of full consciousness, yet not before a heady mix of dreams, hallucinations, memories, meditations—a consciousness both giving itself over to free motion and reviewing perceptions critically as they come. This is a complex and eerily true psychological state into which "In Limbo" ventures, and it cannot be said that many poems in the symbolist tradition have caught that condition as aptly as Wilbur does here. But what seems special about this poem is its patience, a patience out of keeping with symbolist and imagist traditions as they took shape in late nineteenth century France, and as poets like Bly practice forms of them today. "In Limbo" takes four eleven-line stanzas to work itself up to its major imaginative leap, and it is a vortex image of the first water. It is not Wilbur's way to plunge like a pearl diver, straight into the unconscious for deep-water riches. His own kind of imagism takes heed of the psychological landscapes from which the deep images come, and he seems to accept as axiomatic that the image itself cannot and should not be distinguished from the process by which the mind comes upon it. Never in his poetry does he pull a deep image out of context and dress it up as some spontaneous, perfect inspiration of a hyperconscious mind, rather than as an experience of dizziness, fatigue, astonishment or shock, or as here, of gradual descent from full wakefulness down into sleep and dreams. One always has to "get there."

But why? Certainly an insistence on context erodes the authority of deep images, keeps open the possibility, even the likelihood, that what presents itself is not inspiration but giddiness, from a mind whose connections are tripping almost at random in the small-hour ways of consciousness. Wilbur can go first-class as a dreamer, yet with no feigned innocence, no pretended childlike trust in dreams. Such skeptical virtuosity can be infuriating or more threatening, as craft, than Wilbur's stylistic contrariness, his insistence on formal prosody or on introducing his "dead-beat" self and "half-kindled mind" here in nearly perfect iambic pentameters. What we find in the deep dream might be inspiration, might be some richer, better truth, might be empty craziness: we cannot be sure one way or another—and Wilbur will let us neither trust nor doubt too much. What to call this kind of epistemology, these dens of consciousness? Skeptical transcendentalism? Domestic postimagism? Whatever one likes: the point is to recognize that Wilbur is again where he likes to be, in sparsely settled places between favored migration routes of American poetry in this century and between two of those states of mind which I suggested at the opening of this chapter, conditions which the culture may define or take for granted, but which human beings may live among, rather than within.

But "In Limbo" is classic Wilbur in several other ways: like his "Ballade for the Duke of Orléans," it is a tour de force, but here the strategy is concealed rather than flamboyant virtuosity. The stylistic acrobatics, wordplay and technical balancing acts here are finer than in the "Ballade," but it takes more care to find them out, precisely because here they are subordinated to the portrait of a mind in fatigue, unrest, and stages of sleep—and not themselves the center of attention in a poem partly about the inadequacies of poetry. Rather, this is an underground, covert art, something like the unimaginable maze of modern reinforced concrete under Cologne's enormous cathedral—artifice that seems to do better than plain, undisturbed earth in keeping all upright. "In Limbo" starts with iambic pentameter blank verse, the meter growing more complex as a mind moves out of wakefulness and into reverie and dream.

The opening lines of the third stanza read like a final mustering of consciousness before a plunge over the edge into dream—one more deep breath of the mind before surrender and submergence. The laborious syntax adds to that sense; and the break from parentheticals and compoundings is the breaking of the dam, the defeat of hope that this self is going to integrate somehow, on this night, or perhaps on any other. The mind which wills that all its own selves "parley and atone" is answered by a voice that is and is not the speaker's—and the battle

23

may apparently be lost. Whether such "losing" can be in any sense genuine, in a poem so crafted and with its best moments ahead of it, is a problem to return to when this closer look is done. The speaker has called for "parley" and instead has got himself a cacophony; attention in this stanza is on language and its mysterious connections to mind. Mysteries they stay, as mysteries do in Wilbur's verse: that is, profoundly explored yet not smoothly resolved, by recourse either to firm belief or firm refusal. Much is at stake here, for a flood of his poems show that language is what Wilbur trusts to improvise ways through experience; and now, in the hypnagogic state, language, as a last safety net of the mind, is fraying apart, and in the confusion one cannot even be sure of failure as failure. This voice that both is and is not his own "replies" either with capitulation or with studied silence. Are the mutterings of the mind closer somehow to truth—truth of the mind and of experience alike—than is wakeful speech, or only a primal mess of consciousness, which wakeful language artfully and compulsively conceals? The stanza spins on the syntactic ambiguities of the last three lines, a blurring that seems right as an expression of both the psychological and ontological state of the speaker. And there are interesting spreads of meaning here in the use of "invent." Does such inventing have to do only with language, as a secondary effort *after* the soul is mended, in some wordless, a priori way—or is the idea of mended souls itself a contrivance of language? We are and we are not, believing and disbelieving in the coherence and reality of the self, making and reading handsome poems which organize experience and response to it, wondering, at least from time to time, whether such making is not merely variations on some shapeless infant howl, a howl demanding what cannot be given: some trustworthy shape for ourselves and our lives.

The infant howl both is and is not the self; it is both the speaker's own voice, preceding and casting its doubt upon all speech; and it is some other infant, perhaps in a nursery nearby, breaking into and melding with dream and meditation. Wilbur sees to it that symbolic presences in his poems have some status in the physical and psychological surroundings of his speaker. This is no hypothetical or archetypal infant, though the child's signification may be as grand as that of any child in Blake. The Wilbur consciousness never loses track completely of where it began its journey. The place of origin, the everyday, phenomenal world, energizes and transforms whatever the unconscious, or the imagination, or the puzzling forces of the mind come up with later on. This bizarre continuity is not safe tethering of the poetic imagination, refusal to take the leap of the visionary. "In Limbo" demonstrates how, in Wilbur's poetry, the half-perceived, half-remembered wakeful world he puts so much faith in makes some wildness wilder.

So to guess the circumstances as well as one can: the time is shortly before dawn; the speaker, drifting in and out of sleep, lies in bed with his wife; there may be a child somewhere nearby, either in his own house or within earshot. One can surmise that this speaker—to drop the ceremony: biographical clues in the poem point to Wilbur himself—may be lying on his back, as evidenced by the up-to-the-sky imaginings, the Cinema Vascello memory, half-imagined, half-remembered, and the image that follows it, forming the heart of the poem. This "long susurrus" seems to have its start in a helix of cirrus clouds seen through predawn eyes, perhaps through an eastern window. Here is where the poem's crucial image starts, but it moves far from that, toward—not to but toward—something that might be a religious, mystical event. A shift in language here allows the advent of quasi-visions. The questions this groggy-clairvoyant mind is now asking itself pick up scriptural overtones. "Is it I?" resonates with the crisis at the Last Supper, which would mean nothing, were it not that the third line of the stanza recalls both the Emmaus story and Eliot's echoing of it in "The Waste Land." Again, this is psychological sense as well as poet's artifice: a mind awhirl in uncertainties, about even its own reality and worth, might grope by chance or design toward the spiritual and back to religious and mythological troves which years of living have provided. And so the poem has mustered itself for a leap into both a personal and a cultural deep image, growing out of the history and the diversity of the man and his time. It seems to come from much that the poet knows and has been—and from a single long glance at a morning sky.

Deftness in word choice again works in harmony with studied imprecision: the "clockwise or counterclockwise" uncertainty seems an accurately inaccurate piece of physical observation, for in the grogginess of dawn, one often cannot tell whether some twisting mass of cirrus clouds, high and oddly lit by rising sunlight, winds this way or that—and this talk of clock and counterclock rings once more, in a gracefully offhand way, with the foregoing experience of veering uncertainly back and forth through masses of time. "Flagellate" in comparison seems more studied, one of those Wilburesque black holes which draw many significations into one. And what converges here? The flagella form of the spermatozoa, the ecstasy and the pain of love, faith, birth, death; and the mystery, always the mystery, of whether suffering and the wordless cry (the infant howl come back again) are meaningless masochism, pain with some holier purpose, or some

twisting approach toward something—for in botanical parlance a fla-
gellum is a shoot, a runner. Everything comes together, from the first
moment of life to the last, from animal sexuality to the loftiest aspiration; yet such convergence, much as it pleases the aesthetic mind, is
only part of a revelation. The god behind it all, who dreams us, is only
heard, not seen like the portentous sky-high floods of air—and heard
by a consciousness that cannot identify its own breathing for sure, nor
place the other sounds that intrude into the predawn hour. To see for an
instant into the life of things is not to have answers; the best visionary
poets, including Herbert, Blake, Hopkins, have commonly known
where to stop, have recognized a difference between seeing deeper
shapes in the world and professing to have found whence they come.

The light that brings the self back to the world of the familiar and
the "true" comes laden with irony—yet the portent of that irony is
uncertainty, not denial of the truth of the waking world. "Condenses"
is a powerful verb, calling up those odd physical processes by which
something seems to come of nothing, substance out of not-so-thin air.
And what condenses out is not a mundane bedroom, but details which
seem Daliesque, poised between dream and wakefulness. "Curtains, a
clock, a mirror": without diving for metaphoric significance, one can
see here components of a surrealist still life, and if one must have
conventional symbols, one can find them too, as the curtain, clock, and
mirror signify what the poem has been about—death and concealed
truths, time, the self. "Frame" is yet another of Wilbur's peculiar yet
ordinary-sounding word choices, a confluence of meanings drawing
together and intertwining like that long susurrus. To be framed is to be
defined, or as it were, condensed and coalesced; it is also to be bordered, or circumscribed, and in common speech it means to be be-
trayed, deceived, undone by design or circumstance. All such meanings condense here, just as a few more come together in "certain,"
which in tricky, everyday English usage means both what it says and
the opposite: the day is certain, meaning true, as opposed to dubious
night and shifting dream, even though we use expressions like "a
certain day" when memory fails and we cannot recollect, for certain,
which one.

As the last word-susurrus of "In Limbo," "homelessly at home"
must be up to the task of closing a difficult poem, and indeed it is. I find
"homelessly at home" a better phrase upon which to build an elemen-
tary sense of Wilbur's achievement, of his idea of poetry and the human
condition, than "difficult balance," a catchphrase which his fine and
famous poem, "Love Calls Us to the Things of This World," has
caused some critics to feature. Wilbur's poems are often prodigiously

balanced, and frequently that balancing is technically difficult; and one can say that the position of consciousness, between ordinary experience and dubious revelation, requires the poet—requires everyone—to do balancing acts in making sense of what we encounter. But that phrase does not catch the emotional price which must be paid in living, and in writing verse that attempts to engage, in sufficient ways, with the marrow of our experience. Disconnection from the world, from the self, has to do with more than secrets which lurk at the borders of perception, more than the truth, or lack of it, in our best imaginings. Identity itself is a difficult balance, perhaps even an act of faith, a constant process of imagining—and what evades is an understanding of time and the personal past. It is not a matter of seeing angels dancing in the laundry outside the window, but of who does the seeing—and whether the poem as an expression of selfhood really expresses a self at all, or merely contrives a persona out of language and a hodgepodge of perception and memory. Though it means so much in a Wilbur poem, order is possibly only a pernicious habit, and such questions are not put to rest by pulling the lampchain and returning to light and the treacherous routines of wakefulness. That "first birdsong" mentioned in the poem's last line strikes a well-read friend of mine as banal—and so it is, if one hears in it only faint, forced consolations, like the last violin strains of some late Romantic coda. But those who sleep with the windows open in springtime know that birdsongs are there, and are what they are, part of every good, malign, or indifferent morning that dawns. Consoling or otherwise, they are part of the cycle and habit of consciousness. The nightmare will not go away, and it is not forced to; the disorder which threatens is not merely aesthetic, nor something exterior—and to miss that anxiety and its root cause is to miss much about the mind which Wilbur's poems can explore.

This is a Wilbur way of speaking the language of his contemporaries, speaking in a voice shared by Jarrell, Roethke, Bishop, Berryman, yet showing here a melding of artifice and passion that makes the voice unmistakably his own. Knowing the poems of this century so well, Wilbur draws upon that tradition not as a mimic but as that truer sort of revolutionary who affirms himself in full cognizance of what has been said and done before, what possibilities have been broached and sounded. Readers can amuse themselves at length in tracing the presence of this or that British, American, French, or Russian master in his work and commenting not on his variations, but on his personalizations of those strong voices. Yet there is also Richard Wilbur the ventriloquist: along with poems which ring with his own sound, one finds in his collections verse which, playfully or otherwise, or playfully *and* otherwise, contrives to sound like someone else, some single mentor or (putative) aesthetic adversary from his own or the collective past.

Sometimes that Other, when he shows up, is Robert Frost, and it makes sense to include in this first overview of Wilbur a look at this favorite way of his of conversing with his fathers (or mothers: sometimes he seems to address Emily Dickinson) in their own words and ways. In *Walking to Sleep* there is a short poem called "Seed Leaves," with the epigraph "*Homage to R. F.*"—and it is worth asking what the big or little idea might be in putting on a Frost mask here:

> Here something stubborn comes,
> Dislodging the earth crumbs
> And making crusty rubble.
> It comes up bending double,
> And looks like a green staple.
> It could be seedling maple,
> Or artichoke, or bean.
> That remains to be seen.
>
> Forced to make choice of ends,
> The stalk in time unbends,
> Shakes off the seed-case, heaves
> Aloft, and spreads two leaves
> Which still display no sure
> And special signature.
> Toothless and fat, they keep
> The oval form of sleep.
>
> This plant would like to grow
> And yet be embryo;
> Increase, and yet escape
> The doom of taking shape;
> Be vaguely vast, and climb
> To the tip end of time
> With all of space to fill,
> Like boundless Igdrasil
> That has the stars for fruit.
>
> But something at the root
> More urgent than that urge
> Bids two true leaves emerge,
> And now the plant, resigned
> To being self-defined

Before it can commence
With the great universe,
Takes aim at all the sky
And starts to ramify.

This might look like an exercise, a good one, but an exercise nonetheless, and once again one sees the virtuosity, that so-perfect display of skill which bothers some readers. If the conventional wisdom is that poems should reveal dark seriousness on a first look, profundity right there for the taking, then "Seed Leaves" does not play such a game. It is patently homage to Frost's prosody from a close disciple: Wilbur's wife Charlee recalls late evenings in Cambridge when she and the younger poet lounged on the floor at Frost's house, reciting to the now-old man poem after poem from his own work.[11]

And so this short homage poem could have a simple intent, coming from a writer who knows R. F.'s work inside out; yet there seems a focus here upon two of Frost's especially troublesome poems about the shape and sorrow of existence. The echoes in the opening two lines of "Seed Leaves" indicate that this poem would begin its vigil where Frost's "Putting in the Seed" leaves off:

How Love burns through the Putting in the Seed
On through the watching for that early birth
When, just as the soil tarnishes with weed,
The sturdy seedling with arched body comes
Shouldering its way and shedding the earth crumbs.

"Putting in the Seed" has classic themes about youth and age, and the struggle to leave off mourning and regain, for an instant at least, one's old enthusiasm for renewal. Nonetheless, the cadences of Wilbur's poem, and the problem directly addressed in it, seem to reply to a different work by Frost. "Nothing Gold Can Stay" is one of Frost's best-known short works about springtime and seeds and new growth. The tone seems darker, and the perspective on the cycles of life simpler and more absolute:

Nature's first green is gold,
Her hardest hue to hold.
Her early leaf's a flower;
But only so an hour.
Then leaf subsides to leaf.
So Eden sank to grief,
So dawn goes down to day.
Nothing gold can stay.

This poem sits awkwardly in the consciousness the way Frost poems sometimes do—the way that, by his own declaration, they were meant to. Especially "hard to get rid of" is the vexing mixture of offhandedness with something like Victorian sentimentality, a fusion of Emily Dickinson with perhaps a touch of Emmeline Grangerford. The poem's final observation is a "moral" that seems to imply everything and almost nothing, an important or trivial truth that we can take or leave. It is a poem that itself, in other words, would like to grow and yet be embryo, would be wise yet also be what it ostensibly is, a quick, sharp recognition about leaves in springtime. Do these fallings-off from gold to green signify anything, or not? Frost seems to avoid implications, leaving questions floating in the air having to do with whether leaves, growth, life, and poems count at all. To read Frost is to grow familiar with such casually offered enigmas; but with such recognitions, what is one to do? This question is not casual, for it concerns the predicament of a reader of poems, now in the wake of the moderns: the individual consciousness trying for some motion beyond these aching modernist dead ends. The problem is how one *continues* to think in the wake of the likes of Frost, without slipping off toward sentimental consolations on one side, suspect or inhuman metaphysics on another, or repetitious ironies leading nowhere at all. Starting with his own new leaves, Frost moves swiftly to a perspective from which, it seems, one must exit either into homily or cynicism. One way out of the Frost trap is to play Frost a bit longer—to backtrack and look again at the motive for all this, but perhaps more carefully than Frost does. This is, after all, how a star student can pay homage to the master, by going with refreshed eyes into problems which the teacher has found and mapped out. Such is the homage that Richard Wilbur may intend in "Seed Leaves."

So Frost's generalized "first green" becomes one specific yet unspecified plant, one case in point, watched with a little patience and imagination. One loses golden innocence; one takes an inexorable first step toward mortality, toward doom; but what is gained in that process is definition. Without an identity of one's own, nothing can be done, and "ramify" is yet another of these word vortexes which catch both the physical and the figurative truth in a single utterance. Ramify means, literally, to spread out into branches like a tree, but in another contemporary usage—as it turns up, for example, in newspaper editorials and political commentary—it means to have complications, subdivisions; in other words, to achieve an identity.

A basic question about such a "homage" poem is where, stylistically, it becomes Wilbur's and not Robert Frost's. At some point, "Seed Leaves" has to outgrow the oval form of sleep in the bosom of the father. The poem is perfect enough as such slumber for the first two stanzas; but something new begins to happen in the third, as the sound changes. The form itself has tested its bounds a little: the foregoing stanzas are regular arrangements, four rhymed couplets apiece—but the third set has an extra line, odd, rhyming with nothing that goes before. In itself, that is little as an alteration of the poem's voice, but what makes a telling difference, in this same stanza, is this sudden "boundless Igdrasil." Wilbur has simplified the conventional spelling to make the Norse world-tree rhetorically possible in a modern English poem, but spelled smoothly or not, Yggdrasil is not the sort of allusion which sprouts in Frost's major verse. Eden, yes; but Frost favored the classical and the Judeo-Christian branches of our heritage, and in his great years he showed little interest in the Viking exotic. "Igdrasil" is not better than Eden as a moment of poetry, yet it is a *reply* to Eden; it suggests a different imaginative orientation to myth itself. The myth of the Fall, evoked in both Frost's poem and this one, is not answered here by a myth of rising, transfiguration, resurrection: Igdrasil comes from a mythology darker than the Judeo-Christian one. Fatality is fatality, and the poem does not deal in smooth consolations. But perhaps we do not merely *sink* to grief; going up may be part of the coming down. "Seed Leaves" does not refute; it extends, and in a sense it outgrows Robert Frost. By the end it has grown into being Wilbur's poem, his prosody, and his own meditation on fate and the natural world.

A look at one poem more will complete this overview, an introduction to how Richard Wilbur has defined himself as a contemporary poet; set himself close to some traditions, apart from others; and created his special presence, both as a keeper of certain faiths and as a creator of powerful new voices and perspectives. But because he is sometimes cast as the last Girondiste, impeding a postwar movement which was beginning to look to William Carlos Williams,[12] rather than to Eliot, or Frost, or Auden, or Stevens as elders, it is worth finishing with a look at one of Wilbur's poem-conversations with Williams and his circle.[13] When Williams was alive, the two poets knew and understood one another as artists and had an amiable relationship; lore has it that behind the younger man's back, Williams once declared to Denise Levertov, "Wilbur is wrong, but Wilbur is good!"—which to people who listened to Williams's opinions seemed like high praise, better certainly than being recognized as innocuously in step. Awkward for those who would imagine the postwar scene as rancorous quarrels about the directions poetry should take, there is no hint of dislike here to exploit, and one cannot assume anything offhand about Wilbur's short poem "Stop" (from the 1961 collection *Advice to a Prophet*), in which Wilbur seems to rebuild Williams's red wheelbarrow into a blue baggage truck:

> In grimy winter dusk
> We slowed for a concrete platform;
> The pillars passed more slowly;
> A paper bag leapt up.
>
> The train banged to a standstill.
> Brake-steam rose and parted.
> Three chipped-at blocks of ice
> Sprawled on a baggage-truck.
>
> Out in that glum, cold air
> The broken ice lay glintless,
> But the truck was painted blue
> On side, wheels, and tongue,
>
> A purple, glowering blue
> Like the phosphorus of Lethe
> Or Queen Persephone's gaze
> In th numb fields of the dark.

Taken out of the volume, this would be difficult to spot as a Wilbur poem, and it sounds like nothing looked at before in these pages. The unrhymed verses are irregular, with stress overshadowing the poetic foot as an ordering principle. Further, the opening three stanzas seem to play by an important Williams rule: emphasis on the thing. The only direct sign of an intermediating consciousness, or imaginative interference between subject and object lies in the choice of "glum," midline of the ninth line. Otherwise everything seems to fit: the setting is static, decayed urban; the ice seems a variation on Williams's treasured broken bottles—and one wonders what Wilbur's point is beyond some I-can-do-it demonstration, some resistance to being typecast as the different sort of poet.

Considering the politics of poetry in the early sixties—"Stop" first appeared in *The New Yorker* in 1961—Wilbur may have been taking a chance here as he whistle-stops through a Williams landscape, the Passaic County of the mind. If Wilbur means to try out Williams's way of looking at the world, the direct, unadorned, "concrete" expression of the thing observed, then he needs to give that poetic vision more than four brief stanzas. These declarative statements about some un-named railroad siding may read like an exercise after too many hours in

the Grove Press and New Directions paperbacks; the imaginative stillness remains imitation William Carlos Williams—that is until Wilbur
begins igniting metaphors in the final stanza. In these four lines the
poem seems to turn the tables on certain habits of early postmodernism; it moves suddenly into, of all things, classical metaphor, not as a
way of lighting up this stubborn nothingness with false fire from a
naive imagination, but rather of outdoing the blank dark at its own
game, finding images which express that absolute, appalling dark
better than can the scene in itself. The feel of these images is strange:
they are essentially the whole poem, a haiku moment to which all that
comes before is prologue, and as such they need to be something of a
payoff. But they do not bring or will order out of chaos, and they
certainly do not illuminate or console.

The phosphorescent glow of the waters of Lethe is something of
an improvement on classical myth, which does not attest, as far as I can
discover, that any of Hell's rivers are salt water, although for symbolic
reasons it seems right that they should be. But the aesthetic effect here,
out beyond symbolism, is to make darkness darker; the artist knows
that a faint glimmer of light only makes midnight water more black.
And with a similar imaginative leap, Persephone becomes a Golden
Age analogue for Stevens's snow man, or Frost in his desert places and
snowy woods, or Williams himself in the vacant lots between Paterson
walls. Persephone, after all, is the snow-girl in the myth of her abduc-
tion to the underworld, both in the season change her rape brings on
and in the few emotions poets allow her as they retell her story. Her
anguished mother Ceres holds the attention in Ovid; what Persephone,
whom Golding describes as a creature of "sillie simplenesse," thinks of
all this, if she thinks at all, is a mystery one must solve as one likes.
Williams does not care about her either. *Kora in Hell,* an early collection
of improvisations, comes back to Kora, or Persephone, once in a while
as an emblem of his own frustration, of pent-up energies waiting for a
change in the weather, a change in poetry and consciousness. But
Persephone seems only a prop in a wide-veering performance about the
"tough winter months" of Williams's own artistic and personal life, and
here, as in nearly every mention of her rape, Persephone is seen, yet she
never sees. Wilbur's two lines, fixed upon her seeing, hardly constitute
a breakthrough in imagining the story of the violated maiden—but the
final concentration upon her eyes, rather than on the emptiness she
must look at as Hades's consort, has a small effect which nonetheless
makes this a Wilbur poem, rather than a Williams variation. Wilbur
sees her as having the mind of winter, whether or not that is due to her
intrinsic stupidity or to her shock at the violence which has come upon

her. The nothing inside looks at the nothing without, and the lonely place becomes lonelier. But in this difficult world, consciousness is both possible and present, and imagination and interpretation have their place. The mythic and the metaphoric traditions are not undone by the sensory experience and the feeling of vastation they have to contend with; the intermediating human consciousness is there, and however deep the silence it keeps, it bears witness and makes a mysterious difference.

As the title for this chapter indicates, I take the closing words of "In Limbo" as saying much about Wilbur's overall idea of himself, his time, and his condition as an artist; when compared to his perceptions, certain rawer, louder sorts of alienation can seem more facile, and even, sometimes, less honest. It is not hard—at least as a rhetorical gesture— to slam doors on traditions of expression, on faith and the steadier shapes of love, or on the truth that, like it or not, language and the fabric of thinking come in some measure from an all-too-inadequate past. To succumb to that past, to sacrifice to it whatever is unique in the individual consciousness, might be cowardice or confirmed desperation; to turn away from it can be to frustrate one's own voice, or even to lose it, and achieve only a feigned, unresonant sort of originality. Our voice is replete with other voices, whether we like it or not; and our recognitions can be sharper, more validly ours, when they imaginatively answer, challenge, or converse with the mind of the culture which we inherit, and which is always in some way ourselves. Language fails—that is a given. But it gives us some of the words we need to name that failure, and to reach some imaginative dominion over it. Stevens, Donne, Frost, Yeats, Ovid, Lowell, Dickinson, Jarrell, Williams, the Renaissance balladeers—all of them, such as they are, loom in the way we think and feel.

Richard Wilbur's conversations with the past and the present range much more widely than these few, and plenty of other writers will need to be remembered in the process of entering Wilbur's poetry. But engage as he might with poets living and dead, elegantly allusive as his surfaces might often be, those other voices and times seem to make his own words, his own condition, more distinct, and not in noodling academic ways. If every age in our literary history has its blind spots, its irrationalities, then Wilbur's is a voice which suggests that what we overlook is not simple at all, that paradoxes we dismiss are sometimes ones which hide secrets, that the self and the act of poetry are never exhausted, but tougher and richer than we imagine. There is darkness in Wilbur: like Persephone's gaze in those numb fields, the presence of tradition, the conspicuous art, can make loneliness more absolute, darkness darker, the uncertainty of our situation more mordant. His writing is complex, and if one of the shortcuts of our times is to assume that complexity and intensity are by nature at odds with one another, then Wilbur can teach us something about nature and poetry. Wilbur is a poet of *our* times, in many valid meanings of the phrase, yet there is nothing typical about his voice. It takes time to learn to hear him, to understand not only what he thinks and feels, but the proportions and balances of that consciousness, the catalytic effect that these perceptions have upon one another. A good place to continue that process is with the small components, his ideas about the nature and power of language itself.

2. Words

While we acknowledge his erudition and urbanity, we regretfully liken his mildness to the amiable normality of the bourgeois citizen. Emergencies are absent in his poems; he is unseduced by the romantic equation of knowledge and power; he seldom rails at the world. Suspicious of grandiose gestures, of parading the ego, he mediates experience through reason.[1]

He is a bell too conscious of its clapper, clapper-happy. Pert but proper, always safe rather than sorry, his poetry is completely without risks, a prize pupil's performance. His ideas are always cut exactly to the size of his poems; he is never puzzled. And the ideas are all sentiments, aware of their potential high-minded emotional value and determined to snuggle into it.[2]

AFTER Richard Wilbur had won many of the major prizes, much fame, and the poetry chair at Wesleyan—one of the plum academic jobs for poets in the late fifties—this was the sound of a backlash that perhaps inevitably set in. Charges like these came out of a political-aesthetic milieu which has changed or dissipated since. But whether such commentary is dated or not, and whether or not two captious decades of criticism have made a lasting difference to American poetry, cannot be answered satisfactorily if one has in mind "proving" Wilbur's poetry dangerous or puzzled enough for university English departments; seduced, abandoned, and anti-bourgeois enough for the *New York Times*. My subject in this chapter is Wilbur's astonishing use of language—especially his famous wordplay—because that use in itself may be as daring an experiment in poetry as we have seen in the past four decades. One thing seems sure: Wilbur's experimentation with words is not some handsome machine for delivering safe messages or dressing up comfortable or commonplace observations, but rather a labor to recover the power of words as magical, incantatory, creative forces. His famous wordplay seems to be the essence of his imaginative transcendence of the world, as well as his reconciliation, such as it is, *with* the world. If we cannot understand this, the seriousness of Wilbur's wordplay, we cannot appreciate what he is doing. But no new book is needed to tell us that Wilbur is one of the most accomplished wordsmiths of our time, that what he works among the fine gold fibers of the English language is so sharp, so perfect, that like some supremely wrought baroque salt dish, the result dumbfounds some connoisseurs and moves or outrages others. A discussion which would get down into minute particulars of the achievement should try to account, at first or at least in passing, for the genius; decide at least provisionally whether it is cold reason and fortunate apprenticeship, or has something urgent to do with human life as it now must be lived.

I suggest that the latter is indeed true: that there is much in the biography—what we can know of it without intruding too far into the privacy of a working writer—to show the force of what Wilbur tells his daughter Ellen in his poem "The Writer," that finding the right words is always a matter of life and death. What Wilbur has been willing to tell people about his past—growing up on New Jersey farms as the son of a landscape and portrait painter, hopping freights and bumming across America as a young man, dabbling with radical politics among the big-city leftists at the end of the Depression, and four years at conservative, pricey Amherst College—the story so far does not proclaim the word as a power to which a young artist dedicated himself from early days.[3] In fact Wilbur's accounts of himself make him out as a literary sort, but in an irresolute, rough-and-tumble way; he became a famous poet by accident and by someone else's ruse. Graduating as a top student from Amherst, as editor of the college paper, and with a handful of poems published in *Touchstone,* the student literary magazine, Wilbur was gobbled up by the United States Army, which in the months just after Pearl Harbor had great need of bright, robust young men. The Army professionalized Wilbur's business with language, and that relationship may have changed his life if it did not, strictly speaking, save him:

> My Amherst class has always been very close-knit, partly because it lost so many in the Second World War. Even before our commencement, some had volunteered and had died in action. My own girding for war consisted in taking a Government correspondence-course in cryptography, barbarously practicing Morse Code transmission on my honeymoon, and joining the Enlisted Reserve Corps immediately thereafter. . . . Reporting for duty at Fort Dix, I was assigned to cryptographic training, and thereafter sent on to a secret cryptanalytic camp in the woods of Virginia, where (as I later discovered) my progress into cryptanalysis was

cut short by adverse security reports from the CIC and FBI. It was
quite true that I held leftist views and had radical friends, and that I
had been so stupid as to keep a volume of Marx in my foot-locker;
but then as now I had an uncomplicated love of my country, and I
was naively amazed to learn that my service record was stamped
"Suspected of Disloyalty." For some reason, the Army then gave
me a course in commando techniques, after which I was sent
overseas with a company of other undesirables, amiable bookies
or bootleggers for the most part. Arriving, by way of Africa, in a
replacement depot at Naples, I found myself profiting by another's ill-luck: a cryptographer in the 36th Infantry Division had
just gone insane, and the divisional signal company was willing to
overlook my disloyalty. I served with the 36th at Cassino and
Anzio, in the invasion of Southern France, and on through the
Siegfried Line.[4]

So for a while it was cryptograms and language tricks, a peculiar education at federal expense. The Thirty-sixth, however, was in the thick of
combat through the next three years of war: the bloody landing at
Anzio, the crater-to-crater fight up mountainsides and through the
wreck of Benedict's monastery—brutal campaigns, and they seem to
have changed things utterly. Wilbur told Stanley Kunitz that it was
infantry combat which caused him to begin to "versify in earnest"[5] and
to read Poe seriously, as an escape from the realities of battle. It is one of
the ironies of our poetic season that Wilbur never has dealt directly,
graphically, and at length with that experience, and that the most
harrowing war poems we have had from Americans were often penned
by people who watched history unfold on newsreels. Wilbur came
back from the European Theater of Operations hungry, wanting literature as he never had before, and he went almost straight to Harvard on
a fellowship—straight to the American city which would be a center
for the postwar revival in verse.

To reconstruct Cambridge in the late forties, with its energy and
importance to the refreshment of culture in this country, is more
difficult than imagining the truth of the Third Army's ordeal, because
the history of bookshop and cafe encounters, reading room uproar, and
after-hours life still has to be pieced together out of lore and recollections. There is no reliable account as yet of these years in this place, and
the contemporary reader must do something of a trick to imagine a
time when, after the long remove of the war, the hunger for refreshment was everywhere, taste was eclectic and unfactionalized, and people apparently wanted to *know* rather than to classify and pass judgment. A few generalizations can be made safely: many of the writers

who mattered then and later were on the scene or passed through frequently; poetry readings, in something like their modern shape, seem to have begun at Harvard after the war; and young people interested in letters did not lack for excellent company. The internecine warfare seems to have begun somewhat later—perhaps with the readings of *Howl* at the City Lights Bookshop in the middle fifties, or perhaps at some of the postwar conferences, where factions of later on may have begun to take shape.[6] From any perspective, for a few years after the war there was rambunctious peace in American letters, and much of the action was in the streets and flats around the Harvard campus. When Wallace Stevens, on the borders of old age, came to the university in 1947 to give a talk called "Three Academic Pieces," he was shocked to find himself the focus of great attention. Wilbur remembers the evening:

> I don't think Stevens had any idea of what kind of celebrity had suddenly developed for his poems among the graduate students and young people interested in poetry. Of course, the interest wasn't confined to such people. I don't think he had any idea what he was letting himself in for, in agreeing to come to Harvard on that occasion. We all crowded into Room D in Emerson Hall, which was a philosophy classroom suitable for holding maybe one hundred people. It was full an hour before the reading. F. O. Matthiessen, who was introducing Stevens and in charge of arrangements, came in and told us to move to Sever Hall. Everyone rushed over there in a rather impolite way. People were pushing and shoving. Sever soon filled up, and once again it was announced that we were going to move to the big hall in the lower part of the Fogg Museum. By that time, nobody in the audience had any manners left, and people were pushing old ladies aside and rushing across the places where it said DO NOT STEP ON THE GRASS. And there was a great jostling crowd that poured through the door of the Fogg Museum. I had never seen Stevens. I don't know whether I'd seen pictures of him, but I knew which one Stevens was: he was the man standing there aghast as something like a Yale-Harvard game crowd flowed past him on its way to that big basement lecture hall. I can remember that André du Bouchet, who is now so well known a French poet, was then a very young man doing a bit of graduate work at Harvard and running from room to room to try to hear Wallace Stevens.[7]

The reading was a new ceremony that could work, draw crowds, and Cambridge was abuzz with poets willing to read. Frost had owned a house on Brattle Street in Cambridge since 1941; in those postwar years he came there on a seasonal circuit that ran through Dartmouth and Amherst, to teach, do readings at the Sanders Theater, and expound for his circle of admirers, and this is where he and Wilbur first met, probably in 1948. In a room on the top floor of the Widener Library a group of twenty or so poets and critics met, off and on, to talk about each other's poems: among the visitors were Delmore Schwartz, John Ciardi, John Holmes, Archibald MacLeish, Richard Eberhart, Leslie Fiedler, Ruth Stone, and Jack Sweeney. In those same years, at Eberhart's house, Wilbur met young Robert Lowell, and more dialogue informally organized: Lowell, Wilbur, Eberhart, Elizabeth Bishop, Kenneth Rexroth, and Lloyd Frankenburg.[8] Wilbur recalls that in that time before the great schism, it was Bishop who, among his contemporaries, had the single greatest influence upon him, who taught him much of what he calls "the joy of putting a poem together." Up and down the East Coast the action moved, but Cambridge was never out of it. For several years, until the building burned down in 1956, there was the Poets' Theatre, whose funding may have always been fly-by-night, but whose contributing talent included William Alfred, Richard Wilbur, and a young Edward Gorey as set designer and playbill illustrator; Wilbur's Molière translations began for that stage with *The Misanthrope,* which premiered there in 1955.

Refreshed by the example of R. P. Blackmur, whose new essays were a focus for interest in college towns up and down the coast, Wilbur came to Harvard with ambitions to be a scholar and critic, not a versemaker: the first big project was to be a book-length study of Poe. But as I have said, he was blindsided into another line of work by his wife Charlee, who lifted the sheaf of his poems from the drawer where he kept them and showed them to André du Bouchet, a friend from Amherst, editor of a little magazine called *Foreground,* and a talent hunter for the press of Reynal and Hitchcock. Wilbur has told a succession of interviewers what du Bouchet did next:

> He took them home with him and reappeared at our apartment about two hours later, rushed in, and, with a marvelous display of Gallic fervor, wrapped his arms around me, kissed me on both cheeks, and declared me a poet. He then sent my poems to Reynal and Hitchcock. Much to my surprise they wrote back that they would like to publish a book. I guess I had the most painless introduction to publication any writer's ever had.[9]

Six poems appeared in *Foreground* in the spring of 1946, and three more in *Accent* that same season. *The Beautiful Changes* followed in 1947, and a career as a poet accelerated from there.

I have sketched in this history only to suggest that there are at least two pathways one can follow in trying to explain the status and power which words are accorded, not only in Wilbur's poems, but also in his ideas of reality and a human being's place in its midst. One can put on a show tracing Wilbur's literary place and connections—they are profuse—to the American, British, French, Irish, or Latin rhetorical legacies of the past two thousand years; and if one wants to stay at home in our own century, one can unearth plenty of relationships between Wilbur's ideas about language and, say, Mallarmé's pronouncements about words as incantations, Pound's vortices, Frost's compressions of so many possibilities of signification into so few flat, ordinary-looking lines, or Stevens's sudden climbs and dives from the grand style to the vernacular and back again. If Wilbur's reputation holds, there will be plenty of work for students who want to trace these inheritances. But another pathway to understanding this side of the poetry runs through human experience, and I have given that its place because the poet-tradition line of discourse can make this poet, and perhaps any poet, seem perversely disconnected from ordinary life, and because it goes without saying that Wilbur's poems strive for such connection. If family, academe, language study, literary magazines, graduate school, and Village coffee bars are all there in his work, then so is firsthand experience with the cataclysm of this century, with things falling apart, or being blown apart, for real. Though they turn up often in his published essays, his regrets about the modern condition are mildly expressed: in "Poetry and Happiness," he speculates that the generalized misery among modern poets "may lie in the obligatory eccentricity, nowadays, of each poet's world, in the fact that our society has no sufficient cultural heart from which to write," and that "in the full sense of the word 'culture'—the sense that has to do with the humane unity of a whole people—our nation is impoverished."[10] But then he goes back to the task of the essay to suggest how things might be put right, reconstructed, and how poets and an impoverished culture might yet do something for each other. The poet's need, he says in the same essay, is to fabricate "a common and inclusive language in which all things are connected." Wilbur started writing poetry in combat; he became a poet in truth, when after the smoke had cleared and the grief given way to some species of calm, civilization began to rebuild itself.

Words are a means to the healing of the culture, of the self, and of the relationship of self to world: the idea may run counter to certain Franco-Russian doctrines about words as loci of *divergence*, rather than convergence, that multiplicities of signification cause poems and people to drift off into disconnections. But generations of writers and artists in this century have known the difficulties of the media in which they work and the failure of culture to be humanely unified. While Wilbur is not refusing that legacy of thought, his astrophysics of language, if it can be called that, may be more complex than these lines of reasoning have conditioned us for. In Wilbur's poems, significations can move away from one another, range high and wide in opposite directions, then somehow reconverge, like rays of light traversing vast distances, following some Einsteinian principle, some secular mystery of the physical sciences. In the right place, in the right poem, meanings find their way home again, and in a cultural sense poems signify once more.

To see what Wilbur's wordplay is meant to be, one must understand Wilbur's speculations about how the imagination can make sense of experience. As some of his readers have observed,[11] Wilbur's long-standing conception or hope is that the mind can reach for cosmic awareness by imaginative and intellectual chance taking. One of his recurring themes is that our best prospects for understanding where in the world we are lie in somehow melding the dreaming with the waking consciousness, in reconciling dim, momentary intimations of something beyond us with full awareness of the *now*. What he is up to can be easily misunderstood in a time when artists often define themselves more roughly, and as a result Wilbur is sometimes sniffed at as "mannered" or (horror of horrors!) "optimistic," which seems to me a condescending and misleading label. Borrowing a phrase from Loren Eiseley, one would do better to call Wilbur a species of "midnight optimist"—for amid the shape shifting of experience, Wilbur's poems, much like his friend Eiseley's brooding essays, can sometimes find grounds for a most-cautious hope that things and life somehow do make sense, perhaps even on their own. For Wilbur those moments, when imaginative engagement with the world sets off a flash like a discovery *in* the world, give cause for keeping faith alive. Wilbur accepts man as a creature who may have a place or a meaning in other realities; yet only by understanding who and where the self is now—as an unstable brew of flesh and spirit—can one hope to understand anything more of one's place in this or any other dimension.

Consequently Wilbur is a nature poet, a superb nature poet, writing about a nature which changes and constantly recreates itself, awakening that wonder in which one seems to transcend, for moments here and there, separation from the general scheme of things. This much a close reader of Wilbur's poetry will grant; and I think that Wilbur's use of language has everything to do with this intention. Words for him can be regenerative forces, catching not just diversity, but suggesting unity that might lie out beyond diversity. A few years ago, when Wilbur spoke of his conception of language in a short essay called "Poetry and the Landscape," he wrote of language as "re-creating the creation, giving each creature a relation to himself," and bringing the speaker "a kind of symbolic control over what lay around him."[12] Just as a balanced imagination might be able to see in the natural world something of both time and timelessness, the right words can conjure up the same kind of encounter. The right *ambiguous* word at the right time provides not proliferation of meaning, not disconcerting or demoralizing *difference,* but *reconvergence* of meaning, many possibilities drawing toward one.

Like much of the major verse since World War II, Wilbur's verse can therefore be the performance of a self-consciously fictive imagination—but it is also an act of hopeful conjuring, done with this stubborn wish that order created in a poem might somehow turn out to be order perceived. Wilbur's wordplay, therefore, embodies hope for our ontological condition, his own role as a careful, vigilant nature poet, and his faith in the restorative power of language itself. I cannot think of three more serious reasons for a poet to play with words. A look at a few poems, spanning about forty years of Wilbur's career, will indicate how this is so; and they will suggest that Wilbur's language, far from being a vehicle for themes, can shift like nature itself from poem to poem and from moment to moment within a poem, reenacting small, dubious miracles of transcendence. Further, Wilbur's use of language has undergone subtle evolution, and lately a radical change, as the poet continues to mature and expand, and a tour from old to newer work will show how that change has come about.

"The Regatta" (1947) is a young man's poem—Wilbur was in his midtwenties when he wrote it—which no one has said much about, perhaps because it may seem a little too young, too word-dizzy, to be taken seriously. Although it might be in some ways overrich, Wilbur's wordplay already shows itself as seeking not to be precious, mechanistic, or show-off. It is not hard to see that "The Regatta" is about a struggle with despair, about evasive intuitions and the stubborn duality of human consciousness and the persistent knack of that consciousness for dreaming up arrangements beneath the flashy and dismal surface of things. We get all this in a short poem about an elderly couple watching a yacht race. It is the multiple meanings of Wilbur's key words, and the fact that all these meanings achieve a common resonance, which make the poem succeed, and which make this pun-loaded, puzzling description of a regatta both handsome and right:

43

A rowdy wind pushed out the sky,
Now swoops the lake and booms in sails;
Sunlight can plummet, when it fails,
Brighten on boats which pitch and fly.

Out on the dock-end, Mrs. Vane,
Seated with friends, lifts lenses to
Delighted eyes, and sweeps the view
Of "galleons" on the "raging main."

A heeling boat invades the glass
To turn a buoy; figures duck
The crossing sail—"There's Midge and Buck!
I know his scarf!"—the sailors pass.

The hotel guests make joking bets,
And Mrs. Vane has turned, inquired
If Mr. Vane is feeling "tired."
He means to answer, but forgets.

She offers him binoculars:
A swift, light thing is slipping on
The bitter waters, always gone
Before the wave can make it hers;

So simply it evades, evades,
So weightless and immune may go,
The free thing does not need to know
How deep the waters are with shades.

It's but a trick; and still one feels
Franchised a little—God knows I
Would be the last alive to cry
To Whatzisname, "I love thy wheels!"

Freedom's a pattern. I am cold.
I don't know what I'm doing here.
And Mrs. Vane says, "Home now, dear."
He rises, does as he is told;
Hugging her arm, he climbs the pier.
Behind him breaks the triumph cheer.

Because there is a great deal of wordplay here, one must be selective in talking about it. But we are off into multiplicity already in the opening line. What are we to make of "pushed out?" Billowed, like the sails in the verse after? Or is it pushed away—suggesting either that our pleasant afternoon is gone, or that it is now made grander than it seemed? Or perhaps the wind pushes out the sky the way one pushes out an old-fashioned light switch, leaving everyone in the dark. In line three the sunlight "fails," perhaps because clouds have swept in, blotting out the sun and making the deep "shades" in the sixth stanza. The rest of the quatrain gives no help, only more possibilities, and no indication of how one should feel about this view from the pier. The wind "booms" in the sails of racing boats, suggesting the deep, ambiguous noise of sheets puffing out, suggesting too the booms on the boats themselves swinging about in response to a freshened wind. If this is becoming a dark afternoon, it is still a fine one for racing. But what does "plummet" suggest, in conjunction with "fails"? There is no trouble with the connotations of light "failing," but to read "plummet" carefully is to run into more ambiguity. The sunlight has dropped quickly, and the boats flying over the water's surface shine in a darkened seascape. "Plummet" does not, in that reading, seem to suggest trouble any more than does "pushed out." Further, "plummet" means more than drop: it means to drop a plumb line, to take measure, sound depths—meanings which also seem to work here. In darkness do we see something more clearly, something besides the darkness itself? Is it possible that light and darkness, order and disorder, are reconciled here somehow, much as the pun on "pitch"—suggesting perhaps dark hulls below bright sails—undoes the "brighten" of the fourth line and makes sense with it, too? At this point in the poem, we have several alleys of contradiction. But with a little patience, "The Regatta" takes us places worth going.

In the second stanza we get a more definite point of view, an elderly Mrs. Vane on the pier, doing a poet's job of bringing imagination to bear on worldly experience. Perhaps her imaginative involvement fits her name—one way or another; perhaps her "galleons on the Spanish main" are a vain fictionalizing of dark, pitchy, flying disorder, or perhaps Mrs. Vane is a truer sort of "vane"—which from the spelling of her name seems a reasonable bet—a sensibility which in its fictions responds rightly to obscure wonders in the landscape, to the winds, if you will, of truth. Mrs. Vane's eyes are "delighted," delighted by the failing of the light, or perhaps by age—and yet "delighted" in the normal sense, able as she is to sit among friends and see things truly, darkness or no. But any such endorsement of Mrs. Vane is swift, evasive; it slips by quickly in the rustle of a word.

To avoid making too much of a modest work, let us move to the fifth stanza, in which the poem begins to look at the day from over the shoulder of Mrs. Vane's husband, a man apparently nearer his end and the end of his hope. Mr. Vane is offered the binoculars, but apparently he does not take them, out of senility, fatigue, or indifference. The imaginative vantage point is everyone's to take or ignore as one will, should one choose to pursue, with the eyes or the imagination, that "swift, light thing" which all but escapes human apprehension. The poem makes the meaning of "light" as elusive and yet as dimly sure as the elusive "thing" it modifies. The passing sailboat is "light" because it gleams on shadowy waters, light because it is a mild and gay thing upon the face of "bitter" waters, a disordered and somber world over which, for the moment, it seems to hold its own. Every path one takes in chasing the sense of this stanza ends up in the same place, though off in a twilit distance. The poem is swept along by ingenious ambiguities—even so, it is not fair to say yet that this is overdone, nor that these are the poem's finest moments. The race after meaning ends with "shades" in line twenty-four, the last mention of the boat race, and the word suggests every sense we customarily attach to it. But the next stanza brings us into the "The Regatta's" little whirlpool of ambiguity:

> It's but a trick; and still one feels
> Franchised a little—God knows I
> Would be the last alive to cry
> To Whatzisname, "I love thy wheels!"

What is but a trick? The boat race itself, using nature to defy nature? Or is it the trick of sight, the way these passing sails tease both the naked and the binoculared eye? Both of these tricks might be meant here—or something else. The poem also speaks of the method of the poem itself, of the "trick" of the poet's language, the "trick" of making a regatta on a windy afternoon work as a metaphor for the human condition and the grounds of human hope. The speaker, this onlooker, feels "franchised a little" not simply by what boats do, but by what words do. The artist's own imagination does what Mrs. Vane is doing, looks carefully at the world and makes something greater out of it, which in turn gives the artist hope, however cautious hope has to be. Yet no sooner has the watcher recognized his own trick of managed ambiguities than the delicate illusion is gone. For a second, creation has been *re*created, a lucky blending of intelligence and fancy has made separate worlds seem one again—and once that instant has passed, artifice leads nowhere. The poem turns self-conscious, and the imagination grows as "cold" as the body on this chilly day. In such a condition, words can still reverberate this way and that, but the effect can be quite different—suggesting painful, static uncertainty, not possibilities of transcendence. "God" and "Whatzisname" play off each other and an array of significations in the last two lines of the stanza, yet take the speaker and the poem nowhere, either spiritually or psychologically. "God knows" is both an affirmation and a shrug of the shoulders, a way of asserting either that God does know, or that he alone might know, or that nobody knows. That irony would be commonplace, were it not for this cry "To Whatzisname," which in this context becomes also both pious and desperate, hopeful and cynical. The darkest reading of "Whatzisname" is that God has been utterly forgotten, that the very idea is something obsolete, learned long ago, and subsequently, perhaps wisely, forgotten. But following a familiar Old Testament line of thinking, "Whatzisname" seems perfect, if a little breezy, as a modern, cautious way of invoking God, Yahweh, the infinite "I am," the Almighty whose name cannot be known—and cannot be spoken.

So the word whirlpool begins to spin: one does and does not cry out to God, who is and is not to praise or blame for the natural world and the human condition—and the cry is suppressed because "God knows" one's joy without its proclamation in the streets, or because the world is ill and there is really no one to hear. Every tack through these lines leads to the same gulf of irony; and to a "feeling" that words and imaginings are "franchised" only so far; and that trying too hard to see, to dream, or to believe will bring one only to a cold aftermath. In the company of the old people, the emotionally drained speaker takes leave from the pier and the poem. The tone now is colder too, almost mechanical; the wordplay is over. For all the skill of the artist as a conjurer, moments of real imaginative engagement come quickly when they will, and slip as quickly away.

"The Regatta" ends with a poet-voice doubting its own magic—having worked it handily. Perhaps, in this early poem, that cleverness Wilbur is often accused of is too obtrusive for one to feel how somber his meditations really can be. There is much beauty in "The Regatta." It is not a game, but a rich, many-sided observation, and a compassionate look at people and nature. This regatta which the imagination makes so much of is a fine boat race, painted as it were in an austere, vigorous, loving, Impressionist way. The poem looks closely at nature as a realm of constant change and mystery and finds some cause to celebrate that mystery. It is easy to discern a young artist's unsure hand in what we already know is a young man's poem, but one should be careful not to miss Wilbur's achievement in language here, or write it off as decoration.

Since the days of "The Regatta," Wilbur's use of wordplay has grown less obtrusive, has come to integrate itself more deeply into the music of his lines. But in the years between *The Beautiful Changes* (1947) and the *New and Collected Poems* (1988), the wordplay continues to be everywhere, and its purposes and its place in Wilbur's style grow ever more clear. "Year's End" (1949) and "Love Calls Us to the Things of This World" (1956) are two poems about flesh and spirit, time and eternity, life and death. One of these poems is elegiac, deliberate, liable to the charge that Wilbur's thoughtfulness can spoil his work. The other is one of the most admired lyrics in the past four decades, a poem full of vigor and spontaneity—yet it is even more astonishing, as far as language is concerned, than "Year's End." In both poems, words from which meanings spread wide are used to call separated worlds into fleeting, almost miraculous union.

Most of the wordplay in "Year's End" is outright punning, puns scattered all down the page in the somberest way. Here are the two opening stanzas:

Now winter downs the dying of the year,
And night is all a settlement of snow;
From the soft street the rooms of houses show
A gathered light, a shapen atmosphere,
Like frozen-over lakes whose ice is thin
And still allows some stirring down within.

I've known the wind by water banks to shake
The late leaves down, which frozen where they fell
And held in ice as dancers in a spell
Fluttered all winter long into a lake;
Graved on the dark in gestures of descent,
They seemed their own most perfect monument.

I count six certifiable puns in "Year's End," and two other words (this use of "soft" and "shapely" in the fourth stanza) which seem broadly evocative. This is not a poem like "The Regatta" about something always eluding us in the everyday world. Because it is about time stopped and held fast in a suddenly arrived eternity, the wordplay here has different magic to work. The "ends of time" must be seen as, or transformed into, events of both destruction and conservation, and must suggest in such duality some silhouette of eternity. Toward the end of the poem the subject shifts to Pompeii and the drama of an everyday world instantly killed and conserved for the ages:

48

And at Pompeii

The little dog lay curled and did not rise
But slept the deeper as the ashes rose
And found the people incomplete, and froze
The random hands, the loose unready eyes
Of men expecting yet another sun
To do the shapely thing they had not done.

The stanza is especially intense, because the point of view is not that of the tourist or the musing armchair intellectual. Wilbur first saw Pompeii under strange circumstances, in the thick of the war, with Pliny's Vesuvius again in full eruption:

> Our six-by-six truck approached Pompeii through a fine, steady fall of whitish flakes, and set us down in a square already carpeted with ash. Some of our party, not caring for archaeology, headed directly for the bars and other comforts of the modern city; but the rest of us thought it more seemly to begin, at least, with a look at the ruins. We found a displaced Greek woman who offered to be our guide, and she took us through the greater part of the excavations, pointing out the wall paintings, deciphering inscriptions, explaining the water system—until at last, just as we reached the Greek Forum, there was a sudden darkening of the air, a thickening in the fall of ashes, and she took fright and left us.
>
> We found our way back to the modern city and established ourselves in a bar, sitting near the window so that we could watch for the return of our truck. The street was now full of natives evacuating the place, wading through the ashes under the usual clumsy burdens of refugees. Sitting there with a brandy bottle and watching such a scene, we felt something like the final tableau of *Idiot's Delight*. There were jokes about how we had better look smart and sit straight, since we might have to hold our poses for centuries.[13]

The conflation of sensations, in this memory, in "Year's End," makes the difference: real fear, a young writer's urgency, yet also a sense of absurdity, and a contemplative detachment from the catastrophic blows of fate, even from one's own mortality. Every bit of wordplay in this poem has a complex job to do, for each pun must suggest both temporality and eternity, finished and unfinished thought, serene and anxious meditations, the world of flesh, time, humanity, everyday confusion, as well as patient possibilities out beyond time.

"Downs" in the first stanza: the word means *fells* as a hunter fells an animal, or *sets down,* as an artist sets down a recognition to deliver it from time and forgetfulness. Or, given the snowy evening, "downs" might mean *packs in down,* wraps up snugly for safekeeping. "Settlement" suggests both a human settlement, a makeshift town made out of snow—and a *final* settlement, a conclusion to worldly turmoil. And "graved" in the stanza after: these falling leaves are both "engraved" and sent to the grave; their death is their transcendence into slow-time, their transformation into a kind of art. "Composedly" in the third stanza, "pause," and "fray," and "wrought" in the last, each allude to time and timelessness, to flesh or strife or passion on one hand, and the creative act, the transcendence of time and flesh, on another. Further, what is true of the puns in "Year's End" is true as well of "soft" and "shapely." The street is soft because it is snow-covered and quiet, because it is vulnerable and mortal. And "shapely": the astonished people of Pompeii lose in an instant their chance to give life artistic shape and finish, even as they are caught by the ash and graved into their own most perfect monuments. There is a wonderful melding here of diction, theme, and subtle observation of the natural world. The poem is a passionate expression of both intelligent anxiety and guarded affirmation, yet an achievement of beauty and unity which seems to leave cleverness behind.

Because "Love Calls Us to the Things of This World" is Wilbur's single most discussed and admired poem, it needs no laborious treatment here. The opening sixteen lines are:

> The eyes open to a cry of pulleys,
> And spirited from sleep, the astounded soul
> Hangs for a moment bodiless and simple
> As false dawn.
>   Outside the open window
> The morning air is all awash with angels.
>
> Some are in bed-sheets, some are in blouses,
> Some are in smocks: but truly there they are.
> Now they are rising together in calm swells
> Of halcyon feeling, filling whatever they wear
> With the deep joy of their impersonal breathing;
>
> Now they are flying in place, conveying
> The terrible speed of their omnipresence, moving
> And staying like white water; and now of a sudden
> They swoon down into so rapt a quiet
> That nobody seems to be there.

People who apparently enjoy little else in Wilbur's work delight in "Love Calls Us" for its gusto and its easy, spontaneous air—and I want to look at the careful wordplay in it for precisely this reason. The poem marks an important development in Wilbur's relationship with words, for here he succeeds as never before in making wordplay look easy. One readily notices the puns on "spirited," "awash," "blessed," "warm," "undone," "dark habits"; but less attention is paid to "astounded," "simple," "truly," "clear," "changed," and other words which suggest an enduring yet changeful harmony of matter and spirit which the waking man senses in his hypnagogic state, and which the poet celebrates with wakeful imagination. The sleeper's first look at the morning is giddy, solipsistic—but "simple" and foolish as he is in his drowsiness, he is worthy of some affectionate treatment, groping as he does for "simple," pure realities beyond the coming maculate and turmoiled day. The angels on the wash line are "truly" there only to someone not quite awake—or is it that they are "truly" there, in some dimension to which wakeful minds cannot find their way? The soul is "astounded" in every sense of the word: it is both stupefied and struck with wonder; the dance of the laundry-angels in the sight of heaven is likewise "clear" in all ways: simple and pure the dancers are, as well as transparent to the point of nonexistence. The poem is full of affectionate word jokes, all of which are "serious," all of which explore a theme of the duality of human existence and the balanced, dual consciousness one might need to see one's place in the world.

In an interview in 1973, Wilbur observed of the Russian poet Andrei Voznesensky, whom he had recently been translating, that "He likes to be playful in the midst of his greatest seriousness or passion, and so do I."[14] "Love Calls Us to the Things of This World" sheds some light on that remark. The poem is at once perfect seriousness and festivity, its language-founded ironies being play much as Huizinga defines it in its highest state, play as the exuberant celebration of mystery. The gaiety of the play heightens the reverence; it does not profane the ceremony. The words we have looked at are more than expressions of contrast between worldly and unworldly realities. The energy and music here are as well suited to holy festivity as their spreads of meaning are to the analytical mind. If the poem's reconciliation of playfulness and seriousness, energy and intellect is a trick, it is a trick which hearkens back to the very beginnings of literature. Wilbur's theme in "Love Calls Us" is not a new one in his poetry, but what is new is the grace with which he uses his rich language, a grace which shows that he has reconciled the play of words with that spontaneity and excitement which sacred play—as a potent modern ceremony—ought to have.

Festivity for the sake of seriousness, the word as a recreative force, the transcendence of diversity and the recovery of lost union, unstable meanings which catch both the shift and the changelessness of the natural world—how far can this kind of poetry go? Perhaps there is a point at which even the most brilliant renewal of language ceases to be renewal, and a technique like this, however ingenious, dead ends in its own cliche. I am grateful that Wilbur has few imitators, as I am grateful that in the last twenty years Wilbur has not fallen into imitating himself. A verse style meant as a recreative force must itself have constant *recreation*, and Wilbur's wordplay has shown both a change and a continuity, like that change-with-continuity he so often admires in nature.

From *Walking to Sleep*, "In a Churchyard" seems a sober return to Gray's "Elegy," yet in this churchyard too, puns and spreads of meaning earn their place. Transformed again from what it was in "Year's End," Wilbur's reechoing language gives this meditation the poised mood it needs to avoid both banal gloom and repulsive artifice, and this wordplay is one with the perceptions, the atmosphere, the scene, the complex of consciousness. The key to the poem's success is that the word games are now more difficult and less obtrusive, the flow of one loaded utterance into the next being not rapid and easy as before, but deliberate, hindered, slow. The meeting of worlds, in both landscape and language, is again the theme; yet here there are no surprising recognitions. The truth of churchyards has to be found through hard imaginative work. The poem has been busy with the churchyard's suggestions of timeless, speechless realities, a "music innocent of time and sound," when the real world intrudes upon the visitor with mysteries yet stranger.

> It shadows all our thought, balked imminence
> Of uncommitted sound,
> And still would tower at the sill of sense
> Were not, as now, its honed abeyance crowned
>
> With a mauled boom of summons far more strange
> Than any stroke unheard,
> Which breaks again with unimagined range
> Through all reverberations of the word,
>
> Pooling the mystery of things that are,
> The buzz of prayer said,
> The scent of grass, the earliest-blooming star,
> These unseen gravestones, and the darker dead.

If there is any sense—much less manifold sense—to be made of "balked imminence / Of uncommitted sound," it does not lie as close to the surface as the significations of the wordplay we have looked at before. Of course "shadows" suggests both the shadows in the twilit churchyard and the shadowing of the speaker's thoughts. But what is this about "balked imminence," "honed abeyance," and "mauled boom"? "Balked" makes sense if it means thwarted; but it also means heaped up or ridged, like the mound of a grave. That would amount to nothing—except that "honed," besides its modern definition (sharpened) has an interesting archaic one. A hone is a stone marker, like a gravestone; and in a Northumbrian dialect it means hesitate, balk. A queer underground coherence here intensifies the usual meanings of these words. This meditation takes place in a churchyard, and the landscape of the churchyard seems to suffuse the language of the meditation. Once more we are met with one of Wilbur's enduring themes, that a way to make sense of our timeless condition is to be intensely aware of the here and the now. The "mauled boom" is both an ambiguous summons of the unknown and the hammering ring of a real church bell in a tower itself suggested by the image of eternities towering at the "sill of sense." This is one elegy in a churchyard which does not leave or forget the churchyard as the meditation deepens, but rather seeks answers within the churchyard world. In this meditation, Wilbur's language has changed its sound, pace, and strategy, but not its essential object: to be a means by which several realms of reality are drawn together. It shows a power which distinguishes genius from sheer style, the power both to transform itself and remain the same.

A move onward in time to *The Mind-Reader* (1976) suggests that the transformation has continued and ramified through another decade. The title of the book is drawn from the dramatic monologue which concludes it. Wilbur remarked around that time that he found himself increasingly interested in writing dramatic monologues,[15] and as one might expect, the shift in rhetorical strategies has caused more changes in his use of language. While "The Mind-Reader" introduces us to a clairvoyant—something of a charlatan—whom Wilbur says he met in Rome many years ago, the poem does not try to catch anything of the language of its Italian persona. Rather, it is a mind-reading of a mind-reader, an attempt to penetrate to the consciousness pure. The theme is familiar: a true visionary, unlike this failed, unhappy one, must adjust his powers of imagination to a world of waking, rational perception, must reach mystical awareness *without* forgetting the truth to be had from commonplace realities. The mind-reader is a gifted visionary, but because he has no use for temporal experience, his quest for the supernal leads only into solipsism; and the frustration which results has ruined his life.

Wordplay in "The Mind-Reader" might therefore have two objects: to convey the duality of the mind-reader's favored hypnagogic state; and to underscore a pathetic irony in his condition. The mind-reader can read nothing beyond himself because he reads himself too closely. The wordplay in the poem is sparing, to be sure, perhaps because Wilbur, to enter this other personality, must modulate his own familiar voice. But when the reverberating words turn up, as they do in crucial phrases, they serve precisely these purposes. They reveal both the mind itself and its fatal mistake.

The opening line of the poem suggests immediately the difference in outlook between the poet and the persona he now assumes. "Some things are truly lost," the speaker assumes as a way of setting out—but the word "truly" is a problem—dangerous expression that it now is, as well as one of Wilbur's favorite loaded terms. One is tempted to doubt this assurance about what is "truly" lost, and not let this metaphysician off without solid proof. The sun-hat, pipe-wrench, and overboard novel he talks about show that he equates true, absolute loss with removal beyond human senses and recollection, with disappearance into an enormous, unfathomable natural world:

> The sun-hat falls,
> With what free flirts and stoops you can imagine,
> Down through that reeling vista or another,
> Unseen by any, even by you or me.
> It is as when a pipe-wrench, catapulted
> From the jounced back of a pick-up truck, dives headlong
> Into a bushy culvert; or a book
> Whose reader is asleep, garbling the story,
> Glides from beneath a steamer chair and yields
> Its flurried pages to the printless sea.

While one can never have this hat, wrench, or book back again, they are "truly" lost only if we accept reality to be the world we can see into, either with our eyes or our dreams. I am not splitting hairs. For thirty years, Wilbur's self-avowed quarrel with Edgar Allan Poe has focused on this point: that the mind which responds solipsistically to the waking world and trusts too much to a world of dreams finds only madness when it seeks transcendence.

The rest of the poem shows us that the speaker lacks interest—and faith—in perceived reality, and that this is the cause of his misery. Consider the pun on "printless" which closes the opening stanza. The speaker's joke epitomizes his own dilemma. To such a mind the sea is "printless" in three ways: the fallen book leaves no imprint, no track on the surface; the sea is itself printless, inscrutable; and it is "printless" meaning inexpressible, for no language, no quantity of print, will penetrate its mysteries. Having given up on making sense of the world he lives in, the mind-reader calls up landscapes and seascapes which, whether real or imagined, are disorderly, ominous, and perfectly obscure. The play on "printless" is matched shortly with a similar pun on "groundless," as the mystic goes on a trek through his own subconscious: the monologue moves from water into the woods, but the effect of the pun, stressing as it does the bewilderment and hopelessness of too much imagination and too little insight, is something we have seen before. The mind-reader is Wilbur's foil, the poet as abject visionary, trapped in a world in which his powerful mind can find no peace:

> Whether or not I put my mind to it,
> The world usurps me ceaselessly; my sixth
> And never-resting sense is a cheap room
> Black with the anger of insomnia,
> Whose wall-boards vibrate with the mutters, plaints,
> And flushings of the race.

These "flushings" suggest the mind-reader's cheap and shabby world, the psychological torments he suffers and witnesses, and the emotional self-indulgence he is fated to hear over and over and make his own dismal theme. In other words, "flushings" catches the predicament of a kind of artist Wilbur struggles not to be, in language which conveys the temperament and ontological stance which holds such a poet in thrall—and in its vividness, the fact that Wilbur has been here himself. There is no smugness in this poem, no hint that Wilbur is window-shopping among desperate sensibilities. If "The Mind-Reader" means nothing else, it suggests that Wilbur knows firsthand about the perils of the imagination, for he haunts with the very condition of mind he warns against. The wordplay in the poem pays homage to powerful consciousness gone wrong. We should note too that the wordplay in the poem is used here not as it is used elsewhere, to celebrate the subtlety and the possibilities of life, but rather to illustrate isolation from life. I can find only one word in the poem that suggests a recognition of any possibility of underlying order; as one might expect, the word turns up as the speaker *almost* reaches a larger awareness:

> Sometimes I wonder if the blame is mine,
> If through a sullen fault of the mind's ear

> I miss a resonance in all their fretting.
> Is there some huge attention, do you think,
> Which suffers us and is inviolate,
> To which all hearts are open, which remarks
> The sparrow's weighty fall, and overhears
> In the worst rancor a deflected sweetness?
> I should be glad to know it.

Fretting: misery and music at once, a music born of misfortune, music one might hear faintly, if one listens very closely and with a certain measure of luck to the real world, and not so fondly to the voices in one's own dreams. In the world itself might lurk that deflected sweetness which the mind-reader should be glad to comprehend, but which his pathetic consciousness will not allow him to achieve. His monologue is a dignified, credible statement of a tragedy of the contemporary imagination, a tragedy which much of the poetry in this century has been about. Here, then, is Wilbur transforming his wordplay to fit voices very different from his own, specifically the voice of that sensibility with which he has passionately, and compassionately, quarreled since the start of his career. The man on the front of *The Mind-Reader's* dust jacket, the silhouette at the cafe table, has Wilbur's shape, as indeed he should; for this mind worn down with detail and misfortune and those perceptions which can break anyone who seeks the "resonance in all their fretting," *is* Wilbur, the other side of the man—not simply the visionary that he struggles against becoming, but the visionary that, for the controlled surfaces, he always is.

In *New Poems* (1987), the word performances seem to have modulated a bit further, which may have to do with differences in the implicit persona of these most recent works. The mind-reader's torment gives a luminous quality to moments of multiple entendre in his monologue; "Love Calls Us" is about morning giddiness; "Year's End" brought together a soldier's surrealistic memories, vignettes of human and prehuman history, and the familiarly disordered perceptions of a New Year's Eve; and "The Regatta" was an uneasy young man's poem about mortality and the dubious promise of a life in art. "Trolling for Blues," in the new collection, is in contrast a small and gentle poem, an older man's return to the waters that have tasked him so long, for another imaginative dive beneath surfaces. The situation is again domestic, undramatic, an excursion after Atlantic bluefish, and some blue-water ruminations, which deepen and ramify Melville-style into slow and shapely wonder, as the trolling mind considers consciousness itself, the uncertain stages of its evolution, and the unsettling diversity of the other minds that seem to prowl the world.

What results is anything but a sideshow of contrived connections. This is another occasion poem which does not forget where it is, and if it has in it certain word vortices in which a jumble of meanings are gathered and whirled into one, then they are properties of fish, water, and the mind. Specifically, there seem to be three centers of language in "Trolling for Blues": mirrors and reflected images, darkness, and deep color:

> As with the dapper terns, or that sole cloud
> Which like a slow-evolving embryo
> Moils in the sky, we make of this keen fish
> Whom fight and beauty have endeared to us
> A mirror of our kind. Setting aside
>
> His unreflectiveness, his flings in air,
> The aberration of his flocking swerve
> To spawning-grounds a hundred miles at sea,
> How clearly, musing to the engine's thrum,
> Do we conceive him as he waits below:
>
> Blue in the water's blue, which is the shade
> Of thought, and in that scintillating flux
> Poised weightless, all attention, yet on edge
> To lunge and seize with sure incisiveness,
> He is a type of coolest intellect,
>
> Or is so to the mind's blue eye until
> He strikes and runs unseen beneath the rip,
> Yanking imagination back and down
> Past recognition to the unlit deep
> Of the glass sponges, of chiasmodon,
>
> Of the old darkness of Devonian dream,
> Phase of a meditation not our own,
> That long mêlée where selves were not, that life
> Merciless, painless, sleepless, unaware,
> From which, in time, unthinkably we rose.

The oddest word choice in the first stanza, "moils," seems an antique expression, loaded with obsolete significations. As a transitive verb it means to be fidgety or restless—a word choice which suggests considerably more about the mood of this speaker than the way of a cloud on the sea. But beyond that signification, "moils" is ancient and slippery, coming down to us loaded with obsolete meanings, in both the transitive and intransitive form. At various times, says the Oxford English Dictionary, "moil" has meant to befoul, to moisten, labor, fatigue, burrow or root up, mangle. These are shadows around the word, and I mention them not only because its conjoining with "embryo" catches the motion of embryos and makes of the cloud another "mirror of our kind," but also because the word choice contributes to an eerie, unstable mingling of the ancient and the new, the timeless and transitory: the theme is inherent in the very language of this poem, language which seems to slide around through time, gathering what it likes from centuries of accreted and abandoned definitions. "Keen," in the same line, works the same way: the bluefish is a smart, sharp, cagey opponent for the sportsman; but "keen" has also meant fierce, savage, aroused in primal ways (one recalls Ophelia's use of it in *Hamlet*), and not necessarily wise at all. The incipient problem in this verse—can fish really think, or can they not?—is forced into the open by the first flat-out pun of the poem, "unreflectiveness" in the sixth line. On a physical plane, the fish loses his unreflectiveness when he jumps from the disguising water and shines in the sea air, like the incandescent rainbow trout in Wilbur's "Ballade for the Duke of Orléans"; and surely the word also means unawareness, the stupid condition of the fish before the bait and the mating instincts make a more or less "conscious" creature of him. Both senses work here because the line before this has raised the problem of the narcissistic imagination, euphorically transforming nature into a mirror for the self, congratulating itself on a real or a spurious comradeship with the scaly folk in the water. The problem lies with what Saul Bellow has called "otherness," and whether any leap of understanding or imagining can ever cross the chasm between creatures. As the crucial verb in the second stanza, "conceive" has half a dozen apt and contradictory meanings which spin around the question of truly knowing: to conceive is to fancy, to create or engender (which plays nicely off the reference to those "spawning-grounds" which the fishers have thought about, if not the fish); it also means to apprehend, to get to the truth through insight or intuition. So one can know the fish—or dream him up out of the lazy-minded wishes and solipsistic musings of an ocean cruise.

This treacherous wordplay about reflection as imaginative breakthrough or absurd daydream subsides for a while after the second stanza, and the spreads of signification organize instead around the colors and sensations of deep water: is it a realm with its own alien mind, or no mind at all? At the opening of the third stanza, "shade" revolves through several shades of meaning: as the "shade / Of thought" it has a classic symbolic value. And shade can be not a color but a hiding place, a deep shadow concealing the Other; more, it can mean a place of privation, of absence, denied the light of intellection—a place, in other words, where "incisiveness" has to do not with the power of mind but of jaws and sharp teeth, the only thing "sure" about it being its absolute simplicity, and intellect "coolest" not in the sense of rationality, of repressed or absent passion, but in the sense of inertia, signifying a mind that radiates no heat or light at all. The stanza continues to praise the bluefish, to assert kinship, and this trolling then as an act of brotherhood, and so on—while under the surfaces of the language lurks the undoing of that fantasy. One strike on the line and the trap is sprung on the imagination: the fight is with something different, primordial, a consciousness either inscrutable or simply not there at all. Down "Past recognition" dives the fish, into deep water, into the unlit deep of the human mind where the conscious self cannot go, where even the "glass sponges" can reflect nothing, not even a feeble illusion of kinship. The "shade of thought," as the middle-dark in which the consciousness can troll, fancying, and fancying itself to be getting somewhere in understanding the world's depths, gives way now to the "old darkness of Devonian dream"—an unknowable blackness too far back in history, and too far down in one's own mind, down in the place where "selves were not," and life was utterly unlike life as we understand or dream it.

This genesis-world of consciousness, from whose bourn no traveler returns, is like the world of absolute sleep into which, in Poe's scheme of things, the mind plunges at the end of dream or nightmare: the only possible transcendence into this condition, to know it truly, is at the price of destruction. If one stops short of that, short of fantasy or madness or some other absolute loss of the self, then an eerie wonderment is what we can manage: at how we came from that state to this, at the continuing presence of the Devonian Other, down in the deep sea, and locked up in the dark confinements of the risen human mind. And so "unthinkably" is the last small word eddy in the poem, conjoining at least three meanings: something unthinkable is appalling, too awful to think about; we rose "unthinkably" because only at some point far beyond the bluefish level did we become selves, have identities, wills, souls worthy of the name; and this evolution unfolded unthinkably because we certainly did not and could not think of it, but came about as the consequence of a "meditation not our own." This seems both a mild and contemporary way of asking Blake's old question about the tiger, to which Blake never found a satisfactory answer either. All three significations work, because each is a part of the whole mind's whole uncertainty: to wonder about what we were and are is also to wonder about the value and status of our own ideas *about* what we were and are. This is not linguistic trickery or metaphysical hoop jumping, but consciousness, suggested with stunning completeness in a single spinning word.

The mind of a poet has more work to do now. It must be aware of an endlessly expanded natural universe, of new conceptions of time, new uncertainties about human consequence; it must be aware of a cultural past and of the limits of culture as a source of strength; above all, it must be aware of awareness, of the delusions and stubborn mysteries of dreaming and knowing. Richard Wilbur has worked long for a new vocabulary to do that work, familiar words in a context which, yes, does *de*familiarize them, yet not in some schematic way; and never so that they lose their commonplace sense. The title poem of his very first collection, *The Beautiful Changes,* closes with these lines:

> the beautiful changes
> In such kind ways,
> Wishing ever to sunder
> Things and things' selves for a second finding, to lose
> For a moment all that it touches back to wonder.

For Richard Wilbur, a poem is words seduced back into the timeless conspiracy.

3. Quarreling with Poe

All that we do
Is touched with ocean, yet we remain
On the shore of what we know.
—"For Dudley"

LITTLE has been done yet, of the right kind of work, to relate Richard Wilbur the scholar and critic to Richard Wilbur the poet. One can find a plausible reason: Wilbur made one remark, in one essay, more than twenty years ago, which seems to have eclipsed the evidence of his other prose. His attention to Edgar Allan Poe, as one of that writer's best students and defenders, has been steady and fruitful since the late fifties: as general editor of the Laurel Poetry Series, he did the Poe volume himself, furnishing it with an extensive, playful, and personally revealing introduction;[1] his 1959 essay "The House of Poe" is regularly cited as one of the best studies to date of symbolic values in both the verse and the tales;[2] in *The New York Review of Books* he published an essay which champions Poe against his academic detractors;[3] and in the early seventies he edited, with a sensitive introduction, a handsome David Godine edition of *The Narrative of Arthur Gordon Pym*.[4] But none of that extraordinary and expert attention to Poe seems to matter; what you always hear about, with regard to Wilbur's own verse, is that remark in a 1966 *Shenendoah* essay called "On My Own Work," in which Wilbur says, without much explanation, that much of it could be read as a quarrel with Edgar Allan Poe.[5] To understanding readers of Wilbur the poet, it should register somehow that his poetry reverberates with allusions to Poe's work and adaptations of Poe motifs. The faulty reasoning which gets in the way seems to be this: that if Richard Wilbur would indeed "quarrel" with Poe at such length and on so many fronts, and if Poe is ensconced now as a great American bard of dark, dangerous imaginative voyages and extravagant visionary flights, then Wilbur must be a poet of sunshine and surface interests, "things of this world" and all that, steering clear of self-test as an imaginative artist, in or near the chasms of vision and dream.

This chapter therefore has an axe to grind: I hope to correct that kind of inference and look at the broad and rich and unschematic way that this Wilbur-Poe quarrel has been going on. Surely one should not assume out of hand that an extended dispute between artists, especially a fight that a living man picks with a dead one, means a confrontation of opposites; if such were the case, who with any sense would bother to quarrel at all? But one need not do much assuming here: how very *un*opposite these poets are can be demonstrated. I shall look at this important, pervasive presence of Poe in Wilbur's poetry, Poe's continuing impact on Wilbur's symbolism, his language, and his understanding of imagination. And I shall indicate how Wilbur's improvisations on Poe can contribute to an understanding of his own honest and courageous vision, as well as to his impact. I have suggested before that as a "contemporary" poet in the truest sense, Wilbur can offer us our fill of harrowing and hopeful possibility, yet remain, through it all, aware of himself and his readers, not as one-way travelers on blind and careening excursions into dream, but as beings who ultimately must forsake dreams and return somehow to daily business of melding the temporal *with* the dream—that course which offers the mind the greatest intensity and the best of sane hopes. No doubt it is Poe who takes us on wilder, more fanciful, and more abandoned dream voyages; that is why Wilbur is drawn to him, and apparently cannot shake an interest in him. Yet on reflection, I do not think it fair to say that Poe is more audacious as an imaginer than Wilbur, the most attentive and skillful of his pupils writing in English in our time.

Though conversations of living poets with the dead, or with their own active contemporaries, are an engrossing subject in which orderly discussions can drown, it would be wrong to pretend that Richard Wilbur's ongoing address to Poe is something easily distinguished from other voices in his poetry, exchanges with other poets and times. Wilbur is an artist, not a debater from a single bench, and there are moments in which his sympathy with transcendental imagining, whether destructive or not, leads to unexpected responses in his own work, amid the give-and-take which postwar poets have so valued. David Kalstone's last book, *Becoming a Poet,* highlights the complex, energizing friendships which grew among certain major poets of that generation, the ways they provoked and sustained one other, even as critics were busy sorting them into rival camps, and even as those rivalries flared for real. Kalstone presents Elizabeth Bishop as a central figure in webs of affection and mutual influence,[6] for in her voice, her long faraway sojourns, her physical and emotional distance from the humid air of American poet circles and university life, and above all in her celebrated craftsmanship, Bishop could play the cool, composed, astonishing Stranger; and figures as diverse as Lowell, Plath, Wilbur, and Roethke have been drawn to her skill and self-evident delight in making poems, poems as wrought and polished artifacts. Kalstone offers Bishop as the preeminent living influence on younger poets of the fifties and sixties, and there is little reason to doubt him, given the evidence of so many letters and a sort of badinage which echoes in some of the best poems she and her friends were to write. Robert Lowell's skunks and Bishop's armadillo, for instance, are two voices in one of these exuberant conversations about small indomitable creatures and hard weather in the soul; and Bishop's letters to Lowell suggest that when she eventually sought to write more boldly and steadily about her own upbringing, she was encouraged by Lowell's daring in the short poems which became the heart of *Life Studies*.

Though Richard Wilbur has not broken confidences about his relationships with contemporaries, it seems that he has been much involved in such conversations, and that Bishop's artistry figures in his own work. If in Wilbur's poems there are dialogues to be overheard with Frost or Edgar Allan Poe, then there may be thoughtful and even passionate replies to Bishop too, exchanges playful and dead serious between equals and friends. Bishop's first published volume, *North and South*, features a polished array of poems about waking up and falling asleep, poems about the sensory (yet not really the psychological) experience of half-consciousness as the day dawns or ends. Handsomely crafted, these poems have a mingled voice, because they carry that classic Bishop tenseness, her imaginative and temperamental self-restraint, into times of the day and the mind when such resistances are assumed to be down. The tonal agon of "Love Lies Sleeping" has much to do with its defensive predawn wakefulness, its meticulous picture of a world half-perceived and fiercely half-created. The lines enact a partial surrender of self to the dawn and its hypnagogic wonders. Yet they give in to neither. The first verbs in the poem have to be read as imperatives:

> Earliest morning, switching all the tracks
> that cross the sky from cinder star to star,
>> coupling the ends of streets
>> to trains of light,
>
> now draw us into daylight in our beds;
> and clear away what presses on the brain:
>> put out the neon shapes
>> that float and swell and glare[7]

About ten years after Bishop's *North and South,* Richard Wilbur published a lyric of awakening which has become his most famous poem, so often discussed that there is little point in parsing it again. But among its pleasures, its affectionate reply to Bishop's morning poems should draw some attention. Bishop's "Love Lies Sleeping" tensely imagines and observes the early morning city, and the poem resists its own opening, its half-awake image of a metropolis apparently as glimpsed through a rain-streaked window. After morning is exhorted to "clear away" the caprices of the unleashed imagination, there follows a real world observed and a dream recollected—not quite in tranquillity:

> Then, in the West, "Boom!" and a cloud of smoke.
>   "Boom!" and the exploding ball
>   of blossom blooms again.
>
> (And all the employees who work in plants
> where such a sound says "Danger," or once said "Death,"
>   turn in their sleep and feel
>   the short hairs bristling
>
> on backs of necks).

Bishop seems to build this poem as America builds and rebuilds its towns—a little fearful of the whole process and of the imaginative violence which everything seems to be founded upon. Her poem ends with a dead man, who in his inverted "open eyes" may see the truth of human experience "revealed," as it is to Poe in his transcendent self-immolations. A dead man's recognitions are beyond reach, however, and the poem keeps its distance, seeing him entirely from without:

> for always to one, or several, morning comes,
> whose head has fallen over the edge of his bed,
>   whose face is turned
>   so that the image of
>
> the city grows down into his open eyes
> inverted and distorted. No. I mean
>   distorted and revealed,
>   if he sees it at all.

"Love Calls Us to the Things of This World" seems in its title a friendly rejoinder to Bishop, and Wilbur's poem recalls some of the material in "Love Lies Sleeping": wash on the line, the water images, the intruding "alarms for the expected"—meaning the impending routines and ravages (what Wilbur calls the "punctual rape") of the coming day, and most notably a complex blessing for all this getting up and daily business. "Scourge them with roses only," says Bishop's poem, "be light as helium." "Bring them down from their ruddy gallows," says Wilbur's waking man, in a kindred spirit. But Wilbur's poem ventures farther in the Poe direction, as it were, than does Bishop's, for the "revelations" in "Love Calls Us" are neither left to the dead nor strongly resisted, as they seem to be in "Love Lies Sleeping." "Love Calls Us" delights in the ridiculous yet wonderful—and just possibly true—revelations that the dawning hours offer the self whose inhibitions are low and whose imagination can roam, like language, momentarily free. Here is another look at the opening lines:

> The eyes open to a cry of pulleys,
> And spirited from sleep, the astounded soul
> Hangs for a moment bodiless and simple
> As false dawn.
>   Outside the open window
> The morning air is all awash with angels.
>
> Some are in bed-sheets, some are in blouses,
> Some are in smocks: but truly there they are.
> Now they are rising together in calm swells
> Of halcyon feeling, filling whatever they wear
> With the deep joy of their impersonal breathing;
>
> Now they are flying in place, conveying
> The terrible speed of their omnipresence, moving
> And staying like white water; and now of a sudden
> They swoon down into so rapt a quiet
> That nobody seems to be there.

Is this poem in any palpable way a response to Bishop, or some species of quarrel? Perhaps many fine modern poems speak to other ones, or in the case of "Love Calls Us," whisper to them with affectionate poise. About what? Here, perhaps, Richard Wilbur has played Poe for his friend Elizabeth Bishop, not insisting, as Bishop's dawn poem would seem to, on wakeful perception and poem-making, but accepting a meld of free dream and careful consciousness in a crucible of "bitter love."

Here is how Wilbur closes his introduction to the Laurel edition of *Poe: Complete Poems* (the italics are mine):

> By the refusal of human emotion and moral concern, by the obscuration of logical and allegorical meaning, *by the symbolic destruction of material fact, by negating all that he could of world and worldly*

self, Poe strove for a poetry of spiritual effect which should seem
"the handiwork of the angels that hover between man and God,"
and move the reader to a moment of that sort of harmonious
intuition which is to be the purifying fire of Earth and the music of
the regathering spheres. *There has never been a grander conception of
poetry, nor a more impoverished one.*[8]

The grandest, yet the most impoverished conception: in this paradox is
an important clue to what Wilbur respects so thoroughly in Poe as to
wish to quarrel with it. Poe's classic symbol for "the destruction of
material fact" is, certainly, the whirlpool or the abyss in the sea of
experience: any use since Poe of the abyss or maelstroms or swirling
destructive winds in American literature has owed him a debt. And the
processes of self- and world-negation, the slipping movement toward
the abyss, generates (according to Wilbur) the essential allegory struc-
turing many of the tales. In "The House of Poe," for example, Wilbur
argues for a reading of "MS. Found in a Bottle" as

> an allegory of the mind's voyage from the waking world into the
> world of dreams, with each main step of the narrative symbolizing
> the passage of the mind from one state to another—from wakeful-
> ness to reverie, from reverie to the hypnagogic state, from the
> hypnagogic state to the deep dream.[9]

For Wilbur, the symbol of the abyss or the whirlpool, and the
problem of the unrestrained imagination yearning for some leap to the
supernal, are building blocks of Poe's house of art. Both, I would add,
are essential to Wilbur's art as well, and when considered in detail, the
same symbol and problem as they present themselves in his work
reveal much about his divergence from and affectionate quarrel with
Poe. First we need to look at the vortex symbol as both of these writers
make use of it; once its implications are clear, the meaning of imagination for Wilbur, and the price that, by his own reckoning, he finds must
be paid in exchange for it, can be more readily understood.

As Wilbur explains it, Poe's cherished motif of world-escape has at
least two opposite effects on the poetic sensibility: a flight back toward
whatever unity was lost at birth must be at the same time a frightening
adventure into the unknown. And in Poe, as in so much romantic and
symbolist verse, the lapse into dream is the great self-surrender (that is,
short of death itself) to the imaginative powers for the voyage beyond
temporality. Accordingly, the release of the imagination is both the
most awful and the most wished-for of consummations. More precisely, it is the *process* of escape which, like dying, holds the terror; it is

the *end* of that process, shrouded like death in near-perfect obscurity, that sustains and excites the hopes of the voyager.

A longed-for transcendence and a terrible doom; a flight into unity with the still essence behind nightmarish reality, and nightmare itself: these opposing fates and contending emotions are all drawn together for Poe in the symbol of the whirlpool, the abyss, the "vertiginous plunge" as Wilbur sometimes calls it. In these varied forms, the symbol pervades the tales as both the final fulfillment of the dream quest and the end of earthly life itself. Here is Wilbur once more in his Introduction:

> The end of Poe's journey-tales is always, more or less obviously, a plunge. The canoe dives dizzily into the valley, the ship enters the whirlpool or the polar gulf on the way to Tartarus or the Earth's womb. Where the scenery and properties of the tale do not permit a giddy and plunging close, Poe *alludes* to the idea. At the end of "King Pest," to give but one of many possible examples, the intoxicated Hugh Tarpaulin is cast into a hogshead of ale and disappears "amid a whirlpool of foam."[10]

Acute as Wilbur may sound here, he can be at the same time quite blunt in his disclaimers: "Poe's aesthetic, Poe's theory of the nature of art," he says in "The House of Poe," "seems to me insane. To say that art should repudiate everything human and earthly, and find its subject in the flickering end of dreams, is hopelessly to narrow the scope and function of art."[11] Skilled as he is at tracking the flight of Poe's imagination over the edge of the most awesome abyss, Wilbur has little taste for irretrievably dropping to the ambiguous bottom. How, therefore, can a symbol such as the whirlpool, so central to the "mechanism of destructive transcendence"[12] that Wilbur has called Poe's art, serve such a poet as Wilbur himself, much less prove a central symbol in some of his own best poetry?

We can begin to assemble an answer by going back about thirty years. From *Things of This World,* "Marginalia" is a poem which has caused interpretive trouble, but knowing of Wilbur's special taste and distaste for Poe helps to explicate the poem's obscurities and to clarify the difficult closing lines. In fact, the title of the poem seems like a good clue from a Poe detective story that one should have Poe squarely in mind, for Poe's use of the word "Marginalia" is the most famous in American literature, and the title of Wilbur's poem may suggest that Poe's ghost or memory can marginalize, which is to say gloss, some of these lines as well. Whatever the truth of that may be, Wilbur's "Marginalia" surely treats qualities of consciousness with which Poe himself is preoccupied. The poem looks again at borderlands between states of awareness, between being and nonbeing, between temporality and some other sort of existence outside of time and the world. "Things concentrate at the edges," the poem begins; we learn that these "things" include the experiences of the hypnagogic state. For Wilbur, the sanest man, the most reluctant visionary, can perceive a "sublime decor"—illusion, perhaps, or perhaps something more than illusion—only when the mind is near some strange edge between the restrained, waking sensibility and the self-loss of deep dream. What recollection a wakeful consciousness should make of such peripheral experience is a mystery. We cannot know, Wilbur asserts, just how closely these "centrifugal" reveries, on the rim of the vortex that draws all beyond time and life, resemble any truth independent of both imagination and worldly experience. The last stanza reads:

> Our riches are centrifugal; men compose
> Daily, unwittingly, their final dreams,
> And those are our own voices whose remote
> Consummate chorus rides on the whirlpool's rim,
>> Past which we flog our sails, toward which we drift,
>> Plying our trades, in hopes of a good drowning.

Now this peculiar "good drowning" and the "hope" that goes with it in the poem's closing line can be both obscure and a little troubling. How is the poem's premise that imaginative experience projects from the self (as the final stanza again seems to assume) to be reconciled with any "hope" at all, save as some last-hour failure of existential nerve? There are ambiguities in the "drowning" as well, for it can be either a final, hyperillusionary instant before complete oblivion, or a passage into some altered and perhaps better condition of being. One can have better luck with the sense, the implications, and the coherence of this last stanza if one recalls the specific situations and symbols that Wilbur adapts here, as well as the sensibilities of Poe's voyagers.

Of the many journeys and plunges in Poe, two seem most strongly suggested by "Marginalia": aboard a phantom derelict rushing toward its doom, the narrator of "MS. Found in a Bottle" finds that his terrors of the whirlpool before him have suddenly transmogrified into something else:

> A curiosity to penetrate the mysteries of these awful regions, predominates even over my despair, and will reconcile me to the most hideous aspect of death. It is evident that we are hurrying onward to some exciting knowledge—some never-to-be imparted secret, whose attainment is destruction.

The wraith-sailors on this doomed ship show signs of achieving a similar mood:

> The crew pace the deck with unquiet and tremulous step; but there is upon their countenance an expression more of the eagerness of hope than of the apathy of despair.

The lone survivor of "A Descent into the Maelstrom" undergoes a like change of heart, even as he begins his drop into the vast destroying whirlpool:

> It may look like boasting—but what I tell you is truth—I began to reflect how magnificent a thing it was to die in such a manner, and how foolish it was in me to think of so paltry a consideration as my own individual life, in view of so wonderful a manifestation of God's power.

Wilbur holds that Poe's voyagers are nearly all embodiments of the visionary mind, the mind that would give itself utterly to the dream experience regardless of the personal cost. And an enormous cost that can be! His mind blanched like his hair, by the terror and hope of his adventure, only the fisherman of "A Descent" returns from Poe's whirlpools. But if we read the closing image of "Marginalia" in light of its literary heritage, it seems that the final turn here—albeit in a limited way, befitting a skeptical age—is toward visionary faith of its own. It sometimes confuses readers that Wilbur will not ignore one bulky fact about the human condition: that one should not, must not give over the self entirely to dreaming pursuit of absolutes, if one would not be utterly lost in dream-world traps of madness and self-deceit—and that pretending to have so surrendered is histrionic fakery. To take such awareness as failure of nerve does "Marginalia" no justice, for to reject madness is by no means to reject the power and promise of dreaming. Close reading suggests that if we take that repeated "which" in the penultimate line to refer either to voices on the rim of the abyss or to the rim itself—rather than, as some have suggested, to mean the plunge[13]—then we are still a ways from the precipice. We know from Poe's "MS." and "A Descent" that the real fall does not begin with crossing the rim, but rather nearer to the heart of the swirl. But we are not far from danger: we have our doom and its ambiguous promises, although no one alive can give us trustworthy previews of either. And like the silent, anxious phantom crew of "MS." we must still go about our daily business, not frozen with fright and extravagant hope. Faith has to be founded on one of those "centrifugal" and fleeting intuitions—or flat-out fictions—that we have found or contrived to explain the mystery, and give some provisional sense to life.

The theme of "Marginalia," that deep dreams and wakeful imaginings are far from being one and the same, enriches the common observation about Wilbur that he prefers the volatile, maculate sublime to static, unsullied beauty. To sail a difficult, doomed, yet (for the time being) steady course on the boundary waters between the waking and the hypnagogic state is, in fact, to choose a changeful and even treacherous world over timeless and inhuman perfection, for at the heart of both the world and the imagination is something whose beauty is instability itself, an endless shifting which can yield up the truly stunning intensity and the greatest hope. The world moves; the physical and natural worlds are worlds of action; the self that witnesses all is a thing of unrest too. Poe's supernal is a place of death, because it is a place where nothing happens and nothing can happen. While one may feel its attraction, no self can go there and remain a self at all.

One more poem about seas and whirlpools will help define how far Wilbur thinks one can honestly, sanely go along Poe's path toward self-obliterating transcendence. In *Things of This World*—the same volume that contains "Marginalia"—a short poem called "The Beacon" again suggests a Wilbur less confident than Poe is of deep dreams as a bridge to some immutable and absolute reality; yet this poem seems somewhat more optimistic than "Marginalia" about what can be glimpsed of subsurface truth if one can look steadily, and luckily, and imagine hard. The creative, projective powers of "our human visions"—that is, those of the sober and self-conscious mind—seem to strike vague yet telling reverberations in an autonomous order beneath or out beyond the chaotic front the world sets before our eyes. Perhaps an imagination that can resist Poe's manic and mystical extremes can indeed find its way into the odd moment of real insight:

> Then in the flashes of darkness it is all gone,
> The flung arms and the hips, meads
> And meridians, all; and the dark of the eye
> Dives for the black pearl
>
> Of the sea-in-itself. Watching the blinded waves
> Compounding their eclipse, we hear their
> Booms, rumors and guttural sucks
> Warn of the pitchy whirl
>
> At the mind's end. All of the sense of the sea
> Is veiled as voices nearly heard
> In morning sleep; nor shall we wake
> At the sea's heart. Rail

At the deaf unbeatable sea, my soul, and weep
Your Alexandrine tears, but look:
The beacon-blaze unsheathing turns
The face of darkness pale

And now with one grand chop gives clearance to
Our human visions

The whirling abyss and the sea that are for Wilbur an always-changing meld of the eternal and the temporal have, in "The Beacon," much the same paradoxical promise that they have in Poe. That paradox is stressed here by several clever ambiguities in Wilbur's diction, among them the clearest reference to the whirlpool itself. The "pitchy whirl / At the minds end," as it is called here, we may understand in any or all of several ways: "pitchy" is the tumultuous motion of the water or, as in "Marginalia," the chorus of voices with which it calls and warns, or its ultimate blackness on this black night; wordplay like this is the familiar Wilbur trademark. Likewise, "the mind's end" can be, as in Wallace Stevens's phrase, either some "end of the mind" in dreamless unconsciousness, or perhaps the limits of the mind (as in, say, Land's End), or the ultimate "end" of the mind with the end of existence.

All of this may recall "Marginalia"; but what "sense of the sea" one might make through this darkness, what hopes for ultimate order one can console oneself with at this harrowing vista seem not entirely a matter of fantasy and fictions. Wilbur's word choice is precise, and what he says is this: that the absolute is not absent but merely "veiled" beneath a disordered surface; and that the beacon of imagination (which seems to be at once human projective power and human insight) will finally come round again, "one grand chop" of its light giving hopes and visions new "clearance"—not the final ambiguity of the poem, but probably the most significant. What sort of "clearance" is this? A moment of clear, deeper insight which accordingly "clears" (or supports and welcomes) further imaginative life? Or is it "clearance" in the sense of *adequate* depth of insight, like the clearance under a low bridge, allowing us to persist for a while in feeling our way along with cautious and vigilant assurance? Unanswerable these questions may be, but the overall tone of the poem is, I think, surprisingly affirmative—and indicates greater faith in an imagination which holds to its tricky course along the edges of waking and dream, the uncharted boundary waters of imagination and cautious vigilance.

One cannot compare the sensibilities of two poets from two different ages without some speculation about the impact of their most powerful ideas on the form and substance of their art, and so far these abyss poems of Wilbur's, each something of a metaphysical treatise, are of some use in that direction. But if Poe's poetry is, as Wilbur has it, "an account of the process of aspiration, and a rationale of the soul's struggle to free itself of earth and move toward the supernal,"[14] and if such aspirations and movement are what Wilbur rejects, then beyond this dickering with Poe over the proportions and limits of such struggle, what is the motive and cue for Wilbur's own most ontological poems? Again the answer has much to do with Poe, and with a certain kinship that has gone unobserved. In the previous chapter I quoted briefly from a miscellaneous book of pronouncements by artists edited years ago by Gyorgy Kepes, a book which contains some of Wilbur's early speculations on "the essential poetic act." It is worth returning to those pronouncements now for a closer look:

> People feel a real unease and separation when confronted by the nameless, and it is perfectly understandable that the first man, set down in the centre of the first landscape, applied himself at once to redeeming it from anonymity. *What had been spoken into being he spoke again, re-creating the creation,* giving each creature a relation to himself, and gaining a kind of symbolic control over what lay around him. (Italics mine)[15]

The stressed phrases echo a familiar and crucial idea of Poe's, most memorably expressed at the climax of his curious prose allegory called "The Power of Words," in which one meets an exquisitely anguished poet-being named Agathos (some species of immortal spirit of the good) as he looks upon the fair "wild star" which he himself once "spoke . . . with a few passionate sentences—into birth" many ages before. This echo may tell us something: in Poe's universe, where the immortal may mingle so freely and devastatingly with mortal experience, the word is the potent, perilous *creative* force which the dreamer-poet shares with supernal powers. For Wilbur, the word is rather the supreme *recreative* force; "the essential poetic act" is not one with the creative powers of reality. It is a symbolic creation or rediscovery of temporal order and beauty, and just possibly, a momentary perception of something beyond temporality. For Poe, the "power of words" is enormous, very real, bewilderingly and frighteningly free of restraint. For Wilbur it is largely—but somehow not entirely—symbolic, dependent upon the imagination's constant interaction with this difficult temporal world, but possibly magical nonetheless. That is, perhaps, a most fundamental distinction to be recognized between the aesthetics of Wilbur and Poe, Wilbur and the major symbolists, Wilbur and a continuing tradition of surrender to language and dream, a distinction delicate enough and, from Wilbur's perspective, unsure enough, to warrant forty years of such compassionate quarreling.

Once we have seen how important Poe can be as teacher, adversary, and soul mate in some of Wilbur's most interesting poems, one may, if one likes, begin tallying up allusions to Poe, echoes of Poe, and hints of echoes of Poe nearly anywhere one looks in Wilbur's collections, although both the surety and the usefulness of such finds will vary. Certainly Poe does show up here and there with special impact. Wilbur's "Bell Speech," for example, is as forthright a reply as I know of, in modern verse, to Poe's "The Bells," and knowing that connection is of use in reading Wilbur's poem. No longer, "Bell Speech" seems to say, do the bells of our cities speak with the rich and varied rhetoric of old, matching their voices to each human event; their new "selfsame toothless voice" suggests to the listener some sublime "language without flaw"—an ambiguous but perhaps powerful language, able (as, for Wilbur, a real language has to be) to reshape worldly turmoil into something which, whether by prophecy or parlor magic, coheres. And quite as surely, Wilbur's contentious celebration "For the New Railway Station in Rome" takes as its foil the morbid passion for Roman ruins that Poe, and the generations that came and sighed after him, so eloquently indulges in his lyric "The Coliseum":

> Rich reliquary
> Of lofty contemplation left to Time
> By buried centuries of pomp and power!
> At length—at length—after so many days
> Of weary pilgrimage and burning thirst
> (Thirst for the springs of lore that in thee lie),
> I kneel, an altered and an humble man,
> Amid thy shadows, and so drink within
> My very soul thy grandeur, gloom, and glory!

It seems plausible that, from the evidence of his language, his expertise with Poe, and his own aesthetic concerns, Wilbur has Poe's lament in mind (for ruins that Poe had never actually seen) when, in enthusiasm for spanking-new Italian grandeur, Wilbur declares:

> Those who with short shadows
> Poked through the stubbled forum pondering on decline,
>   And would not take the sun standing at noon
>   For a good sign;

73

Those pilgrims of defeat
Who brought their injured wills as to a soldiers' home;
Dig them all up now, tell them there's something new
To see in Rome.

But what of "The Beautiful Changes," "Conjuration," The Jug-
gler," "Still, Citizen Sparrow," or many of the others? Are they not,
each in its own way, engaged with Poe's excessive taste for an unearthly
and pristine supernal? Do they not all contend somehow that the true
discovery of the wonder must include, and be based upon, worldly and
maculate experience? No doubt each of these poems could be reex-
amined with Poe in mind; what we would gain from doing so, however, is variable, and it seems better to look at a few poems in which the
rewards are important indeed.

Just as Poe, for Wilbur, is a teller of tales that are in fact symbolist
poetry, Wilbur is now and then a maker of verse tales about the pitfalls
of surrendering to dreams. Among these, "The Undead" is ostensibly
a poem about vampires—suggesting something already of Poe and his
Gothic posterity. Wilbur's are full-steam vampires, possessing many
Hollywood characteristics: "Mirrors fail to perceive them"; they take
to the air as great bats, flapping off into every night in search of human
blood. But just how these poor creatures have reached such perverse
and pathetic "grandeur" has nothing to do with vampire traditions:

Even as children they were late sleepers,
Preferring their dreams, even when quick with monsters,
To the world with all its breakable toys,
Its compacts with the dying;

From the stretched arms of withered trees
They turned, fearing contagion of the mortal,
And even under the plums of summer
Drifted like winter moons.

No contagion has taken these souls but their own bad judgment. They
have dreamed too much, chased after the supernal too hotly, and
refused any reconciliation with a mortal, natural world. Such an identity, such an idea of reality, is not so much in the usual manner of
vampires as in the manner of Poe. Wilbur's undead seem to be driven
by the fervent wish that establishes the mood of the young Poe's lyric
"Dreams":

Oh! that my young life were a lasting dream!
My spirit not awak'ning till the beam

Of an Eternity should bring the morrow.
Yes! tho' that long dream were of hopeless sorrow,
'T were better than the cold reality
Of waking life, to him whose heart must be,
And hath been still, upon the lovely earth,
A chaos of deep passion, from his birth.

That urge for "destructive transcendence" so familiar in Poe becomes, in "The Undead," the "negative frenzy" of the vampire: a
hopeless frenzy, that is, for the negation of worldly reality, of the self,
of all genuine possibilities of existence and understanding. And such
refusal leads only into pathetic paradox:

. . . Think how sad it must be
   To thirst always for a scorned elixir,
     The salt quotidian blood

   Which, if mistrusted, has no savor;
To prey on life forever and not possess it,
   As rock-hollows, tide after tide,
     Glassily strand the sea.

As ably as these closing lines capture the irony Wilbur finds at the
heart of Poe's great ambition—that to seek so fervently for transcendence and imaginative escape from worldly life is, finally, to deny the
self both transcendence *and* life—Wilbur's culminating metaphor is
itself indebted to Poe. The poetic spirit's disaster, its search for just such
immortality, and its end in an appalling stasis and eventual annihilation
constitute, as Wilbur claims, the real subject of "The City in the Sea."[16]
In Wilbur's reading, such stasis and doom are for Poe still preferable to
the mutable world, or to awareness of either scientific or divine truth.
There are lines in "The City in the Sea" from which the close of "The
Undead" may derive:

Not the gaily-jewelled dead
Tempt the waters from their bed;
For no ripples curl, alas!
Along that wilderness of glass—
No swellings tell that winds may be
Upon some far-off happier sea—
No heavings hint that winds have been
On seas less hideously serene.

When an academic writer outlines one poet's conversation with others
about poetry itself and the imagination, that conversation is likely to

75

sound flatter and more scholastic than it really is. While Richard Wilbur is serious in his quarrel with Poe—joining fun to seriousness is one of Wilbur's trademarks, and there is plenty of play in this complex, unprogrammatic dialogue about what constitutes real horror and imaginative excess. The last poem in Part I of *The Mind-Reader,* "Children of Darkness," offers a brisk counterpoint to "The Undead," for in looking hard here at woodland variations on ghouls and grotesquerie, Wilbur builds a poem that is something of a Frankenstein monster. Its body parts include material from Poe's fiction, but also from a book which is in many ways the antithetical work to Poe's in his own time, Henry Thoreau's *Walden.* "Children of Darkness" opens as a species of riddle, the "answer" being mushrooms and the ugly fungi of the spring woods:

> If groves are choirs and sanctuaried fanes,
> What have we here?
> An elm-bole cocks a bloody ear;
> In the oak's shadow lies a strew of brains.
> Wherever, after the deep rains,
>
> The woodlands are morose and reek of punk,
> These gobbets grow—
> Tongue, lobe, hand, hoof or butchered toe
> Amassing on the fallen branch half sunk
> In leaf-mold, or the riddled trunk.

From these evocations of "Black Cat" violence, the poem graduates to sex, for some of the mushrooms as "shameless phalloi rise, / To whose slimed heads come carrion flies." The end of censorship and poet prudery therefore allows Wilbur to beat Poe, for once, at the game of shock. But these lines have other ancestors. In the closing chapters of *Walden* Thoreau offers his own bizarre early spring hymn to the configurations of mud and sand as the frost boils out of the ground:

> As it flows it takes the forms of sappy leaves or vines, making heaps of pulpy sprays a foot or more in depth, and resembling, as you look down on them, the laciniated, lobed, and imbricated thalluses of some lichens; or you are reminded of coral, of leopards' paws or birds' feet, of brains or lungs or bowels, and excrements of all kinds. It is a truly *grotesque* vegetation, . . .

Thoreau gives a test here to the Emersonian principle that there is nothing in nature that strong light cannot make beautiful—which is to say, nothing that has not indwelling beauties of its own. Performing a like experiment in the same season, Wilbur assumes a viewpoint akin to the one he adopts about the vulture in "Still, Citizen Sparrow," the carrion-eater which "has heart to make an end" and "keeps nature new." "Children of Darkness" declares there is nothing frightening in these ugly, odorous, death-eating mushrooms:

> Gargoyles is what they are at worst, and should
> They preen themselves
> On being demons, ghouls, or elves,
> The holy chiaroscuro of the wood
> Still would embrace them. They are good.

One distinction has to be stressed. This closing seems something other than a magisterial refusal to accept that there is evil in the world, that there are terrors out there—or in the mind itself—which are not "gargoyles" at worst. In Wilbur's cosmology, there can be fear aplenty in a handful of dust. The premise of "Children of Darkness" is a recognition that comes in and for this moment in the spring woods, that in its abundant life there is no indwelling malice, and that Thoreau and Emerson are at least sometimes right, that some sort of good reveals itself in a straight-on gaze into nature's nightmares. Sometimes, for Richard Wilbur is a poet of particulars. His wisdom, like Thoreau's before him, is wisdom inseparable from experience, from specific places and times and recollections. This quarrel of Wilbur's is never prosecuted in bumper stickers, in adages for all weathers and seasons of the self. And in fact that insistence in Richard Wilbur's poems on the particularity of wisdom, on the contingency of perception, seems much more at the heart of his quarrel with Poe than the complex benignity of mushrooms, rot, or natural death.

It is true that Wilbur's "Merlin Enthralled" once again uses the motif of "hideously serene" waters to signify the price of complete surrender to deep dream; but the poem's interest goes far beyond that similarity. For not merely does "Merlin Enthralled" meditate on the end of a great artist, and the fate of his art in the triumph of dreaming and what lies at its other shore, the black of oblivious sleep; the poem also celebrates the power and excitement that the dreaming conscious-ness can achieve—so long as the dreamer-artist maintains some grip against the utter erosion of the waking, reasoning, controlling, none-too-trusting side of the mind. And "Merlin Enthralled" provides something of an explanation, in fact, of how the art of one like Poe can be for Wilbur both "grand" and "impoverished" at the same time. In the poem Merlin's great art is Camelot itself, created entirely out of Merlin's ingenious and daring wakeful dream, wonderful and alive because his imagination in creating Arthur and his near-perfect world has sought no self-loss in the trap of the supernal. But as the poem opens, Merlin has succumbed to the lure of Niniane the nymph, born herself of his dreaming imagination and embodying its perils; beyond the hypnagogic state, beyond even the "deep transparent dream," lies the temptation to ultimate oblivion.[17] So far, that line of thinking seems familiar. But what is to become of the living art? Vital and meaningful so long as Merlin neither sought nor found his destructive transcendence, Camelot can no longer be the continuing celebration of growth and change and life. Its fate, without the controlling, understanding, selflessly vigilant imagination, is to become like some quaint relic, the static leavings of a mind which has foregone it, and the kind of melded sensibility upon which it has survived. Surely this art has its magnificence, which can be recalled, honored, preserved—but there will be no more of it from a mind which has moved so far. As the dreaming, creating consciousness passes through the real world on its way into deeper reverie, it may both triumph and defeat itself in the creation of the sublime, as the astonishing conclusion to the poem would have us understand of both Camelot and its wizard:

Arthur upon the road began to weep
And said to Gawen *Remember when this hand*

Once haled a sword from stone; now no less strong
It cannot dream of such a thing to do.
Their mail grew quainter as they clopped along.
The sky became a still and woven blue.   (Emphasis Wilbur's)

Again, this is a moving poem, a reflection about consciousness and its relation to time, history, art; it is not just a cautionary tale about when to come back from dreamland. But the works I have looked at so far in this chapter all have an air of warning to them; is there another side of the coin? In other words, does Wilbur ever see a price to be paid for the aesthetic and visionary stance that he himself, as Wilbur, not Poe, struggles to maintain? Or should one agree with his detractors that Wilbur has, after all, settled for a suspiciously safe and comfortable place of resistance to aesthetic and visionary excess? For an answer to those questions, one can turn to one of Wilbur's longer and darker poems, called "Beowulf," which seems a very important as well as a splendidly atmospheric poem, a retelling of the epic story with brevity, dignity, and power; and at the same time, I think, an insight into the loneliness that comes to precisely the sensibility that Wilbur himself upholds against a world's prevailing taste for one destructive and self-destructive spiritual excess after another.

A case that one should read "Beowulf" as a poem of Wilbur's own condition, or rather of his plight and the plight of anyone who would follow the changing, subtle edges between waking and dream, is founded in the symbolic shape and look of the poem, a shape and a look comprehensible in light of the rest of his poetry, his opinions on Poe, and the fact that the poem will not make much sense any other way. Consider, for example, the Denmark we are landed upon in the opening stanza:

> The land was overmuch like scenery,
> The flowers attentive, the grass too garrulous green;
> In the lake like a dropped kerchief could be seen
> The lark's reflection after the lark was gone;
> The Roman road lay paved too shiningly
> For a road so many men had traveled on.

How understand such a place, no quality of which we recognize from the text of the original epic, except as a world of excessive and perverse dream, a world where imagination, trusted too blindly, has led the inhabitants into dreams which have turned toward nightmare? Indeed, in these "garrulous green," all-too-scenic landscapes Wilbur finds alarming evidence that the rampant dream is poised to betray and undo the unwitting dreamer. He inveighs against such mind landscapes forthrightly in "Walking to Sleep," a long poem which is, in some ways, an extensive, illustrated field guide to survival in the hypnagogic state:

> Let them not be too velvet green, the fields
> Which the deft needle of your eye appoints,
> Nor the old farm past which you make your way
> Too shady-linteled, too instinct with home.
> It is precisely from Potemkin barns
> With their fresh-painted hex signs on the gables,
> Their sparkling gloom within, their stanchion-rattle
> And sweet breath of silage, that there comes
> The trotting cat whose head is but a skull.

To this perverse and haunted world, this land "childish" not merely in its obsessions with dream and nightmare but also in that the monster which besets them is a "child" of those too-free fantasies, comes Beowulf, as a champion fit to do battle with a nightmare. Beowulf, as we come to know him here, has sailed long upon the changing seas of mind and experience. His greatest power is his caution and his self-possession as a visionary, allowing him at once to enter a dream and combat its own allurement and power. In short, Beowulf is himself a dreamer. The difference is that he is wise and wakeful enough

79

not to dream overmuch. Unlike the Danes, therefore, who "wander" to sleep helplessly and leave their defender to fight alone, Beowulf yields to no master in the hypnagogic state; he may pass on through its nightmares to a "rest so deep" as to be open only to those who are both visionary and self-possessed human beings:

> It was a childish country; and a child,
> Grown monstrous, so besieged them in the night
> That all their daytimes were a dream of fright
> That it would come and own them to the bone.
> The hero, to his battle reconciled,
> Promised to meet that monster all alone.

> So then the people wandered to their sleep
> And left him standing in the echoed hall.
> They heard the rafters rattle fit to fall,
> The child departing with a broken groan,
> And found their champion in a rest so deep
> His head lay harder sealed than any stone.

All seems to be well with Beowulf, having freed a world of its own imaginings gone wild, and maintained through thick and thin his own strong but carefully governed imagination. Yet the poem now takes a painfully ironic turn, revealing the predicament which Beowulf (and by inference, the poet who compassionately imagines him) must share with the likes of Poe, quarrel as they might about the aspirations of the mind. Able to sleep sound again without monsters crashing about in their dreams, these Danes now decide that they have had too much of visions of any sort—and so, true men that they are, they swing to an opposite excess. Beowulf's hosts now put on an aesthetic coldness which suspects all imagining; a soulless, passionless, hopeless stance which makes the hero himself the exiled dreamer, embodying the imagination's threat to sanity; and Beowulf finds himself now quite alone, like one of Poe's wandering, solitary, visionary knights:

> The land was overmuch like scenery,
> The lake gave up the lark, but now its song
> Fell to no ear, the flowers too were wrong,
> The day was fresh and pale and swifly old,
> The night put out no smiles upon the sea;
> And the people were strange, the people strangely cold.

> They gave him horse and harness, helmet and mail,
> A jeweled shield, an ancient battle-sword,

Such gifts as are the hero's hard reward
And bid him do again what he has done.
These things he stowed beneath his parting sail,
And wept that he could share them with no son.

For his victory, Beowulf receives his "hard reward," the play upon
words working in every possible way. It is a hard-won reward, of a
hard material nature, itself soulless and bestowed by hardened, cold
folk who now wish to be rid of him. Beowulf's complex sensibility is
and will ever be such that few around him will understand, and fewer
still will try to emulate. And so the life and death of this hero are
touched with pathos as well as victorious joy, with isolation as well as
with the sublime. The poem closes with such stateliness and compassion that, knowing what we do of Wilbur's struggles to maintain a hard
place amid a world which does not well understand his task, we cannot
but be more convinced that Wilbur's Beowulf is one in whom Wilbur
senses something of himself, or anyone who tries now to keep his or
her own best balance between lethal extremes:

He died in his own country a kinless king,
A name heavy with deeds, and mourned as one
Will mourn for the frozen year when it is done.
They buried him next the sea on a thrust of land:
Twelve men rode round his barrow all in a ring,
Singing of him what they could understand.

All that Beowulf has done is touched with ocean, yet in his death
as in his life, he remains on the lonely shore of what he knows. In years
which can seem, like these Danes, to clamor for honesty yet suspect it if
it be not utterly bleak, which clamor for visions and suspect them if
they be not tinged with madness, Wilbur strives to be an artist of both
intense imagination and human self-possession. He is a poet laboring
to speak to people, to speak to an age which can despair of the power
of imaginative flight. On difficult edges and margins, Wilbur seeks
ways to recover the freshness of experience, to stun and stretch our
awareness without seducing or blinding it, to have us feel as the first
language-maker felt, awed and compelled to speech in Wilbur's myth
of the first poem. In his quest for fleeting moments of "symbolic
control," and in his recognition of ourselves as watchful, unsatisfied
creatures, Wilbur creates a beauty and a vision which can seem true
even to a troubled modern spirit, and can excite even a late-century
imagination.

4. Longer Poems

B ECAUSE the short lyric is Wilbur's preferred form, the few poems which run to more than fifty lines stand out, hinting of some special intent. Even these long poems are not long by either traditional or contemporary standards; few of them run beyond the shortest of the *Four Quartets,* or Stevens's "Comedian as the Letter C," to say nothing of *Paterson,* or *Howl,* or many other expansive and treasured works in the American canon of this century. It would be tidy to trace Wilbur's habit of brevity back to some lesson learned from Poe, namely the famous principle advanced in "The Philosophy of Composition," that intense poems should heed the ravages of interrupted reading and the restless consciousness of the modern reader, and should therefore run their course in one sitting. But a better guess lies in a different direction. Wilbur's poetry is a poetry of transforming moments and momentary transformations: classic Wilbur is a boy's ten seconds of dizziness after digging a deep hole on a hot morning, or a half-asleep sensibility "seeing" angels dancing for an instant on the laundry line outside a bedroom window. Driven underground by bright-light rationalism, ponderous fact, and the fiercely skeptical instincts of postmodernity, the intractable human imagination endures like some endangered predator by making sudden forays against the sober, school-taught, suspicious self. Moods and small epiphanies come and go—mostly they go—and out of the range of them the contemporary consciousness might never achieve any lasting transcendental wisdom, nor plausible, hard-wearing metaphors for the cycles of history, for noumenal realities, or for the holiness or godlessness of human experience. From instant to hopeful instant, one has to feel one's way along; and so poems which struggle to work out something, moving with evident labor and pain from perception to prophecy, and arriving at last at ambitious pronouncements on human experience or the poet's art itself—such poems would seem philosophically and temperamentally out of Richard Wilbur's line.

Even so, scattered through the Wilbur collections are poems different from the others in their sheer extent and in their evident ambitions. As far as I can tell they have never been anthologized together or discussed as a group, as longer poems of Eliot, Pound, Bishop, Rich, and Ashbery are sometimes gathered and offered to the reading public as heavy lessons in an artist's or an age's ethos and voice. For in Wilbur's longer poems other and surprising Richard Wilburs seem to turn up, different from those who present themselves elsewhere. These poems do not define the sensibility so much as extend it, or even at times escape from it; abandoning Wilbur's celebrated compression, they can narrate, even meander; they can assume strange voices. With stubbornness they may probe recent history in its ugliest shape; sometimes they ruminate on difficult and dangerous problems of seeing and knowing. One quality, however, seems evident in most of these poems: that read more or less on its own, each transfigures the portrait of this poet, and thus seems to run counter to modern and postmodern assumptions about the long poem as work which *culminates* discourse, rather than alters it radically. Of course these poems cannot and should not be looked at by themselves, as they do depend heavily on a context of other verse—Wilbur's and other people's—to give them sense and proportion, and to set them in bold relief. These longer poems are problem poems in several ways, and to read them requires a process of closing in.

The 143-line poem "Walking to Sleep" gives its name to the substantial 1968 collection—in which this title work is placed near the end. And what comes before it has been, generally speaking, vigilant, precise, and eminently finished: every preceding poem has evidently "arrived" somewhere. "Seed Leaves" has said astute things about Frost and his differences from Wilbur's sensibility; "In a Churchyard," the anxious dialogue with Gray and the suspicious, wonderful process of English and American elegies, disturbs in measured ways; "Complaint" seems a gracious, tranquil, and antique form, a playful dispute with the muse of poetry, a comic plea in Renaissance dress and adorned with courtly-love conceits. After all that, one can understand why "Walking to Sleep" has caused critics to hang fire.[1] It seems ungainly, blurry; it does not seem to arrive anywhere, and two-thirds of the way along it offers some very odd lines, given that Wilbur is not known as a poet who makes open war on the importance of his own discourse:

> What, are you still awake?
> Then you must risk another tack and footing.
> Forget what I have said.

And there the poem apparently starts over again. Other lines also stand out incongruously in a poem woven of incongruities:

>   Your concern
> Is not to be detained by dread, or by
> Such dear acceptances as would entail it,
> But to pursue an ever-dimming course
> Of pure transition, . . .

It is fair to say that "transition" is a watchword for this long poem. The dream show which follows this passage, the hallucinations that will not keep still, and the experiences that flow into each other in ways that are not quite senseless, focus attention on what we now like to call process. But picking out the poem's chief conceit explains only weakly the mysterious tone of "Walking to Sleep." If this poem delicately presents an anomalous condition, of freedom in and from the imagination, then the cool, witty tone which overlies this poem's surface, and its apparently bemused way of looking skeptically on the very advice it offers, are potentially two paradoxes too many. Again, one can contrive an excuse: the trick to maintaining this suspended state, between too much control over the imaginative faculty and too much surrender to it, lies in *not* knowing where one is, psychologically, epistemologically, and tonally. Yet that may infer too much "management" in a poem which supposedly has something to do with the wilderness of the hypnagogic state, and which nonetheless celebrates the improvisations and open-endedness of the erring mind. Forget what I too have said: more may be at stake in "Walking to Sleep" than this. It is well to take a breath, begin at the beginning, and find the poem's concealed voices, and its larger, darker, and better resonances.

"Walking to Sleep" opens with one of those glint-in-the-eye advisories which one might associate with Frost; yet seriously or in jest, Frost never suggests such a journey as this, entirely out of the natural and waking world, and the instruction to "Step off assuredly into the blank of your mind" seems to reject Wilbur's imaginative praxis in the poems that come before this one in the book. Our old friend Poe certainly has the sensibility for stepping off assuredly into perilous reverie, but Wilbur has always done that sort of thing more cautiously, and in that difference, as we have seen, lies some of the quarrel which Wilbur has urged between them. The escape word from this apparent paradox might be *blank:* perhaps one can safely voyage off into the unconscious, the hallucination, the supernal, or the nightmare, if one is sufficiently tired, or indifferent, or merely stupid enough to stay out of danger. But no mind can stay blank for long, and these wry opening lines give little hint whether this anomalous condition of mind is to be sounded, celebrated, satirized—or sought for in vain. In other words, is all this going to turn visionary, or mock-visionary, or take some other path? Is this to be an encounter with some Wilbur voice other than the ones we know, or a lesson against unwavering rationalism and refusals to "cut loose"? The opening similes are apt bits of observation, ambiguous in their feel:

> As a queen sits down, knowing that a chair will be there,
> Or a general raises his hand and is given the field-glasses

In both these lines, something grand and something banal or even lu-dicrous are mixed; and in a parallel way, the initially crisp five-stress meter seems to go soft as each line finishes up. In beginning to sit down where there may be no chair at all—yet—a queen gracefully and si-lently asserts her authority, and at the same time she risks a pratfall, trusting as she does not only to the loyalty but to the agility and vig-ilance of her retainers. The metaphor may have a grand air to it, but a comic one too. "Potemkin barns," in line fifteen, replies to this opening verse, recalling that even powerful queens, who can sit down wherever they like, nonetheless can be profoundly hoodwinked, as Potemkin's fake towns fooled the Empress of All the Russias. The second line's shift to the "organizational behavior" of staff officers amounts to a quick drop toward the prosaic, enhanced by the ordinariness of language in both of these verses. If this opening affirms in some manner the sov-ereignty of self, there is no hint thus far whether these confident ven-tures of the mind are sublime or ridiculous—or whether the very wish of the dreaming consciousness to discriminate *between* the sublime and the absurd, in voyages into the unconscious mind, is absurd in itself.

After the first of the poem's short rhapsodies of dream mixing and melding, during which the blank of the mind fills, as a matter of course, with landscapes from the id, or the noumenal, or someplace else, "Walking to Sleep" launches into an extended warning label, which seems as dubiously earnest as the poem's beginning. Counsel like this, to dream half-awake, with "numb and grudging circumspec-tion . . . unless you overdo it," amounts to a kind of bear-market romanticism. Offering complex instruction in the craft of irrationality, these verses are laced or land-mined with half-jokes, sustaining the *un*certainty as to whether any of this counsel is seriously proffered or no. This bit of finger wagging—

> Try to remember this: what you project
> Is what you will perceive; what you perceive
> With any passion, be it love or terror,
> May take on whims and powers of its own.

85

—may speak in psychoanalytic or mystical commonplaces, but these verses also seem a parody of lines they recall from Wordsworth, the lines from "Tintern Abbey" which define the essential poetic act for him, for other Romantics, and for many poets since:

> Therefore am I still
> A lover of the meadows and the woods,
> And mountains; and of all that we behold
> From this green earth; of all the mighty world
> Of eye, and ear,—both what they half create,
> And what perceive; well pleased to recognise
> In nature and the language of the sense,
> The anchor of my purest thoughts, the nurse,
> The guide, the guardian of my heart, and soul
> Of all my moral being.

"Walking to Sleep"'s apparent caution against Wordsworthian optimism evades a deeper mystery: if the self cannot be anchored somehow by the interaction of imagination and sensory experience, then who is this "you" that is doing all this vivid hypnagogic perceiving and projecting? Something at the core of the self? Some indwelling otherness, monstrous and destructive? Some elusive *part* of the self, perhaps, in better tune with the truth than "you" are, wakeful or not? And there is always the other, consummately postmodern possibility, that there is no "you" at all, only an array of cultural habits willed or fooled into some travesty of specialness and form. Well, which shall it be? The way out of the dilemma—or perhaps deeper into it—lies through the amusing and unsettling image that comes next, again couched in words characteristically bald, for this poem, yet out of character for Wilbur's work:

> What you must manage is to bring to mind
> A landscape not worth looking at, some bleak
> Champaign at dead November's end, its grass
> As dry as lichen, and its lichens grey,
> Such glumly simple country that a glance
> Of flat indifference from time to time
> Will stabilize it.

The comic edge to this first: it might be that *Champaign* is capitalized here not merely through the luck of occurring at the start of a line, and that there is a joke of sorts, rather than just a flourish of diction. Having lately been on the national reading circuit, Wilbur had seen this Illinois college town up close—and this line may work as another small double entendre, about the late November look of one generic midwestern city, and perhaps also about the walking sleep of daily experience, including the catatonic life of poets on tour through the academic cornfields. There are plenty of dull dreamscapes out there, complete and ready-to-wear; and one can indeed cultivate such stupefying reveries without much imaginative energy or originality. Yet "champaign," with no capital *C,* has other, richer associations: it was, for instance, a favorite word of Thomas Hardy, who found power and strange dualities in it as he described the empty yet evocative heaths of his county of Wessex, a landscape both drab and magical, pregnant with significations, but charged also with that condition of culture and mind which in one unforgettable sentence he called "unhope."

The champaign or Champaign dreamscape forces into the open the droll, disturbing question which shadows this section: what good to anyone is a crash course in drab, sedate imaginings? The ostensible reason, that such practices will coax one onward into nightmare-less sleep, makes little sense as the stuff of poetry; the poem portrays sanity itself as an uneasy balance, cautious patrols in disputed zones between mundanity and dullness on one side, horrors on the other. There are mustering reasons, in other words, for thinking of "Walking to Sleep" as Richard Wilbur's "Skunk Hour," his look into ways that the mind hangs on, by trickery and luck, to its composure on the edge of madness—were the poem not so patently or damnably witty at every second turn. Among these plausible snippets of nightmare are exquisitely ludicrous lines that read as if filched from a federal how-to manual:

> Should that occur, adjust to circumstances
> And carry on, taking these few precautions:
>
> . . . .
>
> Regardless of its seeming size, or what
> May first impress you as its style or function,
> The abrupt structure which involves you now
> Will improvise like vapor.

These verses seem flat, and one wants better reasons why than some excuse about tonal dislocations to match imaginative ones. Possibly what is parodied here is didacticism itself, the comfortable idea that there are any ground rules for holding at bay whatever monsters our reveries and sixth-sense experience of life deliver to us, that there are easy, impartable ways for "coping," as the saying goes, with imaginative predicaments. This ungainly advice may militate against advice about consciousness itself—and the hallucinations interspersed among these clumsy verses have much the same effect. They are good night-mares, delivered with economy, speed, and accuracy; idiosyncratic but eerily familiar, they take us straight to where we are not supposed to go—while they imply that our solicitous and variously sane and sober narrator has gone over his own edge again and again.

Thus one approaches a center of humanity in "Walking to Sleep," approaches its completeness as an imagining of the hypnagogic state in both its timeless and culture-dependent forms, and its manifold and bizarre status in the modern self. Like some of these lines, the culture may have grown wise or patronizing in its talk about its own dreams—and for all that, it knows little about what value to assign to intense, personal imaginative experience. Wordsworth, Keats, Freud, Poe, and perhaps even Lady Macbeth: the hopes, the terrors, the clinical sup-positions seem to fold together here, or rather to meld and compose some comprehensive and paradoxical description of what it is to feel the power of dream, and to try, without absolute success, to achieve some relationship to it.

The latter half of "Walking to Sleep" has many wonderful images, every one of which is injured when talked about alone, for despite their brilliance by themselves, the conjoining and the clashing of these moments make for the haunting effect. How could a poem which builds or dives to a disruptively comic image like this—

> . . . pursue an ever-dimming course
> Of pure transition, treading as in water
> Past crumbling tufa, down cloacal halls
> Of boarded-up hotels, through attics full
> Of glassy taxidermy, moping on
> Like a drugged fire-inspector.

—recover its composure, or rather lose it again, in a refreshed, roman-tic evocation of dreams and their wonderful and sinister possibilities? As he does for the crucial image of "All That Is," Wilbur reaches out beyond the Western tradition to bring this recovery about:

> Still, if you are in luck, you may be granted,
> As, inland, one can sometimes smell the sea,
> A moment's perfect carelessness, in which
> To stumble a few steps and sink to sleep
> In the same clearing where, in the old story,
> A holy man discovered Vishnu sleeping,
> Wrapped in his maya, dreaming by a pool
> On whose calm face all images whatever
> Lay clear, unfathomed, taken as they came.

88

Taken as they came—but what does that mean? Not perfect rationality, surely, nor even calm, perhaps. The dreamworld is not a measurable basement of an inspectable house; the self can neither command the imagination, succumb to it, trust it, dismiss it, nor mechanically work out one of those "balances" with which Wilbur is sometimes miscredited. The "advice" of "Walking to Sleep" is not to go mad, and not to go sane, and not to listen to any advice but some indwelling, self-conserving ground sense that is or is not there to begin with, or which comes—how? Perhaps as grace comes: when the psyche can welcome it, though its advent can neither be compelled nor foretold.

And so by a process of turn and turn again, of reason and dream and urbane wit uneasily indulged, "Walking to Sleep" finds its way to a state of mind that is and is not tenable, does and does not make sense, bring peace, or console. One might recall more validly now Lowell's back-steps condition at the very end of "Skunk Hour," or Bishop's turmoiled serenity before her absurd, portentous wooden "Monument" that does and does not defy the erosions of time and its own anonymity. Neither temperament nor rhetorical nor intellectual style can reduce the mystery of the imagination's consequence, define or validate the act of poetry better for our time, or make easy equations from the quandaries of selfhood. There is no dearth of disordered poems about the multiplicity of the self and the uncertain shape and value of experience; there are few, however, which also express well the enduring presence—wise, foolish, courageous, craven, or whatever—of intelligence, composure, humor, and unextinguished light.

I have made a case that "Walking to Sleep" is about something difficult and important, the shifting relationship of the self to its own imaginative life. To examine now any poem on a more bounded subject must seem like a move downhill. On paper, at least, a summary of what "The Agent" is "about" would make it seem a work in the same league. The telling differences, however, are that in "The Agent" the analytical distance is maintained straight through, that Wilbur does not seem drawn here into the whirlpool of his own imaginative constructs, and that those constructs seem to come all from the same file of modern history and popular culture. "The Agent" anchors a trio of poems in the "Thyme" section of *Walking to Sleep:* their shared subject is self-loss in imaginative habit rather than imaginative free rein, and as such they seem a kind of counterweight to Wilbur's long poem on dreaming abjectly and giving way to the Poe forces within. One of the poems in this set, "The Mechanist," is a symbolist glimpse at a new-style techno-vulgarian who reduces all experience to his own drab terms of weight and measure, the closing paradox being that in a dark inversion of a Stevens premise, the world itself may be changed for the worse by the way such people gaze at it. In a similar vein, "Playboy" is a light, good-humored poem about the confounding of love and beauty by lust, dreams of power, and corrupted art. In a stockroom, a goldbricking adolescent gawks at a *Playboy* magazine foldout, and everything goes wrong; the fantasy of manhood is a fantasy of domin- ion, of exploitation, of woman as yet another mass-marketed Ameri- can commodity. The poem is not tragic or darkly prophetic, for the boy (who is not explored as a character) might eventually escape the musty warehouse of his own mind when he grows up a bit and his hormones cool. But the theme once more is psychological fixity, the lost or diminished flex and beauty of consciousness, when brutal and contrived externality wars upon it for too long. These poems are short satires, somewhat facile and brittle, and "The Agent" has work to do, to give dignity and purpose to this array of poems about pernicious mentalities walking the streets of our Thyme-time, making and con- suming the popular culture, intruding into public life, leering at the world's fragile beauty.

"The Agent" has distinguished kin, which prove that this kind of narrative, an abstractified story-poem about familiar yet nameless modern catastrophes, can be very fine: written around the same time, Anthony Hecht's " 'Behold the Lilies of the Field' " similarly blurs time and place, variously understates and dramatizes to make an ancient, forgotten atrocity (the humiliation and flaying of the Emperor Valerian by the Sassanid king Shapur I) an event which succeeds in shocking us, not only with horror but also with embarrassment, for this poem plays hard on the cynical, impotent acceptance of the barbarity in every blessed human day.[2] In Wilbur's poem, a meticulously coached and remanufactured someone has been parachuted into the pastoral heart of an unspecified, apparently peaceful country, which seems to be some- where around the Elbe: it could be Czechoslovakia, or Poland, or a Baltic state overrun by Stalin, any place that has suffered a like disaster in the last seventy years. To gain every advantage—apparently he has spent years rising to high rank in the local army—this infiltrator has given everything up, including himself. Taking up new language, new folkways, immersing himself in the life and the psychology of the people he schemes to betray, he has forgotten where he has stashed his real identity, and his apparently permanent self-loss matters more here than the onslaught which dooms the nation.

Wilbur's narrative of that attack is skillful, suggesting not only the grainy nightmare of old war newsreels, or details of combat and the sweep of armies as he knew them, but also the eerie mix of sick fulfillment and cold alienation in the agent's mind as he watches the

moment he has spent so much time and life working for—his country-
men bearing down upon the capital of the place that has taken him in:

> But now a torn
> Blare, like the clearing of a monstrous throat,
> Rolls from those fields which vanish toward the border;
> Dark tanks and half-tracks come, breasting the wheat,
> And after them, in combat scatterment,
> Dark infantry. He can already spy
> Their cold familiar eyes, their bodies heavy
> With the bulk foods of home, and so remembers
> A gravel playground full of lonely wind,
> The warmth of a wet bed. How hard it is,
> He thinks, to be cheated of a fated life
> In a deep *patria,* and so to be
> A foundling never lost, a pure impostor
> Faithless to everything.

One of the potent effects of the poem lies in this assault of the massive,
"bulk" indefinite, for it plays off against the mild but pervasive defi-
niteness about the invaded place: the change from peace to war, from
culture to occupied, overrun country, is a change from color to black
and white, from sharp focus to blur. The contrasting passages are a
picture-show of foreground details, florid postcards of an old land one
cannot quite identify:

> Hid under hay, he listened to the ching
> Of harness and the sound of rim-struck stones.
> And then that train-ride!—all compartments filled
> With folk returning from the holiday,
> From bonfire-jumping, dancing in a round,
> And tying amulets of mistletoe.
> Like some collector steeped in catalogues
> Who finds at last in some dim shop or attic
> A Martinique *tête-bêche* imperforate
> Or still unbroken egg by Fabergé,
> He took possession, prizing the foreknown
> Half-Tartar eyes, the slurring of the schwa,
> The braids and lederhosen, and the near-
> Telepathy of shrugs and eyebrow-cockings
> In which the nuance of their speeches lay.

Subtle as the waves of bombers, an idea that sweeps over the poem is
this: that by transforming or counterfeiting himself so utterly and long,
this agent has sentenced himself to inescapable nonexistence, not only

as a citizen, but also as a self. Whether or not his own advancing troops will shoot him, as he fears, in a sense matters not at all, for we see him not as a human being with a personality and full emotional range. He is a distant, anomalous creature, whose identity has already been self-scrambled to the point of abolition: "a pure impostor / Faithless to everything."

All this is potentially rich material: this is modern, anticulture, one-dimensional man, the totalitarian-bureaucratic mind, the organizational man-creature all in one; and to some degree the Agent is anyone who subordinates the true self and will for the advancement of petty or large-scale design. This is also the stuff of movies, particularly the infiltrator films of the sixties when Wilbur wrote this. One thinks of Jack Hawkins in *The Two-Headed Spy,* Oskar Werner in *Decision before Dawn,* William Holden in *The Counterfeit Traitor,* and so on—all agents on *our* side, opposing the totalitarian aggressors themselves. None of these films offers much character development beyond a desire to do good, strike a blow for justice, family, democracy—and so the psychological price of being such a spy is hardly an overworked theme. But the gross circumstances are, and the poem does not seem to establish itself sufficiently as something really different from the Hollywood line. The man who has become nothing is troubling, yet not much more than that, the paradox being that his nonexistence, his "fuddled lostness," impersonalizes him so much as to make the poem itself seem cool abstraction; and the very fact that the moment is sensational, the Hollywood climax of such spy stories, also seems to interfere with a sense that the agent, though not a man of this people or that, is nonetheless one of *us:*

> An ill thought strikes him:
> What if these soldiers, through some chance or blunder,
> Have not been briefed about him and his mission?
> What will they make of him—a nervous man
> In farmer's costume, speaking a precious accent,
> Who cannot name the streets of his own town?
> Would they not, after all, be right to shoot him?
> He shrinks against a trunk and waits to see.

The effect of the closing is irony, not suspense, and this is drier, grimmer irony than one might expect from such a poet. Wilbur is surely within his rights to speak in a Vietnam era mood, yet it is the basic conception of "The Agent," rather than the mood, which causes difficulty. Wilbur strikes another blow for culture here, and for the value of everyday experience—another affirmation that our selves are given shape and sustained by the small particulars of place, language, friends, much that is often ignored in intellectualized constructs of identity; beyond that, the poem seems to resonate only with the thud of bombs falling on distant, nameless towns. It is contemporary, and it rings true, and good poems about the onward sweep of bureaucratized totalitarianism and life in regulated, cultureless superstates comprise a shorter list than such urgencies seem to demand, perhaps because over the past sixty years the sentiments of some of our best poets have, for a time, been wooed to other sides. Oddly enough, the limited resonance of "The Agent" might have to do with a diminished power of poetry itself, as we have refashioned the genre and read it in this century, to face such menace to the poetic sensibility as Wilbur identifies here.

I think Wilbur has much more success with "On the Marginal Way," which is placed a few pages before in the same volume, among a set of nature meditations titled "In the Field". There are contexts and overshadowing precedents to contend with here too, for this is a beach poem, and though there are many such, "On the Marginal Way" seems to reckon with the most famous of the mode. "Dover Beach" is among a handful of poems that seem to survive any anthological winnowing when the motive is to find an eloquent center of the Victorian temper and keys to origins of the modern voice. Friends tell me that "the" Marginal Way is a popular walk by the ocean's edge near Ogunquit, Maine, and that this tourist spot is probably what Wilbur has in mind here. But Matthew Arnold, on the other side of the water, still has to be reckoned with, as he is arguably the grand master of seaside meditations—an important someone for any latter-day beach monologue to address, and perhaps of necessity ease or force out of the way, especially when some of the themes are similar. They certainly are here: the grand and small motions of time and nature, the uncertain witness of the cosmos to human suffering, the dubious battle of contemporary experience. In poetry, and certainly in the visual arts since Monet and Winslow Homer, the shore has been made a place apart from narrow topicality, where the worldly mess farther inland, if it obtrudes at all, does so abstractly, with diminished force; and the cadence of wind and wave offer advantages for making slow, thoughtful, and even melancholy art. But one evident danger about beach monologues is triteness, some failure to budge Arnold, or the bad paintings and the banal greeting cards that have come before and since. Can anything fresh be said from this much-visited inspiration point?

One interesting quality of "On the Marginal Way" is that at first it seems a little jaded, a little weary of looking at sea and shore—and then surprised that one can still be surprised by one more stretch of it. The speaker is caught off guard by the first reflex of his own conscious-ness—and right away the poem moves wryly into new territory:

> Another cove of shale,
> But the beach here is rubbled with strange rock
>   That is sleek, fluent, and taffy-pale.
> I stare, reminded with a little shock
> How, by a shore in Spain, George Borrow saw
> A hundred women basking in the raw.

This does not seem like something that would have occurred to Ar-nold; and in a sense George Borrow, Victorian missionary, tourist, writer of loose and baggy adventure novels, is here as a stand-in for Arnold himself, in that Borrow seems to represent (ready for breezy Borrowing) an imagination lively and unpredictable and pious—a rich sensibility which is not yet balked and "freighted" by insistent visual experiences and metaphors of later days. Borrow roams the imagina-tive universe offered him by his time as we must roam ours: even his id has a nineteenth-century academic sanction to it. His dream of a hun-dred naked women has the ponderous, opulent, innocent quality of a mannered painting by, say, Ingres, whose legions of golden-toned Ottoman nudes seem now as droll as they do exotic or pornographic. And Borrow's immunity to this "too abundant view" has a comic quality of its own: the fly's-eye reference makes him seem more defi-cient in hormones or psychological makeup than saintly in spirit.[3]

But beyond the joke at the missionary's expense, and at the ex-pense of outmoded styles of lust, the implication seems to be that to every age there are temptations, perils especially right for each time and mind—and that while it is safe and amusing for a contemporary self to glimpse this "strange rock" of a world through the vision of someone long gone, the challenge is different when one takes the responsibility of seeing for oneself, as someone with the imaginative burdens of now. That implication builds as the poem moves diffidently forward in time, toward the present rather than directly to it. The third and fourth stanzas seem to hesitate all over the place, the language turning vaguer, disordered, as well as repetitious: we have "some" twice, "murdered" twice, "anyhow" used in a way to suggest careless speech and labored rhyme as much as scattered bodies. Even the fine-art reference seems odd, and perhaps wrong: this panoramically conceived desert-town massacre smacks more of Delacroix than Géricault, whose masterwork features dead and dying western Europeans, not vistas of battle-killed Arabs and Greeks, and nothing in the way of rape. There might be some stylistic advantages here to saying "Géricault" instead: his name sounds better in the line, and his dead look considerably deader—but these are feeble excuses for such a choice. Something more is afoot. The conflation or confounding of these artists is not like Keats's notorious "stout Cortez" mistake, for were the voice of this poem to slip deftly onward here to Delacroix, there would be altogether too much serenity in these verses. The sensibility of "On the Marginal Way" is moving hesitantly toward some recognition already lurking in the unconscious—and connoisseurship *cannot* do the job of keeping that recognition away or making it tractable. Géricault's holocaust is the real thing; Delacroix's is not—and any confusion among painters here suggests consciousness in the process of caving in to terrible memories, to what we all must remember now in ways too hideously serene. The rose-colored light quickly fails, and the compelled remembrance overcomes the art-critic rationality, unleashing mental images that not even half-mad Géricault could imagine. Here is "shade" again, a word Wilbur often experiments with: shade as diminishing light, as further darkening of the spirits, as the common shade or ghost of all these dead, who grow more real by the second—yet the mundanity of this language choice (Wilbur has used "shade" this way in poems as far back as "The Regatta") may signify a giving up, for a while, of decorous talk or tactful allusion. What has been submerged in the consciousness now rises to the surface, breaking free of Victorian decorum, of the mannerisms of art, of the restraints of poetry, of the fragile barriers that protect sanity and the continuance of imagining:

> But now the vision of a colder lust
> Clears, as the wind goes chill and all is greyed
> By a swift cloud that drags a carrion shade.
>
>   If these are bodies still,
> Theirs is a death too dead to look asleep,
>   Like that of Auschwitz' final kill,
> Poor slaty flesh abandoned in a heap
> And then, like sea-rocks buried by a wave,
> Bulldozed at last into a common grave.

Now all of this began with some rocks, and the poem's leap to Auschwitz is a dangerous move for several reasons. When some tally is made of the worst excesses of postwar poetry, the facile evocation of the Holocaust as metaphor, say, for adolescent pain or suburban neurosis, might count heavily. This poem has some explaining to do of its own state of mind and of itself as a poem of these years. One does not think of Wilbur thinking of Auschwitz. The ugliness that he has seen he usually talks about more obliquely, and therefore this black fourth stanza has to work as something more than a Delacroix of dramatized seriousness or self-indulgence.

One needs to be convinced, in other words, that this speaker cannot think of rocks as bodies without eventually thinking of *those* bodies. In other words, this must convince as compulsion, not as gesture. And this comes about in the move away, in a flash, from the recognition. The way the poem presses on so quickly to something else—the consolations of geology—helps make the grimmest shade valid. With nothing of the peculiar attraction which sometimes comes through when, say, Joan Didion looks at a corpse, Wilbur recoils, as the mind must, not to forget everything and continue in banal optimism, but to continue at all—neither to lose one's reason, as the last catastrophe, nor *pretend* to lose it either, which for a poem would be quite as fatal. And so with neither callousness nor morbid delight the poem presses on to the refuge of time and ancient, soulless violence upon the earth. The fright of "the" time, human-scale time, finds some measure of repose in time itself: geological fact is clean, and the rock of immediate reality, looked at again *as* rock, pulls the mind back, not just from fancy or unspeakable human memory, but from regions of consciousness where one can only pretend to linger without going mad:

> It is not tricks of sense
> But the time's fright within me which distracts
>   Least fancies into violence
> And makes my thought take cover in the facts,
> As now it does, remembering how the bed
> Of layered rock two miles above my head
>
>   Hove ages up and broke
> Soundless asunder, when the shrinking skin
>   Of Earth, blacked out by steam and smoke,
> Gave passage to the muddled fire within, . . .

"Soundless" is a vital word in this array, for in it are gathered both the peace and the disquiet of thinking about prehuman history and this place. The word calls up the old schoolchild conundrum about whether there is sound where there are no ears to hear; yet "soundless" suggests other things besides: the indifference of the universe to its own trauma, the forgetfulness of history, the narrowness of human conceptions of violence, of time, of consequence. Perhaps one hears nothing clearly or for long—not the voice of the age, not poetry, not even our own pain. The earth-science cadenza which follows plays through tens of millions of years of another holocaust, and the language of war, of the body, geology, and Genesis meld for a vertiginous effect. The sentences refuse to stop; time itself refuses to bear witness to convulsive event, and only a scattering of experts really apprehends when these things were, and for how long. How "brief" was the "dike's brief chasm?" A few minutes, or a few million years? If by both geological and Old Testament reckoning man has been here but one evening in the expanse of earthly time, then what to make of this vast history which precedes and overshadows our own, and which seems to bulldoze us and our tragedies into some other forgotten common grave? This dizzying intensity winds up in a kind of rest, with the Bible language seeming to win, for the moment—the sun has come out again, and it becomes easier to think of Eve and Adam, of transfigurations, and the chance that the latest inheritors of the scene—the three true girls on the woman-forms of the rock, and the speaker himself—are somehow rightful, consequential; that all this upheaval, human and otherwise, has had them in mind. The poem begins to cool, like the aging earth and this stranded stone, and below consciousness the mind contemplates its own highs and lows, loses itself like the passing gull. It is one of Wilbur's unusual skills that he respects and represents well the cadences of the mind, and can suggest in a poem not merely what burdens or props the contemporary self, but what it is really like to think in such painful and open-ended ways. I think that the relative quiescence of the tenth stanza validates what has happened, psychologically, in the three that precede it, much as the taking cover in the sixth stanza, and the lightness of the first two, make the concentration camp memory between them plausible and valid rather than a contrived crisis. But somehow this poem has to end, and this almost thoughtless composure after the primordial earthquakes is the prelude to the poem's last crisis.

"On the Marginal Way" seems poised to declare something unironically grand, something public. These hit-and-run addresses to horror and history have forced the issue, and some kind of closing perspective seems to be in the offing. The contemporary grand overview, the prophetic dramatic monologue rarely now suggests, for itself or any reader, some way back into the world, some escape from the dark. When one reaches such a brink, there is often a black benediction—"a savage servility / slides by on grease"—and then the poem and the reader are left standing on Beacon Street, looking for a ride home.[4] True to his understanding of who we are, what we are, and the status of poetry with regard to the self, Wilbur tries to get us off the beach and back into the difficult balance of sanity; and the psychological cadences, at least, of his last verses seem right. "But somehow," Ishmael says after a stretch of dismal thinking in a New Bedford chapel, "somehow I grew merry again";[5] somehow one does come down from Mount Etna or the battlements of Elsinore and heroically, wisely, stupidly, or cravenly rejoin the living, finding or concocting reasons to enjoy or at least endure the rest of the day. Wilbur portrays this settling of the mind much as Melville does (and as Shakespeare did before them both): the mind can be overtaken by perceptions and moods other than ones it works itself into, and "joy" is something that even latter-day prophets can be heir to. "Blurting" is an axial word in the final stanza, although the wordplay in "manhood" may be showier. When one blurts, one might speak either fondly held truths or arrant stupidities—the blurted utterance reveals the element of the irrational, or, perhaps, some wisdom surpassing conscious understanding, comes into the mind through some unguarded back door:

> And like a breaking thought
> Joy for a moment floods into the mind,
>   Blurting that all things shall be brought
> To the full state and stature of their kind,
> By what has found the manhood of this stone.
> May that vast motive wash and wash our own.

Our own stone, manhood, motive? Any or all of these readings seem possible, as the poem finally loosens its grip on natural and historical fact, precise thinking, even precise wishing. There is no hint here that in this eventual or wished for coming to fullness, any cosmic witness would be borne for human suffering. What consolation there is, finally, must come of that image in the preceding stanza of the flying gull which "Loses himself at moments, white in white"—in other words, a kind of self-transcendence, some immersion in a larger scheme of things. The poem ends with a release, an almost mindless hope in the rhythms of ages, because on its own, mind has failed. Is this a willed return to faith? Psychological exhaustion? Is the poem poised to drift way into unironic variations on "Shantih, Shantih, Shantih"? What one concludes about such problems has to do with a good deal more than Wilbur's poetics; the issue is ultimately what one accepts as valid in the mind's engagement, and disengagement, with the problem of if and how the mind itself matters at all.

"On the Marginal Way" brings to the fore another challenge in reading Richard Wilbur, a need to decide, and constantly *redecide*, what weight to give the Judeo-Christian allusions, iconography, and religiously connected vocabulary which reveal themselves throughout his poems. Obvious or oblique, this language and mythology are always nearby, entering the verse through many doors. Suffusing the vast poetic tradition with which Wilbur interacts, and from which he so ingeniously draws, this discourse provides ways to express those human crises which Christianity and other faiths confront, and some remembrance that despite the moral and psychological disruptions of the given moment, the heritage of us all is profoundly spiritual, the religious legacy wide and strong and beckoning. The sheer familiarity of the language assists the mind, religious or otherwise, in facing and naming experience which without such language might be beyond comprehension, even beyond the reach of words and dreams.

In "On the Marginal Way" such mythology reverberates in the final, difficult stanza: the burst of joy, the "wash" of the soul or the human motive by some "vast" obscure purpose—these self-evidently suggest redemption through a species of baptism, and looking backwards through the poem one can easily locate other such presences. For example, there may be a classic Christian icon concealed in the white bird, a gull in this case, vanishing up into the white sky. But the exhilarating difficulty of the stanza and the complex moral and epistemological predicament which the poem faces are *not* to be reduced or resolved, I think, by tallying the faint or forthright religious echoes in the poem's voice. The danger with overdoing Judeo-Christian allusions in Wilbur is the same danger which can overshadow a reading of Eliot, Auden, Lowell, or Bishop: such allusions can become an escape hatch, toward which interpretation can edge whenever a crisis in a poem is obdurate and great. The baptism-like ending of "On the Marginal Way" might make the yearned-for redemption at the ending eerily familiar or consoling and Christian-*like,* but finally it does not seem Christian in substance, and it is not affirmed in any final gesture of faith—just as the mind-reader's closing allusion to "The sparrow's weighty fall" does not make him an emblem for God or a plausible Christ-figure, but only a self-pitying charlatan who would perhaps like to imagine himself as divine or martyred. One could write a long book which did nothing but catalogue this side of Wilbur's discourse, this stream of language and symbol which expresses important values in his imagination, his heritage, his dread, and his hope. But because this is only part of his eloquence, sensibility and range, to read too much into the religious vocabulary of his poems is, I think, to reduce and confine his achievement unfairly, and portray his vision as more bounded and safe than it is. We should hear and attend to the religious voices of Richard Wilbur, yet not at the expense of everything else.

From the same volume, "In the Field" has some dramatic progressions which recall "On the Marginal Way," but the attention is concentrated more on consciousness itself. There is a passage by Arthur Symons which, in seeking to explain, early on, the mind of the symbolist movement in nineteenth-century France, says something to be found in few other discussions of the modern or postmodern condition, something akin in spirit to this and other of Wilbur's meditative poems:

> Knowing so much less than nothing, for we are entrapped in smiling and many-coloured appearances, our life may seem to be but a little space of leisure, in which it will be the necessary business of each of us to speculate on what is so rapidly becoming the past and so rapidly becoming the future, that scarcely existing present which is after all our only possession. Yet, as the present passes from us, hardly to be enjoyed except as memory or as hope, and only with an at best partial recognition of the uncertainty or inutility of both, it is with a kind of terror that we wake up, every now and then, to the whole knowledge of our ignorance, and to some perception of where it is leading us. To live through a single day with that overpowering consciousness of our real position, which, in the moments in which alone it mercifully comes, is like blinding light or the thrust of a flaming sword, would drive any man out of his senses. It is our hesitations, the excuses of our hearts, the compromises of our intelligence, which save us. We can forget so much, we can bear suspense with so fortunate an evasion of its real issues; we are so admirably finite.[6]

"In the Field" is about the thrust of that flaming sword. The poem's cadences and progressions look like those of "Marginal Way": taking a short, domestic excursion into nature to contemplate it serenely, the speaker eventually has to grope through a cultural heritage for ways to explain and feel a part of what he sees; here again, what he comes up with fails to bring peace, and so once more he turns to scientific fact, which makes his world only scarier. Mechanically, "In the Field" is the simpler of the two poems, with quatrains that march neatly down the page, diction that is less florid, and images that distinguish themselves for apt compression. Even so, the difference in the ultimate subject—the ecliptic track of the mind, rather than the patterns and slow-time of the physical universe—gives this dramatic monologue a different feel. As this field-speaker thinks about himself thinking, he presents his own little failed profundities with bemusement, edged with a certain scorn—a tone which is bolstered by the consistent economy of word and image here. The poem stresses the very familiarity of these paths of consciousness, and in finding them wanting engages in a certain sympathetic talk with the likes of Poe, or any romantic or modern sensibility that rages (as Poe does, for example, in the sonnet "To Science") that the comely, comprehensible universe that mythology gave us has been overthrown by a wisdom which sustains neither poetry nor hope. The speaker and his companion think in old ruts: going out into a field on a starry night, they look first for the Big Dipper and then for other constellations one learns to recognize at summer camp or in grammar school. This starlit chat is followed by more lightweight erudition: from mythology they move on to freshman astronomy, telling each other that over the eons, the eternal skies have stretched and squeezed "like cat's cradles turned," and that north to the Ancient Egyptians was not Polaris, but a star in Draco. Perhaps everyone has been on such a walk at one time or another, the essence of which is dealing, numbly, glibly, with facts about time and distance which ought to prostrate the mind—were we not so admirably finite, so self-conservingly obtuse about the import of all this. The biggest chance taken by "In the Field" has to do with letting the first ten quatrains run at a mental low idle, catching our bizarre ability to look straight at the infinite, at the imagination-shattering fact, and react with near-perfect banality:

> Whether that might be so
>
> We could not say, but trued
> Our talk awhile to words of the real sky,
>   Chatting of class or magnitude,
>   Star-clusters, nebulae,
>
>   And how Antares, huge
> As Mars' big roundhouse swing, and more, was fled
>   As in some rimless centrifuge
>   Into a blink of red.

This is ordinary evening-talk—and when "the nip of fear" finally catches up with the "schoolbook thoughts," there is no leap to high awareness. One feels the late-night edge of the sword and goes to bed in silence, back to the false light, the false security signified by the bed-lamp shining from the house window. The poem now comes somewhere close to the zero-point that Jarrell reaches in one of his best poems, "90 North," a dream of absolute vastation in which wisdom, schoolbook or otherwise, reveals itself as pain. Jarrell closes with precisely that, leaving us there in absolute waste:

I see at last that all the knowledge

I wrung from the darkness—that the darkness flung me—
Is worthless as ignorance: nothing comes from nothing,
The darkness from the darkness. Pain comes from the darkness
And we call it wisdom. It is pain.[7]

True to his own way, Wilbur continues his poem into how one manages the morning after. Therefore "In the Field" takes a complex moral and cultural gamble, matching the structural one mentioned earlier: following night with day in such a poem sounds suspicious, suggests consolations from flowers and trees and chirping birds, ways out of a spiritual bind from which poets of the past thirty years have had little luck returning. I do not suspect that Wilbur frets over philosophical and aesthetic fashion, but it may be important for the fate of the poem that the garden fields the speaker and his companion venture into the next morning are more Pascalian than Wordsworthian. The hawkweed and daisies are comforting, yes, but these "chasms of the grass" recall the second abyss into which Pascal plunges his readers in his *Pensées,* the endless universe of the small. The carryover of star language to describe these daylit fields does not foster congruence; nor is there any overworked parallel between these "galaxies / Of flowers" and the skies of the night before.

The poem unfolds into three stanzas of sheer seeing to establish this field as a field, not as a metaphysical escape clause. In fact the morning scene escapes the reasoning and the imagining faculties quite as successfully as did the infinities of night. Only then comes the long, driving, cadence-crumbling sentence running through three stanzas to close out the poem. The one "unbounded thing we know" is "the heart's wish for life," and that wish itself, sufficient or otherwise, is the abiding firsthand experience of the infinite, unmediated by schoolbooks, planetaria, botany, or poetry. Consoling or not, that is the sort of perception that one can have even at Jarrell's North Pole of the spirit; it forces nothing upon the self, upon science, upon anything else in the world as we have known it and are coming to know it differently. "In the Field" is a poem about what Stevens would call mere being, before and beyond intellectual or cultural interference; and the loaded word of the last stanza, *peremptory,* which sometimes means overpowering, sometimes obnoxious, conveys both the pleasure and the rage of recognizing in this experience something at the core of the human condition. This is a modest poem, which comes to an awareness likewise modest, yet unassailable, amid and against the dark of the evening.

To come to "In the Field" from the longer poems of Wilbur's first two collections is to sense a rising of his confidence, of his trust in silence and in sparing explanations; by contrast, "Castles and Distances," in *Ceremony* and "Water Walker" in *The Beautiful Changes,* seem more uneasy in their structure and thoughtfulness, though "Water Walker" has the advantage of being one of the few poems Wilbur has written dealing at least in part with his own early life, his freight-hopping adventures as a young man wandering the United States. "Castles and Distances" is in comparison an Audenesque poem, an elaborate rumination on the structure of landscapes, on the need that order and wildness have for each other, on a paradoxical mix of love and predation that suffuses the world of animals and men, the need to master what one can of the world and yet submit to it meekly. For good reason, Hill is enthusiastic about the poem.[8] Its language is lush, alliterative, resounding with puns and spreads of meaning; its observations are subtle, its historical and literary allusions done with characteristic grace. It all works, except that, compared to most of Wilbur's other long poems, nobody seems to be home. Written twenty years later, "The Fourth of July," as we shall see, has some resemblances to it, yet the venture in the later poem seems bolder, if only because an occasion poem about American history and prospects lures the contemporary reader toward his own soap box. By contrast almost no one now would dispute what a poet has to say about King James I, the conversion of St. Hubert, or what it might be like to gaze out the windows of Versailles. "Castles and Distances" is lovely and serene—a Renoir tulip field, or a valley scene by George Inness. It reads like two of Wilbur's short, thoughtful poems seamed together, and the complete or composite work does not venture out on any razor's edge, as his extended works often do.

As the second poem in *The Beautiful Changes,* "Water Walker" does take a risk, yet it works up to it in a wary way: not coyness but diffidence, not show-off performance but uneasy indirection. The opening three stanzas assemble heterogeneous stuff, as if for a display of wit, of ingenious connection among the nameless infidel cited at the first, and caddis flies, and St. Paul on his evangelical tour, and someplace in Virginia, recalled from a young man's memories. But one source of surprise in these first thirty lines comes of the fact that the connections are not really getting made at all, and that the drama here is of a mind trying to get hold of something and not succeeding. The hesitations and the near misses are built into the sound of those lines which, set off by themselves, away from the stanzas proper, recall not Frost so much as Eliot in "Prufrock" or *Ash Wednesday,* the Eliot voice which doubts the worth of its own compulsive reasoning. These are the lines which, strung out islandlike among the four opening stanzas, suggest a stammering of the mind: "There is something they mean," "Always alike and unlike," "I thought if I should begin."

But despite a Prufrockian shyness that such verses convey, something more direct and colloquial in the middle of the second stanza seems to call attention to certain limits in the poetry of wit. The talk has moved from infidels to caddis flies:

> There is something they mean
>
> By breaking from water and flying
> Lightly some hours in air,
> Then to the water-top dropping,
> Floating their heirs and dying:
> It's like
> Paulsaul the Jew born in Tarshish, who when at bay on the steps
> With Hebrew intrigued those Jewsotted Jews
> Crowding to stone and strike;

That quick "It's like" draws attention to its own failure, for by the end of the stanza one has no clear idea what "it" refers to, or how "it" is like anything that follows: a Calvinist somersault of interpretation is required to get from waterbugs to Paul, or to his ministry or his Gentile-Jewness, or whatever the simile might encompass. The very next line, "Always alike and unlike," provides an escape, but only by a kind of shrug, a giving-up on the comparison, or at least on making it clear. Paul was not stoned to death by anybody, and so the connection with dying caddis flies cannot in a strict sense work; and after such a build-up, this vatic paradox seems weak, does not satisfy. And it is not meant to. The snapshot of Paul's life is well chosen, for it recalls a crowd sotted with its own identity, tired of itself and its own finitude, angrily impatient with one of its own who has tried to tell them something and finally *failed*. In other words, it remembers Paul as a visionary poet whose own words have let him down also, who could not at that time speak fully what he saw: the multiple realities that the self must inhabit, the truths which escape the grasp of language.

The intermediate zone that the poem speaks of, "where air / Mists into water," rings familiar to people who have read Wilbur's early poems—this realm between, this cherished state-between-states is the condition which by its existence, or at least its possibility, offers a prospect that we are more in touch with truth than ordinary life on solid surfaces might lead one to suppose. But up to this point the poem sounds a little *unnerved* by the prospect of such double life; a self that is always alike and unlike, that walks around full of discords, deep-set conflicts, deeply uncertain as to just what and where in the world it is, is perhaps a self without an identity, or at least without an identity that language can express. Paulsaul is a shapeshifter, playing Jew to the Jews, Greek to the Greeks, and Roman too, when that role serves him; and there is little encouragement in seeing the greatest Apostle change thus, for who then was this Paul? For a culture and a religious tradition founded upon a concern with the integrity of self, such changefulness can be as daunting a prospect as unregenerate fixity.

After the first stanza, "Water Walker" veers back and forth between those two ideas of identity—as something set and safe, and as something impalpable, out beyond doctrines, beliefs, or continuities. And played off against Paulsaul is private experience, specifically two recollected nights, one somewhere in the summer sleep of Virginia, the other in a small town in Illinois—private recognitions of the allurement and the danger of establishing a self too firmly. Again, what disturbs and intensifies the poem is that there is something unresolved, uninterpreted about these memories; the incongruities spreading through them are not to be explained away, and the poem makes no gesture to do so. The Virginia house: whether the place really did belong to his family, whether he really was "home" in any sense, or instead trying out some fantasy born in a daze of wandering, is not to be known here; and the Illinois town, remembered in more of this not-quite-right diction, seems a place both consoling and unnerving for being sure. Why are the remembered trees *Japanese* maples and not, say, sycamores or some other species that belongs on these prairies? Why "lawnsprays and tricycles," an odd linking to represent the spirit of the sleeping place? The benediction for Geneseo is "Shyly things said what they meant"—followed directly by another meditation on Paul, not by any effort to say what these mundane things did mean, shyly or otherwise. Unless, that is, these things meant only a life too bounded and knowable, a world too certain. This is life underwater, life as the armored larva, not as the complete creature. At least in retrospect, the poem's amazing leap from insect larvae to Geneseo seems to work well.

Some of the best effects in "Water Walker" unfold in just this way—backwards, taking on strongest resonance when one gets to the end of them and tries a retrospective, reconsidering view. For example, the two lines that follow the Geneseo section make more sense when the syntax is reversed:

Shyly things said what they meant:

An old man stitching a tent
Could have been Saul in Tharsos,
Loved and revered;

Coming abruptly into the poem, the old man appears first as something else seen or dreamed from that Illinois porch, who reminds the speaker of Paul as Paul was before his conversion. But turning the lines around works better: Paul could have made Tarsus (or Tharsos or Tarshish, as the town's name slips and shifts like the man) and tentmaking his identity, his refuge, could have accepted "tentmaker" as all the selfhood he needed. But one does not get that on the first try, moving forward through the poem; and this need to watch out, as it were, for the undertow of these lines draws one into a wavering reading, like the back-and-forth psychological condition, the yearnings now for stability and closure, now for freedom, for changefulness, that the poem is very much about.

The last third of "Water Walker" grows even more resistant to any start-to-finish reading, with ostensibly free associations changing the subject again and again. "His wasn't light company" refers to Paul, but in the next two lines:

> Still pearled with water, to be
>
> Ravished by air makes him grow

the "he" in question is evidently not Paul this time, or at least not Paul first and foremost, but the growing larva of the caddis fly, which has not been mentioned for about twenty lines—and again the reader has to do some water walking of his own to keep up with this and other shifts that follow. From here on out the poem plunges into the whirlpool of the speaker's own selfhood, into the mystery which cannot be solved and which can hardly be expressed. And the syntax becomes Teutonically complicated, going round and round like the self thinking about the self. For about ten lines the speaker sounds a little like Tennyson's Ulysses set down on Forty-second Street, congratulating himself a little for being a part of all that he has met, boasting mildly of his own restlessness; but the commanding tone gives way under the pressure of external nonsense, or rather the sound and fury so general that nonsense cannot be told from the genuine issue:

> I hold
> Here in my head Maine's bit speech, lithe laughter of Mobile
>   blacks,
> Opinions of salesmen, ripe tones of priests,
> Plaints of the bought and sold:
>
> Can I rest and observe unfold
>
> The imminent singletax state,

> The Negro rebellion, the rise
> Of the nudist cult, the return
> Of the Habsburgs, . . .

So far so good; but the conclusion of this windy sentence is baroque enough to suit the Habsburgs:

> And praise
> The spirit and not the cause, and neatly precipitate
> What is not doctrine, what is not bound
> To enclosured ground; what stays?

In sorting this out, one finds it makes better sense to link "precipitate" and "To enclosured ground," rather than the latter phrase with "bound"; in other words, the theme here seems to be an anxiety that after the hectic self-consuming life, there may be nothing left but doctrine and dust, that we are, or that we become, nothing more than an array of received ideas. If the enclosured ground of the grave takes most of us, then what stays? This is conventional fear, surely; yet the struggle by which it is finally expressed does more than dress up a commonplace. Confusion, deep uncertainty, is the dark side of duality: to affirm, as Wilbur so often does, that the complete self lives in more than one world, that it needs the nurture of both the sure and the changeful, is to lose track of what it is, to stammer on the idea of identity. The last two stanzas are among Wilbur's darkest, allowing no way out of the quandary. Paul is remembered at his worst, as the saint of vengeance; the shapeshifting evangelist passes through a terrible incarnation. And the final, five-verse sentence of "Water Walker" is yet another syntactic back flip. "Who learns" turns out to be neither a question nor the start of one, but rather the subject of "cannot go home," and "the dilemma" stands far from its verb, "returns," set off in the same sort of periodic structure. That "who" should be read as "whosoever" only adds to the difficulty of making this out, and the stanza has to be read, like most of the others, from the first musical measure: "Da capo da capo" as the closing verse both observes and instructs. No benedictions here, no consolations; this is one of Wilbur's most affecting poems on the unresolvable dilemma of knowing who one really is, and on the price one pays for affirming anything, within or without, beyond the solid, safe, unsatisfactory places of the world and the mind. A hard poem, for the rightest of reasons.

But can there be forgiveness, now, for occasional verse? When Wilbur became Poet Laureate of the United States, he reassured his public that

he was not thereby required to become the American Southey, crank-
ing out poems for royal birthdays and the dedication of civic projects.
Among his longer poems, however, we find an ambitious venture into
this neighborhood, a poem written well before he took over the laureate's office in the Library of Congress. And given the custom of the
time, a strange venture it seems. For of all the modes of American
poetry, which of them is more "out" now than an Independence Day
ode? Thanks in part to MacLeish's civic spirits and to Jarrell's ferocious
attacks on what they wrought,[9] the public poem has been in disrepute
since the Second World War—except for some choice invective against
the state; and long before, toward the turn of this century, the Fourth of
July poem was already going down to exhaustion along with iced milk
at picnics and the senator's three-hour commemorative speech. In this
fallen, poem-as-gesture world, a title like "the Fourth of July" seems an
incitement to trouble, and one is induced to read if only to see if and
how the poem will avoid the brink of banality. One is set up, in other
words, for a performance, something more like the wit poem which
"Water Walker" expressly was not; and with its ostentatiously odd first
line, "The Fourth of July" seems poised to deliver: "Liddell, the Oxford lexicographer."

The plan apparently is to surprise the Fourth from a fresh direction, avoiding the trappings of the picnic speech and opening instead
with what seems a mysterious event, couched in fairly mundane language. The first half of the first stanza is a mild literary in-joke, which
"outs" clearly enough in the figurative diction which adorns the stanza.
Mr. Dodgson is Lewis Carroll, and the opening alludes to the afternoon of 4 July 1862 on which, while boating on the Thames, he regaled
Alice Liddell with the tales which later became *Alice's Adventures in
Wonderland*. But perhaps the effect is better if one is not in the racket of
English literature, if one does not recall offhand who this Liddell was or
what these two young daughters and Dodgson signify. The importance of this afternoon can then dawn in the consciousness and suggest
more poignantly that great changes within it, decisive battles in the
history of the imagination, are fought along the quieter, unwatched
streams of life, and come clear to the mind itself only later. The same
effect holds true for the reference to Grant in the following stanza:
whether or not he was churning out cigar smoke and battle strategies in
the same hour that the Mad Hatter took shape is unclear from the
historical record; but during that summer, perhaps the darkest season
of the Civil War, grant was around Memphis, working out his outlandish plan to take the apparently impregnable fortress town of Vicksburg. Vicksburg did surrender on 4 July 1863, after a long campaign

through swamps and meandering rivers, a break away from his own supply lines, and tactics which violated every rule in the West Point books. The strategy becomes "brilliant" months after, when after a bitter campaign it actually brought a Union victory. And so the sense of these two opening stanzas extends farther than a contrast between the fantasizing mathematician and the pragmatic soldier. Both of these people, perhaps at the same moment, are engaged in pure imagining, in abstract thought, in enterprises which make their mark on history and the culture only with the passage of time. Out of the same sunshine, one consciousness forges a great children's story; another reinvents war.

This is ingenious, yet holiday declamation nonetheless. An amazing and ironic difference observed, great physical and psychological distances bridged, with a building implication that we, as the audience, should see some sort of wholeness where we once saw disconnection— this still seems the stuff of the holiday orator. What counteracts that, in these first stanzas, is a small matter: the fact that these stanzas are numbered, contrary to Wilbur's usual way. The gesture is a little peculiar in its implications. One might think of Emerson's essays, or Ruskin's, and the British ecclesiastical habit of numbering paragraph blocs in published sermons as a sign that the thinking is shifting significantly, while continuing in some grand, concealed, yet logical way. But it also recalls Stevens in his academic mandarin voice, supremely detached from the paradoxes he observes in the human condition. Wilbur's language here is unbuoyant, unrhetorical: these great moments of imagining are not celebrated, but recollected in cool tones. Dodgson dealt in "fool's gold," stories worthless (at the time), which in their foolery made fun of his own profession and faith in reason; Grant's ultimate scheme did not topple Vicksburg "like a house of cards"; it resulted in "wallowed guns," frustrations, doubts, losses, and a long siege before the city fell. In other words, what seems absent from this declamation is what is crucial: conviction, enthusiasm, whether real or forced. Like the two imaginative turning points that they are about, these stanzas are a long lit fuse, perceptions whose significance, as yet obscured, will eventually need to come clear. The suspense, however, has to do with whether the tone of the poem can itself muster any excitement over what it presents.

The first line of the third stanza does not offer much hope in that direction: "The sun is not a concept but a star." That sounds like a Stevens verse, Stevens as mandarin, dealing in reality as the fatal X, and the poem seems to be heading at high speed away from consolations and shapely connections. What had been mustering, apparently, was

109

some address to the imagination as catalytic force, as a kind of chlorophyl, transforming the primal, holy power of light into individualized, world-altering shapes. But the conviction has gone out of such ideas by the third stanza, and one faces again the Stevens question of how the random "points and waves" of reality are ordered into spatial and temporal relationships, into time, history, and ironic symmetries, as on this bygone Fourth—arrangements so delighted in by the tranquil reflective mind. Under all the clever juxtapositions of the classic Fourth poem opens an abyss of nothingness, treacherously bridged by the designs of language. That is the dark reading of the third stanza's first six lines. Even so, the question they ask is not nihilistically rhetorical, and "saves appearances" is a Wilbur design that works several ways. The order of the world perceived is made-up, cosmetic—perhaps; or perhaps "appearances," phenomenal reality, are saved by some grand arcanum, a Platonic something that really does create and sustain designs *out there,* makes them entities beyond delusions of order, dreams in our inadequate Western heads. Wilbur looks about him for allies in keeping that hope alive and finds them immediately in the people he is talking about, both of whom must have recognized that imagining is an act both of will and of faith. Alice's "termless wood" refers to this well-known passage in *Through the Looking Glass:*

> "This must be the wood," she said thoughtfully to her self, "where things have no names. I wonder what'll become of *my* name when I go in? I shouldn't like to lose it at all—because they'd have to give me another, and it would be almost certain to be an ugly one. But then the fun would be, trying to find the creature that had got my old name! . . .
>
> . . . She was rambling on in this way when she reached the wood: it looked very cool and shady. "Well, at any rate it's a great comfort," she said as she stepped under the trees, "after being so hot, to get into the—into the—into *what?*" she went on, rather surprised at not being able to think of the word. "I mean to get under the—under the—under *this,* you know!" putting her hand on the trunk of the tree. "What does it call itself, I wonder? I do believe it's got no name—why, to be sure it hasn't!"[10]

Although language gives names and a measure of order, these trees are *there,* not linguistic constructs. Alice lacks the words to give thanks, to celebrate, rather than words to create trees out of points and waves. Mind and the natural order (or disorder) have complex business with each other. Without Grant's imagination, the swamps around Vicksburg are chaotic, an impenetrable wallow, but they nonetheless exist, beyond the fictions of consciousness—and one gets on by accepting the "grand arcanum" as a mysterious presence and by dreaming in some wakeful harmony with its rules. The stanza does not overthrow the Stevens line which begins it; instead it observes what the contemporary mind makes, of necessity, out of its recognitions. We take our sun "star" in two ways: as a blind ball of hot gases, throwing off its waves of radiation; and as the star of old, a thing of order, purpose, even guidance, as we continue its business of organizing the world.

Language, while not everything, is something; this poem, we recall, is dedicated to "*I. A. R.*" which signifies I. A. Richards, who spent much of his life exploring the dubious and shifting connections of spoken and written words to represented fact. And when language fails, identity is threatened, if the identity depends overmuch on words to resolve the world. Tragedy is the subject of the next stanza, tragedy in a fairly strict sense, for in the pain and loss something is recognized about the relationship of the physical world to our linguistic constructs. The great Swedish naturalist and classifier Linnaeus ("tree-named" because his real name, von Linné, means *linden*) devised words for the termless wood, giving us the way of genus and species, the "branchy" way of speaking—and seeing or imposing—the interconnectedness of forms of life. In his old age, Linnaeus lost his powers of recall: words failed him, and with them went his world, for it was a thing "made," like Grant's Vicksburg campaign, like Dodgson's story of a trip down the rabbit hole, like the heavily wrought poem we are in the midst of reading. If we trust too much to artifice, we are terribly vulnerable to wallowed guns and wallowed minds. And so the stanza's campaign ends in a retreat, back into Stevens. This "fire-fledged knowledge" that one approaches wordlessly, intuitively, this side of consciousness that resists language, classification, logic, structure, may come in part from the "fire-fangled feathers" that close the last stanza in *The Palm at the End of the Mind,* the closing celebration of "mere being" and the end of rational, inquiring talk. We speak in theorems and ideologies; we live on hunches, distrusting, for our own safety, our own words.

But the thought cannot be allowed to end with that doubt of thinking, and in fact the sentence comes to no finish for a full stanza more. Wilbur's axiom, that things are never as simple as they appear to the eye or the mind, drives him onward and back to the other sort of mental life, the conscious, methodical, wordy imagining that requires not hunches but some better proof. Copernicus could not let his dream of the solar system be a caucus race, where everyone wins, all have prizes, and responsibilities to fact are left behind. Imagining is risky business; one's constructs can fail and doom the dreamer with them; the recourse is to test what we can in the "fitting-rooms of fact"—an image cleverly fashioned from the stuff of the mundane. The poem here begins its returning arc, back to the problem held so elaborately in abeyance since the beginning, the common significance of the Fourth of July. The poem has a rendezvous with public speech of the Mac-Leishean sort, and in keeping that appointment it finishes up quickly. Perhaps too quickly:

> And honor to these States,
> Which come to see that black men too are men,
> Beginning, after troubled sleep, debates,
> Great bloodshed, and a century's delay,
> To mean what once we said upon this day.

This may be one of those unusual instances in Wilbur's work where the fitting-room thought overbalances the termless, intuitive sensibility: where the crowning idea may look good on paper, or after too much reflection. The point—unhappily one can use that word here—is that the republic is finally taking its opening words to heart, the ones about all men being created equal, and that as a culture we are reconciling our dream stuff with reality, remaking the truth to fit the word and the idea. And so we move from Dodgson to Grant, from hatter-mad visions to resolutions. This is all fine, schematically, a finale that Edward Everett, who orated at Gettysburg for two forgotten hours before Lincoln's address, might have thought grand. The trouble seems to be with the proportions. The crisis in our history gets four lines, half as much as Linneaus's senility, less than Copernicus's familiar business with the solar system, and less than either Lewis Carroll or General Grant get for an afternoon's work. Alice's tea party is more vividly remembered than the "great bloodshed"; Dodgson's hayrick amusements are better explained than the century's delay in making social equality the truth. And the final line, with its suspicious "we," cannot but ring with patrician complacency, oratory from the bandstand, in the park, in the all-white part of town.

Perhaps "The Fourth of July" is at its end a failure. It is a match for high stakes with the likes of Everett, and Everett ultimately wins. It is troubling to see Wilbur lapse, however briefly, into a voice that rings hollow, not convincing in what he says about the national day and its changing significance. The poem's quiescence in the third and fourth stanzas is refreshing and new, as commemorative poems go; but at the closing the escape from windy convention, the move back toward genuine profundity and sincerity, has gone awry. The struggle to achieve real liberty for all is perhaps not a subject that a poet, any poet, can address now for more than a few lines, the matter having been talked to pollution by politicians and loudmouth opportunists; but recognizing that problem does not make the imbalance go away, or these few breezy words adequate to their job. Maybe the form is exhausted after all. But what is also troubling in this, one of the later poems, is the possibility that in Wilbur's complex, poised consciousness, logic can get an upper hand on intuition, threatening to overshadow that disorderly sense which can keep even the most mannered poems from decaying into tracts. A long poem takes a chance; what hurts about "The Fourth" is how a great promise seems unfulfilled at the very last.

A better poem, perhaps the very best of Wilbur's longer works, is "The Mind-Reader," rightfully the title work of the 1976 collection, a poem tilted the other way, toward intuitions and the price one pays for them, in both sanity and certainty. Discussing this poem briefly in an earlier chapter, I have said something about its wordsmithing, the unprecedented resonance of its many puns and spreads of meaning. But "The Mind-Reader" is more than a technical feat. It is Wilbur's boldest attempt to write as the sensibility he almost is, or rather as that side of himself which poems like "The Fourth" keep in check. The speaker in this dramatic monologue is a heavy-drinking Italian with powerful intuitions; he has lost the battle with those powers, and they have swept him over the brink into solipsism, obsession, and profound confusion. Too much imagining, and too much trust in the imaginative faculty, have made the mind-reader a desperate man:

> What can be wiped from memory? Not the least
> Meanness, obscenity, humiliation,
> Terror which made you clench your eyes, or pulse
> Of happiness which quickened your despair.
> Nothing can be forgotten, as I am not
> Permitted to forget.

But the poem does not begin this way, with a groan of unhappiness and loss from the other side of the imaginative fence. It begins close to home, gradually moving the reader off into psychological states where other poems in the volume do not go. The first stanza unfolds in the cool modernist discourse of Bishop or Stevens, making its wry concessions to the reader, calling attention here and there to the mix of compulsion and artifice that make a good reverie. All of it seems perfectly mandarin-dispassionate—and the suspense that nonetheless builds here has to do with when or if the poem will move beyond all this hypothesis:

> Some things are truly lost. Think of a sun-hat
> Laid for the moment on a parapet
> While three young women—one, perhaps, in mourning—
> Talk in the crenellate shade. A slight wind plucks
> And budges it; it scuffs to the edge and cartwheels
> Into a giant view of some description:
> Haggard escarpments, if you like, plunge down
> Through mica shimmer to a moss of pines
> Amidst which, here or there, a half-seen river
> Lobs up a blink of light. The sun-hat falls,
> With what free flirts and stoops you can imagine,
> Down through that reeling vista or another,
> Unseen by any, even by you or me.
> It is as when a pipe-wrench, catapulted
> From the jounced back of a pick-up truck, dives headlong
> Into a bushy culvert; or a book
> Whose reader is asleep, garbling the story,
> Glides from beneath a steamer chair and yields
> Its flurried pages to the printless sea.

None of this makes much difference, save that one hears, faintly in all this embellishment, a supposedly reserved and detached teacher getting a bit too caught up in the reeling vista of his own lesson. The first hint of trouble—and it seems to take shape only retrospectively—is the aside about one of the three women being "perhaps in mourning," a nice touch for filling out, say, the foreground of a Pre-Raphaelite landscape, but odd here, when nothing is made of it. The "haggard escarpments," more of the dream stuff that fitted out the near-nightmare tour of "Walking to Sleep" are offered, the speaker says, if *we* like; but there is no problem sensing whose unconscious they gratify, whose drives they serve. These object lessons in the absoluteness of some losses—hats into canyons, books into the "printless" sea—pick up an overtone of wish-dream: the opulent language may be in some ways stock Wilbur, but here it hints at a yearning for such oblivion, an escape from, say, the pain of mourning and the rituals of consolation, from the boredom of pipe-wrench errands and fixings, from the prison house of consciousness. "Lui parla" reads the Italian epigraph to the poem: the mind-reader speaks himself, and speaks to himself. And what one hears thus far is an unacknowledged delight in the "free flirts" of pure escape from himself. That implication comes clearer in the short, taut stanza which follows the reverie:

> It is one thing to escape from consciousness
> As such things do, another to be pent
> In the dream-cache or stony oubliette
> Of someone's head.

There is regret here, or uneasiness, but veiled. As yet there is no clue as to what sorts of things are regrettably pent up in heads: remembered hats, wrenches, and bad novels, or something more, something like the self, turned too much inward, too enamored with fantastic runs of imagination. But there is no lesson here, no instruction such as makes or threatens "The Fourth of July," and the thirty lines that follow are in their brilliance a celebration of enigmatic fragments of memory, the husk of lost dreams, the energy of the mind turned loose. It is hard to find in English verse a sharper, more compressed expression of the moment before a storm hits, the beautiful ominousness that one sees, when very young perhaps, and never forgets:

> And then these voices,
> Querying or replying, came to sound
> Like cries of birds when the leaves race and whiten
> And a black overcast is shelving over.

This may owe roundabout debts to Pound, but *whiten* is the stroke which sends these lines of poetry out on their own. The word is simply great observation, both of the natural moment and its transformation in memory and dream. Leaves in a stormwind—I suspect these are Wilbur's maples as much as they are any Italian poplars—whiten when they are blown so hard that only their backs show; they whiten in the strange half-light before the absolute wet blackness of heavy rain; they whiten in the remembering mind, which strengthens the contrast of light with dark. This is dreaming, and real, obsessive remembering, and not some self-conscious show of dominion over the unconscious. Yet this resonates too with traditions, with poetry of a sort that Wilbur is not supposed to like or understand from the inside. Dramatic monologue or not, this is an imagist moment, and a fine one, echoing with some of the best of that tradition:

> The mind is not a landscape, but if it were
> There would in such case be a tilted moon
> Wheeling beyond the wood through which you groped,
> Its fine spokes breaking in the tangled thickets.

Such lines may recall many moons of the late nineteenth century, but perhaps most of all Conrad's, from a place called Patusan, a dream kingdom where fantasy and self-involvement can be the undoing of noble souls. The hypothetical, imagist woodland merges into very real ones, and the stanza delivers up details known not from remembering poems and good prose, but from wakeful walking. Woodland hikers know the bewildering way that marked trails evaporate into dried-up stream beds, and what it is to come from bright clearings into the black sudden shade of hemlock trees; but neither Frost nor Annie Dillard nor Gary Snyder have seen the woods quite this way, through the medium of this troubled imagination, and as an allegory of its motions. In such memory dreams as these, says our mind-reader, he can find lost things, things whose whereabouts are buried deep in the unconsciousness of the people who have lost them. So there is power in such a surrender to deep dream; one can even make a living at it, if one cannot make a life. Doing the latter is impossible because of what else one comes upon in those haunted woods of the mind along with the old keys and photographs: one rediscovers those lost moments of perception, of feeling, of intensity. The poem slips eerily from talk of retrieved bric-a-brac into a pained acknowledgment of what comes up with it: an overflow of enigma, an outpouring of all that has been experienced, recollected, and dreamed. Quickly the poem becomes a lament for some loss of balance in the consciousness—yet this is no message delivery system for mental health. What strikes home is that these inner landscapes are *right,* depicting beautifully what it is to lose one's grip and slide into an inner chaos, to fall farther than the controlled fall of "Walking to Sleep" ever goes.

Memory being one of the wellsprings of art, no artist is permitted to forget, and from a broader and simpler perspective, perhaps nobody really forgets anything. The puzzle which is forced to the surface here has to do with the uncertain relationship of harrowing memory to second sight, to being a visionary, an artist who not only recalls well but foretells too. The mind-reader seems to take it for granted that the two powers are intertwined, or perhaps one mystery only, and the idea is never questioned in this poem. The mind-reader jumps the gap: "It was not far / From that to this—this corner café table," he says, where he does his prophetic act for pay; but that skips over the key question of the poem. What do obsessive memory, or obsession in a general way, and genius have to do with each other? Is a powerful unconscious a curse or a blessing, junkpile of recollected and wearying trivia, or the giver of some kind of wisdom closed off to the normal or waking mind? The Western tradition of visionary poetry is not being challenged here, but rather entered, probed from within; and the mind-reader is not a caricature of the Other in our psychological and literary life. He speaks with Wilbur's words, and there is no attempt to assume a speech, whether Italian or otherwise, which is not recognizably Wilbur's own voice. Another darkness emerges here, which is not alien: the relationship of the poet to audience is also placed in the foreground by Wilbur's speaking in his own tongue. What do people want from the artist anyway? Prophecy, narcissistic gratification, flattery: there is all of that in the act of reading, whether or not the writer exploits those motives or not. The artist sits at the café table, and an unhappy, self-seeking society comes to him for consolation, for direction, for a spiritual pat on the head:

> They come here, day and night, so many people:
> Sad women of the quarter, dressed in black,
> As to a black confession; blinking clerks
> Who half-suppose that Taurus ruminates
> Upon their destinies; men of affairs
> Down from Milan to clear it with the magus
> Before they buy or sell some stock or other;
> My fellow-drunkards; fashionable folk,
> Mocking and ravenously credulous,
> And skeptics bent on proving me a fraud
> For fear that some small wonder, unexplained,
> Should leave a fissure in the world, and all
> Saint Michael's host come flapping back.

It is not difficult to take this as swinging beyond the ken of mind-readers and their superstitious bourgeois clients. Though the relationship of poet-seer to world has rarely been so uncertain, even formal criticism of poetry has such stuff in it, such insistence that poets "see" when the rest of us cannot, and do the vatic act on demand. Nor perhaps is the elaborate game of judgment, as played by this miscellaneous audience, so different from competitions among critics and poets:

> All that, of course,
> Is trumpery, since nine times out of ten
> What words float up within another's thought
> Surface as soon in mine, unfolding there
> Like paper flowers in a water-glass.
> In the tenth case, I sometimes cheat a little.
> That shocks you? But consider: what I do

Cannot, so most conceive, be done at all,
And when I fail, I am a charlatan
Even to such as I have once astounded—
Whereas a tailor can mis-cut my coat
And be a tailor still. I tell you this
Because you know that I have the gift, the burden.

And so, for self-preservation as well as profit, this man, with a real sixth sense, deals in fortune-cookie messages, evasive and bland prophecy for the skeptical, credulous public he despises. Precisely here is where the gap widens between the mind-reader and Wilbur, where we can see this self presented as a not-I, or at least as a not-I in crucial ways. What the mind-reader may not completely recognize, yet what is clear in his words, is how this contempt for the world is bound up with contempt for himself, that like one of Browning's Italian artists, the trouble in mind is never really faced because the mind itself fobs the trouble off on external realities, competitors, an unappreciative public. There are flickers of rage here at his own consciousness, but the mind always recoils from that, and drifts back to the baseness of "the race" which of course includes him.

It makes no difference that my lies are bald
And my evasions casual. It contents them
Not to have spoken, yet to have been heard.
What more do they deserve, if I could give it,
Mute breathers as they are of selfish hopes
And small anxieties? Faith, justice, valor,
All those reputed rarities of soul
Confirmed in marble by our public statues—
You may be sure that they are rare indeed
Where the soul mopes in private, and I listen.

As a human being, gifted or not, what can one say to the world, and what can one make out of the disorderly stuff of one's own unconscious? Memory, dreams, language, audience—they are burdens, problems, for the consciousness that is compelled to look deeply into self and world, and to speak somehow of what it finds. It is too easy to say that this is only a modern version of the Poe prophetic mentality which Wilbur is sometimes taken as quarreling with in academic ways. What the mind-reader says to his world, at least as a species of prophecy, is evasion, is cheating. What mixes with all that is his powerful intuitive sense of what others are thinking—a poetry of compassion, if you will, or of sympathy, rather than something vision-

ary in the cruder sense. But here is the mind-reader's grave mistake—
that he cannot accept his gift of understanding, of second sight, as
enough, that he must primp it up into the fortune-telling which makes
him a fake: the pathos is that he cannot do otherwise. He is trapped in
his fakery because he has given in to the sheer seductiveness of a special
power, and also because he lacks compassion for other human beings,
and for himself, and any hope that the world as consciously experienced is possibly sufficient or good. It takes no insight to do that, but
faith, and faith is what the mind-reader does not have. He has slipped
into a contempt for life, for experience, for human nature, for his own
mind:

>   . . . my sixth
> And never-resting sense is a cheap room
> Black with the anger of insomnia,
> Whose wall-boards vibrate with the mutters, plaints,
> And flushings of the race.

This is a look into the chasm under Wilbur's feet, or rather under
the rickety bridge of his hope. Only the last line of "The Mind-Reader"
is Italian, which is not a sudden shift into the right language. Rather, it
draws attention to the English, the Wilbur-like English, of everything
else, the insistence of this unique voice that we are *not* gazing at perfect
otherness, but at a darkly familiar side of the self. As I suggested in
chapter 2, there are strong bonds between Richard Wilbur and this
anti-Wilbur whom he imagines, and the poem reveals again this poet's
intimacy with the allurements of destructive transcendence, the border
regions of madness. If that premise will hold, then one can return to a
few difficult lines in "The Mind-Reader," to consider how they work
both antiphonally and deceptively in this strange music:

> Is there some huge attention, do you think,
> Which suffers us and is inviolate,
> To which all hearts are open, which remarks
> The sparrow's weighty fall, and overhears
> In the worst rancor a deflected sweetness?

The surprising line here is the third one, which resounds with the
opening words of the service of the Eucharist in the Anglican church:
"Almighty God, unto whom all hearts are open, all desires known, and
from whom no secrets are hid. . . ." In context this allusion is astonishing—and perhaps risky in other ways, given interpretive practice. I
have observed that Wilbur's poetry can be made a playing field for
games of Find-the-Redemption, scavenger hunts for every possible

religious word or resonation, to be assembled (forcibly, if necessary) into Christian allegories which can take the place of richer, broader, better readings. This poem is no exception: here are words from a mass, an adaptable bird symbol, a *mezzo litro* of (holy?) wine in the closing verse, mention of a "black confession" seventy lines earlier— and if one would connect the dots and have this mind-reader be a Christ figure (or perhaps a Satan, for in this game one has choices), the poem will accommodate. But such constructs from Wilbur's poetry often must ignore the context of these echoes, and particular voices in which they are spoken. Only recall that this poem is *lui parla,* and the allegories begin to rattle: why should a Christ-like or Satanic Italian alcoholic be thinking in the parlance of Anglo-American protestants? He does not; this is conspicuously Wilbur's voice, not a violation of the etiquette of Browningesque monologue, but another indication of who *else* is talking to himself here, whose sensibility is also at stake in this test of the contrary vision. Coming late in the work Richard Wilbur has published to date, "The Mind-Reader" darkens and enriches much that has gone before, and it reveals, as do many of his long poems, a mind still keenly engaged with challenging border regions between selfhood and otherness.

5. Chances

The world of the younger poets, at present, certainly is the world of Richard
Wilbur and safer paler mirror-images of Richard Wilbur—who'd have
thought that the era of the poet in the Grey Flannel Suit was coming?
—Randall Jarrell, letter to Elizabeth Bishop, 1956

WITH SO MUCH cross-wiring in the past thirty years among
avant-garde movements, media caprice and hard sell, and
the rising academic establishments, one has to be quite careful when responding to art which somebody heralds as new. At the
moment, fame accrues to one young painter whose jackpot heresy
involves purchased specimens of "sofa art," the mass-market paintings
of mountain landscapes, clowns, and Parisian street scenes, the kind
bought for fifty dollars or so at shopping malls. Tacking six or eight of
these canvases together, he paints one huge Hollywood cartoon character smack in the midst of them. The resulting artifact or gesture is
construed by certain enthusiasts as witty satire on American kitsch—
and as such it sells. In fact it sells to the antibourgeois connoisseurs at
the Chase Manhattan Bank, which recently paid handsomely for a
piece of this action and published a cover photo of the new treasure on
an "acquisitions brochure" for shareholders.[1] Because few scholastic
and artistic pastimes have been more secure in the modern West than
ridiculing the tastes of the middle classes, the practice has become a
blue-chip cultural industry, a business for which there is as yet no pithy
name. Possibilities may occur to readers, and perhaps grosser examples; the point is that with such a university and media presence in arts
and letters of the United States, and with the sanctioning by influential
professionals of certain species of experimentation, it is not so easy to
discern who, in any mode, is taking chances, venturing with genius or
courage in some actually "new" direction, rather than accommodating
a style or a mentality which might have been fresher, more truly
experimental, twenty-odd years before. Even good museum curators
seem sometimes to forget that Duchamp signed his notorious urinals

and bicycle wheels and snow shovels many decades ago, and writing-center elders in expansive moods can be heard lauding "new voices" that sound uncannily like Robert Creeley, Gary Snyder, Denise Lever-tov, or other poets who have long since come in from the cold, and who at our academic conventions sit at the high table as familiar guests.

All of which sounds like a prelude to a case that Richard Wilbur is one of the few brave experimental voices we have. I have no such scheme in mind; what I want to suggest is that he should be recognized better for his own adventures, certain unpopular, unusual kinds of risk taking. On occasion Wilbur moves in directions almost no one else seems to be taking now, and to see some of his work in this light is to feel a little instructive vertigo about what it is to be adventurous in poetry. And it is to confront, as readers, certain aesthetic and human problems in a fresh way. This chapter deals with a range of works which seem from some perspectives peculiar, either on their own or in light of Wilbur's canon. Wilbur can sound flip, cavalier, irritating; he can march truculently into exhausted modes of poetry, reanimate forms which have long been worn out. He can take up voices which seem inescapably strange to the ear. And he says things, from time to time, which poet heroes on the national circuit are not now encouraged to say. Not all of these experiments work—if they all did, and if failures worked no harm, they would be paltry experiments indeed.

To achieve some conception of Richard Wilbur's courage as a poet and of the quality and originality of some of the artistic, political, and moral chances he takes, one could begin with the religious poems, which by themselves set him off from many of his good contemporaries. For not many other major poets in the past seventy years have written Christmas hymns, classic, straightforward Nativity celebrations with no irony to them, and which work beautifully in a traditional church service. Here is the opening stanza of "A Christmas Hymn," which appeared first in *Advice to a Prophet*—and which appears now in several standard Christian hymnals:

> A stable-lamp is lighted
> Whose glow shall wake the sky;
> The stars shall bend their voices,
> And every stone shall cry.
> And every stone shall cry,
> And straw like gold shall shine;
> A barn shall harbor heaven,
> A stall become a shrine.

"A Christmas Hymn" closes Wilbur's book; the vocal stones make a symmetrical arrangement with "Two Voices in a Meadow," which opens the collection, and in which the last word goes to a trustworthy, comfortable stone in the earth, "under the crib of God," aspiring to nothing but continuity and stability, congratulating itself for being one with the reliable slow-time facts of the universe. So we have God, nativity, and rocks opening and closing the book: handsome, but perhaps only in schematic ways. Spectacular symmetry—one of Wilbur's favorite tactics for running athwart poetic fashion—has come up before as an issue in this discussion; this instance, however, seems guilelessly simple. We begin and end with the rock-side of reality and of the self, those parts of both mind and worldly experience which do not seem to rattle with caprice, doubt, or self-consciousness—which is nature, human and otherwise, in its continuity, a reliable stillness for the world and the self.

And the poems are simple too: Wordsworthian peace pervades the first, and clear, earnest, old-style Protestant order and circularity define the hymn which comes last. The scene and the metaphors which set it going are stock, and center on the all-transfiguring power of Christ's birth. The stones cry out; the straw turns (in a way) to gold; the stable becomes holy; and a small ordinary place provides the "harbor" for everything that matters. One hears Christmas legend here, but also a touch of Wilbur's metaphysics: this is another of those Wilbur occasions when for an instant, through the power of one consciousness (divine or otherwise) things change state, alter their relationship to one another, reveal that "sublime decor" which underlies the known. Man and God perform the same species of miracle, imagination changing the world—and we seem to be in a realm of romantic or transcendental Christianity, which is one reason why the hymn's opening stanzas have an air of being centuries old. The second stanza contains few surprises, moving from Christmas to the Passion, keeping the refrain, calling these roadway stones "heavy, dull, and dumb," for part of the pleasure of a traditional hymn lies in how it ceremoniously affirms the obvious, shores up the footings underneath the extraordinary. There are a few twists here which as yet signify little: the palm cannot strew its own branches, and Christ when he rides through Jerusalem is no child. These are not so much liberties with the Gospels, however, as continuance of the idea that consciousness changes the world, that passionate imagining—sacred defamiliarization, if you will—can amount to seeing things more truly.

While much of this is familiar thinking in the Wilbur canon, here the poem ventures out of secularized metaphysics and into Christian theology. The only peculiar moment in the third stanza is its last line: the "again" may be standard scriptural allusion to a long sequence of violations of the Covenant, but the word suggests cycles as regular and seasonal as the quick passage from Christmas to Easter in this hymn. Odd overtones build up here: refusing God's love is as timeless a process as celebrating his birth, something Christendom does as reliably as gather to sing in late December. We make a round out of rejoicing and forsaking, because it is in the nature of the human mind to see clearly and see nothing at all, in a regular, almost melodic cadence. Again, this is at most a penumbral theme, in a stanza which follows, more or less faithfully, the ritual of berating mankind for its unregenerate ways; but the last stanza seems to bear out suspicions that this Christmas hymn is also, or at least a bit, about miracles of the imagination and how a Christmas created by and in the self is a real Christmas in a theological sense. Any recurring magic is brought about by the singing—of stars, stones, congregations, who not only praise the coming of Christ to earth, but also make that coming possible. The low which is lifted high is everything earthly, including the singing stones and the human heart, because one wishes and dreams it to be so; and the alien worlds that are reconciled here, or intended so to be, may include Wilbur's poetic sensibility, his idea of what it is to imagine, and the traditions of the Christian faith.

Friends of Wilbur say that he has been for many years a member of the Episcopal Church—meaning at least that he goes to services and counts himself part of a congregation. He has not advertised that fact, for reasons that perhaps are obvious, and though his poetry is often charged with the Christian mythology and iconography which lie at the core of the Western poetic tradition, his own verse does not seem to me to resolve its own crises by recourse to theology, church doctrine, or Christianity of either a denominational or generic kind. His short poems on scriptural subjects are together no more than a small-scale heresy, as far as poem fashions go: what the poems observe is human beings, not divinities or miracles; yet they are, some of them, corrosively satiric, because they attack not unbelief but intellectual and spiritual laziness, the mass-marketing of the contemporary condition. His short, light poem "Matthew VIII, 28 ff." for example is a gospel story about the socio-babble of the suburbs and the intellectually hip. The title refers to the moment when Jesus is faced by "demoniacs" spilling out of the Gadarene tombs, "so fierce," says Matthew, "that no one could pass that way." With a word, Jesus orders the demons out of these tormented folk and into a herd of swine, which immediately stampedes over a cliff and into the Sea of Galilee. It all takes a moment in Matthew, and the possessed Gadarenes of Matthew's Gospel, who cry out but once, do not deal in therapy-session or social science twaddle:

Rabbi, we Gadarenes
Are not ascetics; we are fond of wealth and possessions.
Love, as you call it, we obviate by means
Of the planned release of aggressions.

We have deep faith in prosperity.
Soon, it is hoped, we will reach our full potential.
In the light of our gross product, the practice of charity
Is palpably inessential.

As the poem keeps up this tone, the impatience which prowls behind the unctuous voice cannot be missed. These modernized demoniacs talk in bumper stickers about the self and the soul, seem to know all
the answers, yet can neither account for nor relieve their own misery.
Smug, materialistic, pseudological desperation: from a religious perspective or otherwise, that is what being possessed by devils might
mean now. These Gadarenes cannot hear the Rabbi's message because
they are not open to mystery, not aware of a world charged with more
possibilities than their store-bought rational systems allow. This is a
small poem, yet its ironies are heavy; nor does sniping at middle-class
complacency and sophomoric jadedness require much pluck. But beyond the pleasures of expanding and reimagining this moment from
Matthew, there may be a couple of forays here into treacherous ground.
Aside from taking liberties with the Gospel, moving well out beyond
the customary bounds of exegesis (or "applications," as Jonathan Edwards and other Calvinists called their modern lessons from Scripture),
there seems to be fury at sloppy-mindedness, and a rage which could be
construed—wrongly, I think—as against what the religious right calls
secular humanism. The satire is broad here, yet Wilbur's poem respects
certain distinctions in a time which commonly elides them. These are
not agnostic or atheist philosophers that the poem lambastes, but rather
the admen of aesthetic, moral, and theological fashions: people who
take shortcuts through the crises which make life intense; who use
beliefs of one sort or another to get ahead in their professional and social
careers, rather than to challenge or define a self; and who stitch together
flattering but ill-made intellectual garments out of the abused travail of
tougher, braver minds. A good companion piece to this poem is
Wilbur's early fable "Superiorities," which praises both an animal-
brave lout and a silent, stoic Victorian as better than those passengers
who huddle below decks in life, sharing borrowed "prayers" and other
socially sanctioned "proper studies." As "Superiorities" seems to have
it, one can get along either by a rough, lonely path of all-out self-
confrontation, or of rage and fear and intense spirituality, or by riding

some shabby elevator through the used-ideas warehouse of the culture. There is not much doubt as to which journeys Wilbur respects more: how one goes seems to matter more than where exactly one arrives.

Although he is one of the most fully realized and appealing personalities in the four Gospels, Simon called Peter is not a man of many words, and assigning him more voice than the New Testament affords him is a touchy business, for psychological as well as theological reasons. Peter is a physical man who can respond with action, even violence, in crisis, and his waverings of faith, his ups and downs of courage, make him the most puzzling, most vivid personality of the twelve. Speaking for saints is neither an easy nor a humble practice for poets, and a dive into the turmoiled mind of this ancient fisherman is as much a move into alien psychological territory as speaking like an Italian mind-reader. What is going on in "Peter," a kind of freeze-dried dramatic monologue of twenty tight, three-stress, rime-royal lines? The account of Peter's denial of Jesus on the night of the arrest appears in almost the same form in all four Gospels: in three of the four he warms himself by a fire in a courtyard, where he is accosted thrice, by three different people who recognize him. In two Gospels, Luke and John, he has drawn a sword at Jesus' arrest and cut the ear off a slave of the high priest, the only significant act of violence by a disciple in the Passion stories. But also in two Gospels the man called the Rock has fallen asleep at Gethsemane, unable to keep vigil for even one hour with his imperiled savior. "Peter" the poem imagines his own account of that day and night, that swing from weakness to fury to cowardice to humiliation—the transformations which do so much to make the Passion a tale of imaginable people. This short poem, late-Yeatsian in its austerity and hard sounds, is the tale of a would-be saint trapped in his humanity: in his physical nature, his human sloth, his dullness. Fear in this version has nothing to do with his denial of Jesus: the "new wine" of the Last Supper and the late-night fatigue seem to matter more. This can sound therefore like excuses—a common enough sin, yet not, by the scriptural account, one of Peter's on that night. What does he mean by implying that he has slept somehow through the whole business, not just the watch in the garden, but his own assault on the priest's minion, the following of his Master to prison, the questioning and the three denials, and even the recognition that he has fulfilled the prophecy? This cannot make sense or have dignity unless Peter's long sleep is of some other sort, something like a human failure to grasp, with enough intensity, some truth about what we are, and what is always at stake.

The final two stanzas develop an oddly clumsy conceit which

urges this theme along. The self is a kind of prison, a permanent confinement of cowardice, and of unawareness, of failure to rise with brains or spirit to occasions which warrant a waking-up to some decisive or transcendent moment when it comes knocking. Schematically at least, the conceit works well: commonplace enough to befit Peter's "rock" personality, his lack of metaphysical flash, the prison idea bulks naturally in the mind, if only because Jesus, at the poem's dramatized moment, is in Pilate's dungeons. The disciple without shares the plight of the Savior within, and Peter is unable to escape either fate or the moral consequences of his own humanity. Much in the poem militates to keep this ingeniousness from getting out of hand: the trimeter is flat, taciturn, the diction simple, the emotions either checked or understated—fisherman talk keeps the Renaissance symmetries of prosody under control. Peter tries to look at his own grief and humiliation only as a physiological event, carrying the stone prison a step farther—and perhaps one step too far. The last line has a strong, simple ring to it, but the conceit at the end seems beyond the poem's bounds: human identity and corporeal life as a prison confinement, the lashes of the eye as a grille of bars on the prison window, the tear-filled eye socket as the moat around the jail—it all adds up a little too well, if this is supposed to be both a vignette of Jesus' first and favorite disciple and an austere meditation on human frailty.

The near miss indicates a difficulty that Wilbur contends with through several poems on figures from Christian history and legend. The problem is to strike a reconciliation between, on one side, Wilbur's own contemporary, reflexive, paradox-happy sensibility, or the self-conscious poetry which that sensibility makes and favors; and on the other side, the simple fire of these intense, almost unimaginable souls. Wilbur has an easier time and better luck with his talky Gadarenes than with the quiet storm of Peter; in trying to speak for other souls and scriptural folk, one would like to succeed with more than villains and losers, charlatan mind-readers, smug or dejected refusers of belief. Perhaps this is a reason why Wilbur tries his hand with St. Teresa of Avila and John Chrysostom, both of whom an Episcopalian could well leave alone, as figures too passionate and antique for modern folk, Christian or otherwise, to understand sympathetically. Neither of these saints is given a voice in Wilbur's poems. Instead they are imagined closely if briefly as personalities—compassionately in the case of St. John Chrysostom, even more so in the case of St. Teresa. The difference in treatment has less to do with gender or theology than with the fact that John Chrysostom, for all his legendary rage, ultimately believed in *words,* in strong speech, and that through word and speech

127

he created a new self, while Teresa, by Wilbur's reckoning, had to contend with a catastrophe, as it were, of imaginative transcendence, of wordless ecstasy. Thanks to Bernini, St. Teresa of Avila is remembered as something like the Edgar Allan Poe of Renaissance saints, and Wilbur's brief poem challenges that recollection.

The poem about John Chrysostom, echoing the mind of the Early Church evangelist, seems to take sound and cadences in part from Dylan Thomas, whose short career brought him to the first rank quickly for his conjoining of rhetorical precision with what looked on the surface like reckless abandon. The interwoven rhyme scheme of "John Chrysostom" shows a Thomas trademark; and it was also Thomas's way to let lines avalanche through a stanza, as they do here, in one long, building sentence. Of our major poets in this century, Thomas with his rough passion suggests best, perhaps, the archaic energies of this fiery, Greek-speaking church father:

> He who had gone a beast
> Down on his knees and hands
> Remembering lust and murder
> Felt now a gust of grace,
> Lifted his burnished face
> From the psalter of the sands
> And found his thoughts in order
> And cleared his throat at last.

The poem seems to take liberties with the saint's biography: according to standard modern accounts,[2] if John Chrysostom knew "lust and murder" he knew them secondhand. Antioch, the town of his upbringing and early ministry, was a dangerous and wide-open place, but his own youth and schooling apparently passed without mayhem of his own to atone for. The "psalter of the sands" seems to be more than the desert of privacy and privation where any number of prophets have meditated and found their voices. It may mean again the psalter of firsthand earthly experience, where the abstractions of philosophy and theology are tempered and sincerity is tested. Directly or otherwise, Wilbur's John Chrysostom knows common experience, knows sin and the underside of life. The "wildness" in the last line casts a certain shading back upon "dumb" in the line before. Wildness is passion, but sometimes also simplemindedness, animal stupidity; and properly or not, "dumb" in common American speech can mean much the same thing. "John Chrysostom" seems to puzzle over a question more than it sketches an ancient personality. This question has to do with how, as Auden put it, the free man might praise, given what he knows now,

universes and human truths that this early saint could never have
dreamed of—and what capacity for fierce simplicity had to be given up
for such knowledge. In preaching, Chrysostom excelled beyond all
those "gelded priests" because unlike them he had lived intensely; yet
unlike us he knew a world which, compared to our own, was as simple
as sand. "John Chrysostom" does not range far, either in length or in
ambitions: one gets a quick look into his face, as into the enigmatic eyes
of an ancient Byzantine icon; and the problem that such a self poses
down through the man-forgetting centuries is merely spoken, not
pondered for long.

St. Teresa the Spanish Carmelite is contemplated more steadily,
perhaps because her story suggests something less antique, more familiar to the modern consciousness, more possible as a way of being that a
modern self might understand or achieve—perhaps "fall into" is closer
to the mark. For Teresa, as one of the most popular of European saints,
is remembered for her sublime, bizarre, holy-erotic vision—a kind of
Christian version of Poe's *Eureka*—and for a theology founded on this
catastropic moment of imaginative rapture. "Teresa" is a poem with a
cause: it does not quarrel with Teresa, doubt the power or the truth,
whatever its origin, of her mystical breakthrough. The retort in the
poem addresses a culture which recalls her wrongly, as Bernini por-
trayed her in his showboat style, with her eyes closed, mouth open,
submitting to that smirking angel and his little arrow—the Teresa of
almost licentious surrender, not hard sacrifice. That misunderstanding
of her life is perhaps akin to the shortcut transcendentalism Wilbur
found around him in the early seventies, when the poem took shape;
and an impatience with such complacency may be smoldering behind
this brief rewrite of the life of the saint. *After* her vision, Teresa went to
work, led a life of hard menial service in the Spanish outback; but it is
not easy to make flashy sculpture out of that. So Wilbur gives Teresa
some help, putting the middle stanza of his poem through a somer-
saulting analogy, a leap of metaphysical wit to match Bernini's baroque
spectacle:

> Not all cries were the same;
> There was an island in mythology
> Called by the very vowels of her name
>   Where vagrants of the sea,
> Changed by a wand, were made to squeal and cry
> As heavy captives in a witch's sty.

A note at the end of the book tells that this is Circe's island, Aeaea from
The Odyssey, where Ulysses' crew was transformed into swine—a long

jump indeed from Teresa's ecstasy. Yet the poem has opened not with the vision but after it. With her mouth shut and her eyes open, Teresa is in the midst of that unspectacular but urgent business of trying to make human sense of what she has undergone. Just who thinks of Aeaea, herself or the speaker thinking for her, stays unclear, but that may be of small concern. The self-conscious mind knows that the wordless experience, the intuitive recognition, the long vowel-cry, can come from many places within, as well as perhaps from without; and for Wilbur even a saint—perhaps especially a saint—has to wonder about the truth of revelations. The closing stanza tries to get the problem settled, though perhaps less patly than the language might on the surface suggest:

> The proof came soon and plain:
> Visions were true which quickened her to run
> God's barefoot errands in the rocks of Spain
>   Beneath its beating sun,
> And lock the O of ecstasy within
> The tempered consonants of discipline.

The complex significations of "true" have come up before in reading Wilbur's poems, and perhaps one can know instinctively, when seeing the word, that questions about truth are being puzzled over, not finessed. Wilbur seems to be playing pragmatist here, in a William Jamesian way: the world was made better by St. Teresa as a consequence of her vision, for out of that experience, she became a preeminently useful and charitable human being. Therefore the vision was "true" by pragmatic or situational measure—as true, in other words, as a skeptical philosopher can make out. Even so, older ways of judging the "truth" of religious conversion may resonate here too: St. Paul's premise that works are a validation of faith, and American Calvinist recognitions of good deeds as indications, if not always "true" ones, of divine grace. Once again Wilbur seems to address several sides of an old dispute at once. The poem celebrates St. Teresa on both transcendental and existential grounds, for her vision is "true" from either a theological or a utilitarian perspective. The poem apparently evades the question as to which is the right way to think about her. Putting faith to work, Teresa turns out all right one way or another, and her psychological condition is a question too distant to matter. Wilbur's doctrine of disciplined imagining *and* engagement with daily life holds up here in more than one kind of philosophical or theological weather.

But while most of that, as a theme, falls within charted Wilbur domains, there may be something unusual, even presumptuous in the tone of these lines, which like "John Chrysostom" suggest that Wilbur is he who knows the hearts of saints, understands fine points about conversions and divine revelation. If this is a valid inference, it would not be an unusual act of hubris in our time: troubled by a century's aphasia on the subject of goodness and faith, Lowell, Eliot, Pound, Shaw, Kazantzakis, and others have tried some modern reimagining of Jesus himself, of Christian saints or other holy folk, to seek reconciliation between the ungainly, insistent stories of these lives, and modern ideas of what it means to be intelligent, to be fully conscious, or to believe. Having taught the Milton course at Wesleyan for a dozen years, Wilbur has had plenty of experience with the best English practitioner of this trade. But where Milton, Pound, and Lowell grow thunderous, Wilbur can turn uncommonly quiet: even the poem about John Chrysostom's rhetorical fire is only sixteen lines of plain, self-resisting trimeter. More telling is the way that Wilbur's saint poems seem to stalk around their subjects curiously, not coming too close, not presuming that the mystery of these supremely "other" selves can be solved. The attention is not so much on who these saints were as on what they signify—or could now signify—if a contemporary world were to overcome its self-involvement a little and imagine some full measure of humanity into these iconic figures, who task us from the chronicles of our own culture.

Such an enterprise has a high ring to it, and if one objects to saints, one still cannot fault Wilbur for low seriousness here. But with Anglo-American poetry heavily involved in dramatizing the collapse of faith and the erosion of faith in language, and with a public apparently convinced that true poets cannot speak well except from some species of torment, Wilbur's composure and air of geniality have been bothersome, and there are poems in which he seems to flaunt good humor and breeziness in a literary world which (officially at least) has limited patience with such moods. Some other fine poets drink, take peculiar pills, consider suicide, write about doing those things; Wilbur takes himself jogging and dares to write about that. Poetry is supposed to be solemn business; Wilbur can make poems which unregenerately suggest that poetry is also fun. In the building of reputations and the riding of trends, these light poems may be chancier in some ways than the ones about holiness.

"Running"—really three poems in one—could be wrapped up as exhibit A in a case against Wilbur as reprehensibly well adjusted. It dates from the midsixties, about ten years before the practice caught on as an American bourgeois health craze; in *Walking to Sleep* the poems come right after "For Dudley," a quietly unconsoled elegy for Dudley

Fitts. So in a sense "Running" seems a rebuilding from grief and from the failure of thought to allay that grief. Playfully, it presents a version of those allegorical trilogies by Romantic or Pre-Raphaelite painters—youth, maturity, age—with running as the stand-in, as it were, for some more familiar trope like the "voyage" of life. But "Running" gets there gradually: the first poem in the set, "1933," is bright, quick kinesthetics, a memory of the animal pleasure of running bases as a twelve-year-old boy. The memory is specific, of grounds near the Wilbur family farm in North Caldwell, New Jersey; and no grown-up moralizing is appended to the reminiscence. Wilbur plays by a classic rule of post-Romantic poetry, that a thing must be itself before it can be anything else. Here running is running, the mind a delighted blank, and all thought (to borrow a phrase from "A Fire-Truck") blurs to sheer verb. The language is simple, with lots of Anglo-Saxon drawn from the parlance of boys and their sports pages; but the meter is as showboat as a child proud of his speed and style. The quatrain ties together a shifting, leaping 5–3–4–5 meter scheme, with each third line in doubt, loaded with precarious spondees:

> Down the cart-road past Rickard's place,
>
> . . . .
> Took two hard lopes, and at the third
>
> . . . .
> By the bull-pen, and up the lane.

The effect is exuberance recollected in tranquillity, wild energy barely concentrated in the craft of the run. This is nothing much, but deft as a starting point, establishing memory as something unedited and re-affirming moments within memory that neither sadness nor reason nor age can alter or dismiss.

"Patriots' Day" moves ahead a generation: in the second stanza one learns that the restless "we" of this poem is no longer boys playing, but softened "fathers and our little sons," waiting along the road to see the real runners in the Boston Marathon. And so it is only in the second stanza that one knows for sure that years have passed since "1933." Age in these poems comes in jolts, and running is part of what of the last of them calls "the thing which men will not surrender," their belief in their own vitality and power, their faith in the corporeal side of iden-tity and experience. The older voice of "Patriots' Day" is now self-conscious, capable of being "put to shame," and capable also of talking in double-edged words which convey the pain and delight of seeing somebody else run better, somebody else play the hero in your own and your children's eyes. Entering the poem when the runners do, in the third stanza, the metaphors are edged with envy and a bit of resentment:

Dark in the glare, they seemed to thresh in place
Like preening flies upon a window-sill,
Yet gained and grew, and at a cruel pace
Swept by us on their way to Heartbreak Hill—

The pace is cruel to the runners—and cruel to these fathers who can only watch them; Heartbreak Hill, an agonizingly long rise up Commonwealth Avenue toward the end of the race, is a lucky name, certainly, if one wants to look at this marathon as having connections to the classic conception of the good race of life, replete with its own heartbreaks, and find some weightier meaning in Kelley's "champion" style of being "at rest within his run," "stamping on the sun" like a hero out of obscure mythology. But all that seems tertiary to the shift from running to watching, from furious, mindless motion to envious reflection, and the recognition of a process of growing from a child's action into an adult's impatience, and then perhaps to a restful cadence that can take one a long way. These are lightweight recognitions, pleasantly presented; the subsequent shift is to time present and to the perspective of the middle-aged man who jogs now rather than runs, and who is trying to make peace with his own waning speed and endurance and the fact that he must give way to other, better runners.

Whitman's is the voice he echoes for this last poem, called "Dodwells Road" (in the neighborhood of Wilbur's Cummington house). It is an uncustomary voice for Wilbur: irregular, breath-length lines, rhetorical questions and truculent challenges to the reader, showy vernaculars. The breath-cadenced lines have an explanation: our speaker has just finished a run, and with his own breath coming unsteadily, he seems to pitch out verses between gasps. But Whitman is present in more ways than this, and for more reasons. Modest and light as it is, "Dodwells Road" is a poem about age, about reckoning with the ego and with diminishing powers, about a grudging embrace, as it were, for the shape and the onward motions of a worldly adventure that is already beginning to pass one by. "Song of Myself" is a song of *ourselves,* about an aging Whitman, in good health again and a little smug about that, but feeling and celebrating the energies of a humanity wider than his own—the transcendental consolation that comes with accepting mortality.

Described so, this sounds like heavy stuff for a morning run; Wilbur's poem may try Whitman on for size, but it does not dish out Whitmanesque transcendentalism wholesale for the second-wind market. The first poem in the set is about a boy's exuberant egotism, the second about the civil humiliations of being grown up and watching from the sidelines as the dreams pass by; the third, not really a resolution, ruminates on the language and the spirit of that inevitable losing. We do not give up our power. It is taken from us, and the larger world which receives it has perhaps heard enough from the souls of aged men, clapping hands and singing overlong about that loss and how content they are anyway. "Dodwells Road" begins with the kinesthetics of running and being winded, and after this bout with mortality and the creaky habits of poets, the poem goes back to the pure experience. Those opening lines catch what the world looks and sounds like to the senses of someone winded. The scene is edged with dizziness, racing pulse, elevated blood pressure; the rushing streams may not be merely out in the woods, but inside, the thrumming of someone's overtaxed vascular system:

> The wind harsh and cool to my throat,
> A good ache in my rib-cage.
>
> Loud burden of streams at run-off,
> And the sun's rocket frazzled in blown tree-heads:
> Still I am part of that great going,
> Though I stroll now, and am watchful.

Watchful of what? Of himself as well as the world, and of his physical as well as his psychological state: the scene around him is charged with his own exhaustion and the limits to what he sees are patently his own limits too. The reflective powers, however, are in fine shape, and taking off as the man's body slows and cools, they rove through a few perceptions about the hungry hearts of maturing men. The turning-point lines of the poem may have a Beat ancestry, but they show Wilbur-style multiplicity:

> But why in the hell spoil it?
> I make a clean gift of my young running
> To the two boys who break into view.

Spoil it: spoil the expansive mood, the inevitable giving, but also the "clean" thinking, the response uncluttered, unpredicated by anyone else's crisis and words. The world goes its "full tilt" way with or without the blessings of anyone in the midst of it, and poets may need to quit their own poet minds and poet voices for a while to feel shapes and motions which they do not themselves create. In a gentle way, Wilbur comes up against the old paradox of subjectivity, the recognition that as a range of prophets from St. Paul to W. C. Williams has insisted, silence and a kind of self-forgetting are a way out of exhausting, confining circuits of the mind. So the poem at the end goes back to something like pure seeing: if one wants some allegorical arrangement in the chain of being and moving that closes "Dodwells Road," with the old jogger giving way to these leaping and running boys, and they in turn to the dog, and the dog to the flushed pheasant, the symmetries are there for the taking. But this is a poem that seems gently to warn, in the same words, that sometimes it is best to leave grand thinking well alone.

Yet if we want complexity, it is here, and consequential. Consider the reverberations of one quatrain in particular:

> You, whoever you are,
> If you want to walk with me you must step lively.
> I run, too, when the mood offers,
> Though the god of that has left me.

The first two lines could be straight out of "Song of Myself," as a playful, earnest Whitman often prods us in such language to keep up with him on the poem's unpredictable run through prophecies, insights, visions, and horse sense. Yet if these lines in "Dodwells Road" are a poet's voice as well as an aging runner's, who is speaking here, and who is being addressed about what? Is Wilbur nudging his reader, "whoever you are," in Whitman fashion, suggesting that there may be more in this poem, more recognitions or allusions or connections or whatever, than the smooth surfaces of this or other of his lyrics suggest? Is it possible that Wilbur is playing medium for a moment, hearing his "father" Whitman speak to him clearly for once, in Wilbur's own mind, which has been altered or opened by physical exhaustion and a nice day in the woods? Is there a suggestion then that Wilbur as an artist has not "stepped lively" enough yet to understand Whitman well, and that the Whitman way of looking at things is something a formal poet like Wilbur, in middle age, ought to know better? Possible quandaries: looking at the latter two lines of the stanza, one may hear a tone which at least gives shape to the mystery, though nothing may be resolved. "I run, too": like Whitman and his many followers I can go all out for imaginative experience, dream as freely and perilously as anyone else, when the mood offers—though as time goes on I, as an artist, am dreaming less, meditating and crafting more. But one way or another, I am not to be clocked or typed—for old or young, I contain multitudes. Such interpretive possibilities, if indeed they are here, would not fragment "Running" but converge within it. Poets resist their literary fathers and love them; freedom and formality are values that must be affirmed, contended with, and even surrendered when the time is right. "Running" does not constitute *rapprochement* with either Whitman or Williams: the mind has its shifting moods and shapes, its varying responses to the world; Wilbur has picked no quarrel with contemporaries. The poet, for his part, can loaf, and imaginatively and linguistically go wherever he wants. The "Running" poems may be light, but they do not lightly consider how lightness matters in a complete, plausible sensibility, or how hard that fullness is to sustain.

Richard Wilbur's interest in translating ancient and medieval riddles runs back almost thirty years: there are small crops of them in *Advice to a Prophet, The Mind-Reader,* and in the "New Poems" section of the 1988 collection. This last group originally appeared in a 1981 chapbook from The Deerfield Press.[3] From the beginning they have seemed like small lessons in an archaeology of wit, glimpses into the wordplay and the delight of old minds in epistemological and linguistic mysteries, and the odd entanglements that reality, words, and the mind can get into. They sometimes have a scholarly air to them, and come as moments of stillness rather than levity in the galleries of poems which make up these collections. Until recently, Wilbur had said little about this longstanding interest in riddles, but lately he has written a fine essay about their history, their continuing power, and their close connection to Wilbur's own idea of the poem. For like high formality, riddles stream down to us from the primal, Edenic, or Arcadian beginnings of poetry, times when they had "sacred uses, and were a way of approaching the spirits of things":

> If poetry deals in surprise and delayed apprehensions, then the riddle exaggerates an essential characteristic of poetry. If metaphor, the perception of resemblances, is central to poetry, then the riddle operates near that center. If lyric poetry perceives wonder and mystery, so does the riddle. And if poetry may be seen as offering a continuing critique of our sense of order, the riddle has its peculiar aptitude for that.
>
> Thus, though they have long been slighted by common opinion, riddles are irrepressible; they so belong to poetry's nature that if we scan American verse of the last two centuries, riddle and the spirit of riddle crop up surprisingly often.[4]

Delaying this explanation of his interest for so long, forty years into his career, has been for Richard Wilbur perhaps a bit of chance taking in itself. In this same essay, he acknowledges that "many people nowadays, if they think of the riddle at all, consider it a sort of trick question which . . . once clarified, self-destructs, as Rumpelstiltskin did when the miller's daughter spoke his name."[5]

One wonders if this assumed self-destruction has been so self-*contained* when it comes to his own work, and whether these spates of riddling, enigmatic on several levels, have not contributed to misapprehensions about collections in which they have appeared. For most of the riddles in Wilbur's collections are translated from Roman texts or the Latin of the early Middle Ages, and the reality they accordingly suggest, when read in sequence, seems safer and more orderly than Richard Wilbur's own cosmos seems to be. While these riddles by Aldhelm or Symphosius favor surprises and ironic arrangements, and fresh ways of looking at the ordinary, their paradoxes look consolingly formal, smooth turnabouts in a grand and geometric reality. A couple of handsome examples from "Eight Riddles from Symphosius" in *Advice to a Prophet:*

I bite, when bitten; but because I lack
For teeth, no biter scruples to attack,
And many bite me to be bitten back.

Unequal in degree, alike in size,
We make our flight, ascending toward the skies
And rise with those who by our help can rise.

An onion and a flight of stairs are respectively the answers: the riddle world of classical and medieval times is a place where solutions are sure. When Richard Wilbur goes riddling on his own, however, the world glimpsed and represented is not quite so bounded or assuringly arranged. Called simply "A Riddle," from *Walking to Sleep:*

Where far in forest I am laid,
In a place ringed around by stones,
Look for no melancholy shade,
And have no thoughts of buried bones;
For I am bodiless and bright,
And fill this glade with sudden glow;
The leaves are washed in under-light;
Shade lies upon the boughs like snow.

Though the answer here is a campfire, certain possibilities seem to linger in this scene, this woodland transformed, for the moment, by a small fire and an imaginative spark. As with the old riddles, there are symmetries here: firelight comes to these trees of night from precisely the wrong direction, with the shadows above and the glow beneath them, and the man-made fire drives back the gloom and fear of a black evening. But campfires are contrived, and they do not last long; they gleam and are gone, like Arnold's light from the French coast, or Wilbur's "The Beacon," making sudden sense of "the sea-in-itself," for an instant that must be remembered and then must be questioned. This "melancholy shade" is not banished; it just is not looked for, and the "buried bones" all around are not dismissed so much as temporarily denied. Let the campfires go out, and all will be doubtful and disheveled once again; order and surprise in riddles and riddling poems might be flickering firelight, among shadows unimaginably vast.

Part Three of *The Mind-Reader* includes surprises of a different sort, an excursion into facetiousness, wedged between some sober translations of classic French love-and-death poems and gray- or black-humored modern Russians. "Flippancies," the opening poem of the set, consists of two short, discrete satires with no apparent connection, save that they offset and soften each other. The second one seems an abrasive, reductive dig at a poetic main event of the sixties and seventies—not the confessionalism of the gifted few, like Sexton, Lowell, Plath, Hugo, and James Wright, but the derivative agonies of lesser talents, sojourns in the void typed up neatly and submitted to the promotion files. My ironies sound flat, and for that matter, so do Wilbur's in "What's Good for the Soul Is Good for Sales": surely he is entitled to such jibes, and in a way one is gratified to see him return one of the brickbats that Bly and others have aimed at him as a way of gaining space for their own work.[6] Wilbur has rarely returned fire; one such instance, a little poem at least as good as "What's Good for the Soul," was sent as a note to Bly's magazine *kayak,* and remains uncollected:

A POSTCARD FOR BOB BLY

Having extolled a campy magazine
As a "fist" raised against my kind of writing,
What will you tell me now, friend? That you mean
No harm, of course, and would not dream of fighting,
And have but put, in furtherance of your Mission,
A little punch into your disquisition.

Granted that it's a figurative fist;
That critics punch as harmlessly as kittens;
That you have merely slapped me on the wrist
With one of *kayak*'s puce Alaskan mittens;
Nevertheless, when you incite to riot
Against your friend, he is not pleasured by it.[7]

This is a sharp jab, not a roundhouse punch. In contrast, the latter half of "What's Good for the Soul" tries to move quickly through some conventional cues for passion to imply that the packaged misery of much contemporary verse likewise does not really add up, that real and bogus crises are being tossed together into the soul's fire, for the sake of a quick blaze and little heat:

> So it be tristful, tell us what you choose:
> Hangover, Nixon on the TV news,
> God's death, the memory of your rocking-horse,
> Entropy, housework, Buchenwald, divorce,
> Those damned flamingoes in your neighbor's yard . . .
> All hangs together if you take it hard.

The epigram which wraps this up is worth collecting and remembering. But the bulk of the poem seems to be a Woody Allen array of incongruous disasters. This is not a stop-and-think poem but a return salvo, which provides little more than a sense that there is a temper here to be felt sometimes behind the wit. The first poem in the set is a counterbalance because it is reflexive: Wilbur's shot at the game of confessional poetry is offset by a swipe at poet careers, confessional or not, and including his own. The two most recent books occasionally resonate with thought about what art and the stages of life have to do with each other; the joke upon which these eight lines run has to do with carrying the old American "star" metaphor for eminence out to a preposterous astronomical extreme. Much is here: interstellar distances and their effect on radiance, the life cycle of suns, the lower temperature and the great extension of the bright old red giants:

> Then, white with years, live wisely and survive.
> Thus you may be on hand when you arrive,
> And, like Antares, rosily dilate,
> And for a time be gaseous and great.

"Gaseous," the punch word of the joke, needs no explaining, but perhaps one needs to notice behind it, and behind the caricature of poet lives, a certain shiver of futility. Stars blaze for a while in the empty black of space—and how long does their light last when and where it might "arrive"? The dazzling of "future days" might be meaningless, and this reward for being productive and "white-hot" when young, this time as an eminent blowhard, a few years of bulky greatness on the human scene—what is that worth? I do not want to suggest more than a few shadows amid this light and behind this self-announced flippancy; but such shadows seem to be there.

After these come two medieval riddles, followed by two poems entirely new and Wilbur's own: "Rillons, Rillettes" and "The Prisoner of Zenda"—a gourmet poem and a movie poem. "Rillons, Rillettes" is as defiantly airy as Wilbur gets, an Oscar Wilde rumination on, as the opening note says, an "hors d'oeuvre *made up of a mash of pigmeat, usually highly seasoned,*" and beyond that, on thinking deeply about grand and abstract problems. A contradiction in an "Encyclopaedia of Gastronomy," a coffee-table book, is the cue for a ghastly opening joke, some sharp play with French and English end rhymes, and a "solution" to the problem contorted enough to qualify for *Yale French Studies:*

> Does Blois supply, do you suppose,
> The best *Rillettes de Tours,* while those
> Now offered by the chefs of Tours
> Are, by their ancient standards, poor?

So much for modern intellectual life. A close friend of Wilbur, who has known and admired him throughout his career, refers to him as a "peasant" in spirit, unsympathetic to the epistemological and aesthetic maze making that sometimes passes for work in the humanities. Preferring instead complexities of his own device, he seems to suspect anything knocked together out of reasoning alone. Our practicing Anglican can equate the mysteries of the Trinity with those of French pig-pastes because the theme of the poem is that thinking can lead one into vertigo, into a loss of a sense of proportion, into forgetting about the different consequences of problems which come into the ken of the logical mind. We need something else—unspecified here in this humorous poem—to carry us to a point where sausage, theology, and infinity are not all of one weight. One need spend but a little time at academic conferences in the humanities to feel a touch of the same yearning.

The last poem in the trio forms a complement to the first two: coming along with a satire on careers and a gag about the authority of printed words and the rational mind, is a light piece about the limits of "serious" art: while it is not a Warholian joke so self-conscious and extravagant as to claim reverse-spin solemnity for itself, it is pointed and effective in its own way. "The Prisoner of Zenda" muses not on Anthony Hope's novel but on the film—which is not film so much as movie, ham-and-egg Hollywood romance. Tonally, we find out where we are in two quick lines:

> At the end a
> "The Prisoner of Zenda"

If by chance one does not catch on, the second stanza does the same thing, matching "behavia" with "Flavia"—ingenious idiot-rhymes from some New Jersey dialect. There are other caperings between: the first stanza rhymes "star" with "Kerr," recalling one of those non-lessons that every young American once learned who wanted to talk glibly about high-class English actresses. Deborah Kerr does rhyme with star: few people in this country know that without being told, and the fun lies in being teased a little about the trash knowledge Americans accumulate without really wanting to—the thick pseudoculture of modern times. The movie "The Prisoner of Zenda" with Deborah Kerr (pronounced like *star*) and *two* Stewart Grangers belongs in the board game Trivial Pursuit—or does it? Does this artifact, with its "plot so moral," have legitimate claims upon one's attention? Insofar as there is a "moral" to this poem, here it is. All sorts of imaginative contrivances, books, movies, poems, tug at our sleeves, and we must decide how seriously to take each and all of these overtures. This is a silly poem about the endemic silliness of taking poems too seriously; it considers an old chestnut of a movie which both moves us, and moves us to laughter. The last stanza is a handsome triple flip of a joke: how seriously should one take words about not taking words too seriously? There are finally not two, but three Stewart Grangers to account for:

> One redeeming factor,
> However, is that the actor
> Who plays the once-dissolute King
> (Who has learned through suffering
> Not to drink or be mean
> To his future Queen),
> Far from being a stranger,
> Is *also* Stewart Granger.

So there is Stewart Granger as Rassendyll the heroic impostor, Granger as the once-dissolute king, and Granger as the familiar movie actor, the leading man never quite forgotten even as we suspend disbelief, almost successfully, in this far-fetched and lovely tale. It is consoling, a relief from our moral quandary, that the noble Rassendyll gives up his "future Queen" to himself, since Granger is playing both parts; it is also a relief that the film, like this or any poem, never obliterates from the mind all the comforting signs of its own contrivance. The artist that agonizes also edits; and a "somebody," like those unseen hands which organize Elizabeth Bishop's wonderful Esso station, sets things in order, tidies up, puts passion and the noble self-sacrifice on film stock and poems neatly on the printed page. Art, as artifice, is never perfectly grave. And from the kitschy movie or the great poem we can always recover. These three "Flippancies," one on the poet game, one on limits of reason, the last on the intrinsic limits of art, thus work well together as the sort of unconscionable levity that guides reading and makes writing and reading a little more honest as human ventures.

The most identifiable sort of public-speech poetry, political verse, has never died out as a mode practiced by leading American poets, yet it has picked up a kind of etiquette that MacLeish, Frost, and other wartime practitioners would not have countenanced. One can identify these traits without, I hope, resorting to political diatribe of one's own. A reading of Ginsberg, Ferlinghetti, Merwin, Rich, Levertov, and others who spoke out about political matters and public issues in the fifties, sixties, and seventies may suggest the ground rules: a refusal to embrace, at least in published verse, the status quo; a kind of institutionalized Bertrand de Bornism, a passionate rejection of compromise or any moderated way of living with or transforming that status quo; and a rejection of work celebrating or commemorating official holidays, national achievements, bourgeois festivals, or public figures, except for those who have have died catastrophically. Irony and rage are preferred fuels for contemporary public verse. One can trundle out plenty of ironies about such ground rules and build shapely arguments for their urgency or cultural inevitability. But one way or another, in such a situation the poet who celebrates marriages and railroad stations, writes cantatas for superpageants in New York harbor, and pleads for social and political change on the basis of cool-headed common sense, is running against the grain. The cantata for the Statue of Liberty, which Wilbur wrote a few years ago as Poet Laureate, is a case by itself which I shall come to in a moment; but his liberal rather than academic-radical voice in public-issue poetry goes back to the beginning of his career, and this voice has not always been welcome. But there is no point making Wilbur out as a martyr for his unfashionable discourse on public issues; by no measure, partisan or otherwise, is this material among his very best work, and the point of looking at it here is to see what happens when he ventures out into these trampled arenas, and what sort of reconciliation he can achieve between passing public-life concerns and mysteries more durably on his mind.

Though written several years apart, two poems from the early books seem to have duality at their heart: behind each poem's response to the newspapers and the radio is a dilemma about what kind of poet speech can be right for such a time, when year in and year out, the American ear is being drummed to deafness by ugly new voices. From *The Beautiful Changes,* "A Simplification," perhaps by intention, seems to backfire, even in its title. Rhetoric, so the argument has it, has grown simple, weak, and flat; thundering battles between faiths have rotted down to a shrugging agnosticism—and this or any sixteen-line grumbling summary of moral history has to be too simple itself. Gone are the great old boys of ranting, Bryan, the English iconoclasts, an American fury named Brann (who, as Wilbur confesses in a note, was not great at all, but whose name sounds good here); and Jahweh, both as the eloquent and personal head of the human tribe, and the nameless God of good speech, "simply withdrew" from us as once He did from Saul. But the rest of the poem seems a victim of the same curse, for it fails to keep its implicit promise to strike some good blow for the losing cause. Who in blazes are "These foetal- / Voiced people" that Wilbur can not stand to listen to? Dewey and Truman? The Germans in the Nuremberg docket? The Boston City Council? A few now-forgotten poets of the time? It is not hard to imagine what is unsettled in Wilbur's mind with regard to rhetoric, or what the trouble is in getting that said: Brann and Bryan and these "catarrhal Colonels" are stand-ins for big talkers closer to our own time, Pound, Yeats, Eliot, maybe Vachel Lindsay and Wyndham Lewis, maybe others, whose "good round rhetoric" went wrong, spoke for some sinister causes, and in some cases got innocent people killed. The trouble with rhetoric after the war had nothing to do with statue smashing of the seventeenth century or the forgettable Brann who was shot in Waco in 1898; the trouble included the fresh memory of Pound's anti-Semitic broadcasts for Mussolini, Eliot's *After Strange Gods,* and the pro-Hitler sentiments of poets whose enthusiasms for fine language and new worlds drew them, for a time at least, toward the hosts of intolerance and murder. War does its damage to round rhetoric too, and if there is any sentiment behind the inchoate scorn of "A Simplification," that other sentiment seems tristful, frustrated, like Arnold's in "Rugby Chapel," for "A Simplification" seems itself caught between two worlds of discourse— one dead, one powerless as yet to be born.

Once only in *Things of This World,* nine years later, does Wilbur speak out on a worldly issue, and he tries to work past the prophet speech dilemma by going back in time to one of his favorite rhetorical hunting grounds, the Middle Ages. "Speech for the Repeal of the McCarran Act" drops rhyme, drops regularity of meter, in emulation of the plain talk of Old English homilies, especially those of Wulfstan, the eleventh-century Bishop of York whose sermons survive in manuscript. Plainness is the watchword: the very title word of the poem is "speech," not "ode" nor even "verses"; and the strong implication of the poem is that clear thinking, straightforward language, colorful, folksy metaphor, and a respect for plain truth can guide us now, as then, through riptides of domestic and international trouble. The Mc-Carran Act aimed to defend the country against the leftist politics of some postwar refugees; the narrowest intent of Wilbur's "speech" is to proclaim that our own moral and rhetorical health, if we look to it as plain folk in the Anglo-Saxon mode, will give protection against shifty ideas from across the waters. "Let thought be free," he says: what could be plainer than that? A problem with the poem is that it seems more interested in Wulfstan and his colorful ways of speaking than in the Act or the political realities into which this little poem, mannered in its very plainness, must sail. Two of the four short stanzas—the two with the most vivid and original diction—are about things that Wilbur is "not speaking of": rose windows and rail lines devastated by war. The rhetoric seems round all right, but roundabout, reluctant to get into the matter, name names, or move from the gentlemanly and generic to the specific. Again a Pound-fashioned wall seems to loom up, and Wilbur for a host of reasons, historical, aesthetic, and temperamental, does not scale it. In his verse he has kept quiet about politics, about specific infringements on freedom of thought during the McCarthy years, the Kennedy era, the opening years of the Vietnam War; when Lowell and other writers boycotted receptions given at the Johnson White House for the arts, Wilbur was known to put on his tie and go, and on the printed page he was silent about public affairs until 1967—not late for a sixties political conversion, but not at the head of the pack either. When Lyndon Johnson invaded aesthetics, Wilbur retaliated with a quick raid into satire and political commentary.

"A Miltonic Sonnet for Mr. Johnson on His Refusal of Peter Hurd's Official Portrait" is a rare *ad hominem* attack, and it arrives buffered with disclaimers. It is one of only two poems in the canon with a specific date affixed to it (6 January 1967), which conveys the impression that it was written like one of Milton's political sonnets, in a white heat that must be taken into account, and perhaps forgiven; the title's allusion to Milton may ask indulgence in the same way, fury and irony being, after all, a manner one can borrow from the very best sources. And this smacks a little of condescension too: the title takes it for granted that Johnson has not read Milton and will not recognize or understand the style. But for all this handsome combativeness, the poem again proceeds by indirection: most of it is about not Johnson but Jefferson, by whose measure not only Johnson but practically every other president falls short. Most of the opening stanza is a perfect pedestal inscription for a Jefferson monument, in a style that emulates the style of Jefferson's mind and life, elegance with simplicity:

Who drew our Declaration up, who planned
Range and Rotunda with his drawing-hand
And harbored Palestrina in his head,
Who would have wept to see small nations dread
The imposition of our cattle-brand,
With public truth at home mistold or banned,
And in whose term no army's blood was shed.

The shorter second stanza springs the trap: Johnson's grousings that the Capitol, painted in the background of the portrait, is too bright, and that the whole work was too large, are pregnant with ironies that poor Lyndon cannot see, just as he cannot see how history will "render" him. The ironies get the better of sense: "Wait, Sir, and see how time will render you" needs Milton to excuse itself. As Calvinist rage the line works, perhaps, but as counsel, even of a sarcastic sort, it might seem far-fetched. Oh, well: the poem was written in one day, or so we are reminded. Its last six lines are as caustic as Wilbur ever gets in verse, and by the standards of some of his contemporaries—Ferlinghetti, Olson, Wright, and Nemerov come to mind—that is not very caustic at all. Explanations of Wilbur's mildness, in hot political times, will likely depend on one's own politics and sympathy for Wilbur's achievement, and my sympathies are obviously high. But ordinary reasoning can take us some distance in understanding this side of his voice. Watching the mayhem of the sixties, Wilbur's political worries seem to have centered on the saturation bombing of the English language. Anyone who remembers that time in detail recalls incredible linguistic excesses on all sides, the sickening euphemisms of the Pentagon and the State Department, the numbing hyperbole in the resistance movements. And people with longer memory than that have seen, as Wilbur has, language in a ghastly state, speech which violates not only itself and its audience, but also all speech, all ways of saying anything with clarity and power. In troubled times, Wilbur had no apparent reason to "cover his ass," as the expression went: he was a distinguished professor with a good salary at a top New England college. And in the backwards arrangements of the Vietnam era and after, conspicuous restraint could be itself a risky business. If one wants an explanation for Wilbur's apparent composure, one needs to look for it in his allegiances to the English language, rather than to the middle class or the social or political status quo.

History has at least partially absolved him in the case of "For the Student Strikers," a short poem written for the Wesleyan University strike newspaper in the early days of May 1970, when, after the Kent

State and Jackson State killings, many of the nation's important college campuses suspended normal operations for the rest of the spring term and finished the academic year giving and listening to speeches, demonstrating, organizing each other and the local communities, inasmuch as that was possible. The Kent State spring turned out not to be what some of those strike papers called it, the end of reasonable talk, the end of conventional education, the end of complacent American life as we knew it: these campuses opened for business as usual in the fall, and, in the years since, many of them have drifted back to pre-Vietnam pathologies. And so Wilbur's epigrammatic call for the "patient sound / Of your discourse," rather than for "the bullet" and "the blunt / slogan that fuddles the mind" ultimately faces down the brittle extremism of those days and the complacency of these latter ones.

With an edge of self-congratulation, Wilbur notes that the poem was originally thrown into the wastebasket at the *Strike News,* "because it did not flatter the students in the manner to which they were accustomed," but was eventually fished out and published. The I-told-you-so middle-aged voice can be heard in the marginalia, but not in the poem itself. Ever the cause, in the public poetry, is to be clear and to be heard and understood, to find a voice and a perception about the subject, a voice which will be worth hearing when the emotional heat of the moment has died down. That runs counter to postwar practice: when one turns to the Beats, or the confessionals, or the Black Mountain school, or to the continuations and interpollinations of any of these movements in the past ten years, one finds that when the poet speaks to the social or the political side of the world, the dramatized real subject is often the temper of the poet: Ginsberg's anguish, Lowell's black pits of nihilism, Rich's gray sense of disconnection. Whether Lowell has his facts straight on Hiroshima or the Second World War, or Ferlinghetti on the soul of Fidel Castro, or Bly on the truth of combat in Vietnam— none of that matters, as the poems put such issues beside the point. Ferlinghetti's Fidel is not the Fidel of prison camps for homosexuals and political undesirables; he is the Fidel that Ferlinghetti wants, the new Abraham Lincoln he yearns for to shake up and set right a drab bourgeois time, and the fact that Castro has turned out to be in some ways another tropical generalissimo does not embarrass "Fearful Words." Ferlinghetti is most "fearful" about himself, the latent, complacent Yankee imperialist lurking inside, just as Lowell, meditating by the undermined Boston Common, is anxious about the undermining of Robert Lowell, the "savage servility" ineradicable—and deep within.

So political poetry has been able to keep a semblance of honesty in self-conscious times, keep going after the rhetorical excess of the forties. But whom is Wilbur talking to in "Student Strikers," "Johnson's Portrait," or "McCarran Act"? Not to shadows in himself, however much he might address them elsewhere. No, this seems like old-fashioned exhortation, straight wisdom from the bard; but more important, it is common sense and moderation again, of the sort one might live by but not necessarily want to hear from poets. These are minor poems, short rubs against the contemporary grain in the name of good sense and the "trusty reflex" of the ordinary mind. In other words, minor heresies.

Poems about religion, jokes, small verse on domestic pleasures, politics, even some "occasional" poems for big public occasions—dominated by Republicans, no less. An important group of poems to consider, when on the subject of chance taking in Wilbur's poetry, is his array of poems forthrightly about poetry. Two of the more provocative of these are in *The Mind-Reader*. As more of Wilbur's dangerous domesticity, "C Minor" is about the pace, the place, the human metabolics of art; and by itself, it gives a skewed account of his own convictions about contemporary verse. Whether Wilbur writes in "sequences," which require a careful tour like those of Yeats, Williams, or Plath, is a matter I will turn to in the last chapter; but without much trouble one can see that his poems on poetry mean more when they are read in sets, or at least in pairs, to give his complexities and abiding mysteries their due. "C Minor" is another of Wilbur's vexing Dutch-dooryard poems, measured, moderated, stable, sure of itself; it plays off nicely against a more recent daily life poem, called "All That Is," from the 1988 collection, a poem in which poetry works black magic instead of white, not organizing or settling anything, but letting the devil loose.

One cannot say for sure that the allusiveness of "C Minor" is one of the poem's virtues. It recalls Dickinson strongly, but also Stevens, Frost, perhaps Williams, and some of the late poems of MacLeish. But such easy referentiality may look like another round of patient discourse, more common sense against certain art habits of the age, irrationalities which have decomposed into a mulch of fashion. In the early years of the seventies, one standard joke among off-duty music critics and in the "serious" record shops was that "serious music" might be getting too serious for human beings to stand. Academic-affiliated composers and their graduate assistants seemed to be manufacturing deadpan and apparently shapeless tone poems which purported to probe subjects like "Man's Existential Predicament" and "The Death of Values"—each in twenty minutes on a Moog synthesizer. It was a mild iconoclasm then to observe the obvious, that neither Mozart nor Beethoven nor other great classical composers were so unrelievedly serious as this, that Beethoven was known to complete tragic concerti with hunting songs, that Mozart did not forget the saving powers of the minuet. It may be an untaught, vital principle of art, this intuitive understanding of when *not* to be solemn.

"C Minor" seems to refer to the Fifth Symphony, a solemn work from the supreme composer and—by need as well as custom—a capstone work for the evening concert, although thanks to inane programming on some FM stations, one can indeed have it in Dolby stereo first thing in the morning. But one does not want the Fifth for breakfast, or Milton or the Pisan Cantos or the Duino Elegies before coffee; we do not commonly try to teach *King Lear* or the later Yeats to very young people, for some days and lives have to go on for a while before art can give them its riches. These are neither excuses for lightness, nor everyday banalities beneath art's purview; they may constitute, rather, one obdurate truth about the cadences of consciousness; and an art which recognizes those cadences might deserve recognition itself. If this sounds folksy, preachy, too certain, so perhaps does this poem. Its meter gives a model for such cadences, such healthful harmonies: the opening line of each stanza is ragged, prosy, discoverable as iambic pentameter only with some work. Thereafter, each stanza tightens up to cleaner iambs and commonly finishes with a crisp closing trimeter— a line Dickinson could love. Out of the inchoate comes coherence, but not right away; out of domestic life comes consciousness, the best moments we have, and not the other way round. But "C Minor" is a light rejoinder, something provoked, by bad scheduling and cultural pretense—and rejoinders almost never manage to tell even half the story about a sensibility. This is a mildly argumentative poem, not for "lightness" but for proportion, a recognition that we stand strangely on the driveway gravel, hear woodpeckers in the morning, hoe the garden, split the wood, pace around "balked and dissatisfied," and that because all of this does matter to what one thinks and who one is, these experiences require a place in the art that more or less complete people make and value. These are morning-weight ideas; this is a morning poem. Wilbur's poems of evening suggest altogether different relationships between poems, the imagination, the self, and worldly experience.

From the latest collection, "All That Is" returns to a conceit that has apparently been turning over in Wilbur's mind for thirty years: it seems a development of "After the Last Bulletins," a poem about newspapers and night that appeared in *Things of This World* in 1956—a poem about what happens after the C minor symphonies and clear words have "organized" the day we have lived. As the town sleeps, the discarded newspapers spin through the streets and the mind in blasphemous wind gusts, and all the sense we have made of reality spirals in a "fierce noyade" which turns all meaningless, like the echoes in E. M. Forster's Marabar Caves. The next morning, human beings go back to work, living daily life and making their poems about it; and the chaos of the unconscious and the failure of words are almost forgotten, until night comes again. So much for the triumph of Beethoven in the hour before dinner. Stays against confusion turn out to be momentary, which is hardly a surprise to a reader schooled in the modern—yet this is problematic, especially when one bears Wilbur's morning poems in mind. Does an art of words then matter, or does it not? The question is more darkly and soberly posed in "All That Is," in part because the analogy offered for poetry is more demeaning. Bulletins at least have an afternoon's dignity; they can convince the waking world, at least for a while, that the news does matter in some relative way—but where lies the dignity of crossword puzzles? Wilbur has built a career on the astonishing conjunction of words, on the surprising discoveries that lie in bringing incongruities into shape with one another; crossword puzzles do almost the same thing every day, and their surprises and melded words are empty. "All That Is" therefore might seem a reflexive attack, on wordsmithing, on any ordering will or instinct which mankind fumbles with in the twilight; and so this poem, which apparently has not been discussed before, is worth a careful walk-through here, to establish some sort of interpretation and to see how "All That Is" complements the thinking behind some of Wilbur's other poems about poetry.

The order-loving, word-loving, urbanized human race has turned much of the earth into a huge puzzle grid, but not quite all, and certainly not successfully: the poem's fade-in and crepuscular fade-out, which recall moments in famous works of both Stevens and Yeats, dwell on a nature irreducible in its mysteries, transformations, ambiguities. Out beyond the "hedged air" of the "eastern suburbs" of some unnamed metropolis, somewhere in the Western world, midges, bats, swallows flicker in the air as they have for centuries over new chimney tops and wrecked Roman tombs; at the end of the poem attention turns to unseen mushrooms in the regimented shrubs of suburban lawns, the ancient life "As hidden as the webwork of the world," casting spores out into the dark which winged natural things own and human systems neither command nor comprehend. In between, most of the poem is about life on the safe side of the hedges, the cozy, evening world which

149

Wilbur looked at with both nostalgia and a bit of suspicion as long ago as "Year's End." There is comedy in thinking of civilization as laid out like a crossword puzzle and in thinking of all sorts of people settling down at the end of the day to fuss with such a thing. Landscape-as-puzzle, a motif that builds in the first dozen lines, suggests a kind of obsession which seems here to overcome everyone (the speaker included) as the sun sets, the objective correlative being not a triumphant C Minor symphony on the radio, but a silly symphony to capitulate yet another absurd day:

> One passenger
> Already folds his paper to the left-
> Hand lower corner of the puzzles page,
> As elsewhere other hands are doing, whether
> At kitchen tables under frazzled light,
> In plumped-up sickbed, or the easy chair
> Near which a faceted decanter glows.
> Above this séance, in the common dark
> Between the street-lamps and the jotted sky,
> What now takes shape?

The poem's jump shift from top right to lower left, as the paper is folded, is a classic Wilbur pirouette, lightening the mood, forestalling the dark like the streetlamps and the overbright kitchen bulbs; this weekday evening recalls, in the balances it strikes, a certain Sunday Morning in which comforting oranges, peignoirs, and cockatoos are arrayed against those somber sacraments which are underway somewhere else. A ridiculous collective séance is afoot, and the poem seems to remain tonally in neutral, the ironies muted, the point of view ambiguous. Wilbur plays Wallace Stevens for a moment here, the Stevens who, as the jaded, dispassionate tourist of his own imagination, drops mild Wildean jokes here and there on the doorstep of chaos:

> It is a ghostly grille
> Through which, as often, we begin to see
> The confluence of the Oka and the Aare.

This sounds like Stevens, but a Stevens recollected in the giddiness of that hypnagogic state which is such a favorite of Wilbur's—a kind of Stevens double-talk, echoing in a mind on its way into a trance. What follows immediately is more of the same, but more broadly comic: a supreme fiction conjured out of those English words which have their being, for most of us, in crossword puzzles and there alone. If we insist on grand experiences of language to organize our days and close them out, here is what we get, and perhaps deserve:

Does the eye make out
A flight of ernes, rising from aits or aeries,
Whose shadows track across a harsh terrain
Of esker and arête? At waterside,
Does the shocked eeler lay his congers by,
Sighting a Reo driven by an edile?

And so on for a while in this fashion. What grows as a question, underneath this mock-synthesis, is whether any vision, Beethoven's or the evening puzzler's or anyone else's, counts for more than this one. The poem sobers up quickly and grows a bit didactic, declaring that wordsmithing, at least of this random sort in which the mind plays free with the oddest of English lexicons, will not happen upon truth, never make the trip from excess into wisdom. The allusions to Lautréamont and Markandeya would perhaps have warranted endnotes in an earlier Wilbur volume; here they are allusions left arcane to culminate a show of arcana. A symbolist poet who dreamed and dissipated himself into an early grave, Lautréamont seems yet another emblem for Poe, another of those brilliant young sensibilities who is undone in a quest for destructive transcendence. Markandeya, on the other hand, was practically indestructible. A Methuselah figure from Hindu mythology, he has adventures that span ages, seeing much of miracle and mankind, and learning to become part of all that he has met. He dreams, too, but dreams in that wakeful manner which conserves life and confers wisdom:

No, there are no such chance encounters here
As you imagined once, O Lautréamont,
No all-reflecting prism-grain of sand
Nor eyeful such as Markandeya got
When, stumbled into vacancy, he saw
A lambent god reposing on the sea,
Full of the knitted light of all that is.

Such a puzzle, the poem says, "Dreams that there is no puzzle," being a "rite of finitude," and knowing itself ultimately unfit to contain reposing lambent gods or anything else worth knowing. Are poems rites of finitude as well? In a sense: inevitably having to choose words and form, having to imagine *something* and give it shape, they shut doors, throw deadbolts, miss the portentous mushrooms down under the "clipped euonymous" that is every formal utterance—and the webwork of the world lies mostly hidden, even to the best of artists.

"All That Is" echoes with other poems in the Wilbur canon and casts illuminations far back: the trimmed shrub and endangered, precious life concealed beneath it recall a dying ancient creature under the cineraria leaves in "The Death of a Toad," written more than thirty years before—and in light of this newer poem, one can hear in that older one a certain lament for the crude ceremonies and killing structures, not only of civilization, mowers, suburbs, and the mind, but of poetry as well. If Beethoven and some good poems "organize" our days, they do so violently, and they can miss the point—for truth, whatever it is, escapes language, escapes classification, like the spores of the mushroom unseen. But that is not quite right either, for the mushroom here *is* seen, named, classified technically, in fact: "Bred of an old and deep mycelium." The paradox atop the paradox is that the poem, blocked and crosshatched and circumscribed and demeaned as it is, is what notices, names, and in a sense makes the spore-casting mushroom which supposedly escapes the word. The fade-in and fade-out of "All That Is" may suggest life before and after the poetic act, yet these sharp observations are part of a poem about the weak-sightedness of poetry. Thus the successful unsuccess of poems, their miraculous, insufficient recreation of the world, their way of naming things they cannot name at all. A poem for Wilbur is not an order perceived or willed, or a momentary stay against anything: it is something more shifty and complex than any of that. Order, chaos, success, failure— none of these words has worked well to describe the status of modern verse, and this array of poems about the poetic act suggests its anomalous, plasmic nature, its state between states, neither deception nor truth, neither empty puzzle nor inspired art.

As far as I know, only one of Wilbur's poems about poetry has brought—and continues to bring—outright hostile response in print. "Cottage Street, 1953" contains Wilbur's single mention in his verse of a contemporary poet by name, and in the midseventies, the years of *The Mind-Reader,* literary politics made this poet the wrong one to refer to unadoringly. At that time Sylvia Plath's reputation flew extraordinarily high; books and articles about her and her work were spilling from university presses, and ten years after her suicide she had achieved a kind of beatification in American English departments. "Cottage Street" could seem therefore aggressive or envious and bound for trouble, and one wonders what was so at stake as to provoke Wilbur to publish it. Poems discussed above provide some guidance, as do the odd proportions of the poem at hand: poetry which affirms a glimmer of belief cannot debate for itself, nor the artist for it, in face of a "large" refusal. What consolations an honest poem can offer are fragile, transitory, too much so to banish such despair.

But one of the poem's key themes, perhaps more central than the issue of Plath's "unjust" art, is Wilbur's dramatized ineptitude in his relations with her. These stanzas recall an early stage of a long predicament, Wilbur's inexorable role as a success, an artist who has won the laurels quickly and must sit ready in the parlor chair with words of consolation for the young, the aspiring, the unhappy. Ezra Pound hoisted Arnold Bennett as such an establishment father-dummy in "Mr. Nixon"; Wilbur seems to be doing something of that sort here— doing it to himself. He has told interviewers that this remembered afternoon is a composite of several encounters with Sylvia Plath and her mother around that time, and though the latest and best biography of Plath makes sparse mention of her connections with Wilbur,[8] there are records of their proximity and interaction. As a rising star in 1954, Wilbur helped judge the Kathryn Irene Glascock Intercollegiate Poetry Contest, which attracted entries from Mount Holyoke and Smith, where Plath was an undergraduate; in the next year's competition (1955), the judges included John Ciardi and Marianne Moore, and Plath was one of the cowinners.[9] Back in 1953, she had won a term editorship for *Mademoiselle* and had written a piece about "Poetry on Campus," featuring a report on Wilbur and showing evidence of at least one interview. That was also the year of her disappearance from the Plath home in Wellesley, and the subsequent discovery of her suicide attempt, by drug overdose, which made headlines in the Boston papers. One can assume that a spate of small-group readings, writers' workshops, classroom encounters, and other conversations figure into the recollections behind "Cottage Street" as well.

In any case, Sylvia Plath is here as that "brilliant negative" which the "published poet in his happiness," an emerging voice with at least some shred of faith in the value of life and art, can neither answer nor put aside. Philosophically, she is the immovable object, and psychologically a real and dangerous threat. Speaking to them the younger Wilbur makes a fool of himself:

> It is my office to exemplify
> The published poet in his happiness,
> Thus cheering Sylvia, who has wished to die;
> But half-ashamed, and impotent to bless,
>
> I am a stupid life-guard who has found,
> Swept to his shallows by the tide, a girl
> Who, far from shore, has been immensely drowned,
> And stares through water now with eyes of pearl.

Perhaps this sounds inert, even hackneyed. We were warned: the second stanza has informed us, flatly, that this visit, from early on, seemed "strained and long," and the language and the prosody follow suit,

153

down to this pairing of Sylvia with T. S. Eliot's Phlebas, grandsire of so many drowned souls in poetry since the First World War. Though one could say that these stiff quatrains suggest Wilbur's stumbling solicitude at these afternoon tea-therapies, a poem cannot ride on such rationalizations. A more plausible reason for the sound of "Cottage Street" may come from looking at its overall shape, for, clumsily or not, Wilbur makes himself a supporting actor here; these laboring lines, showing so little of his characteristic grace, carry him into the background, leaving two women counterpoised in the afternoon light: Sylvia Plath, and an elderly someone named Edna Ward. The poem tells us that this Ms. Ward—Richard Wilbur's mother-in-law—was a woman of stoicism and grace, of culture and sensitivity, who lived eighty-eight years with "Such grace and courage as permit no tears." Fair enough: life brings plenty of experience with such quiet folk who live with dignity and composure and who are not stupid, not unaware of darkness all around; and their laconic perseverance might be as profound as somebody else's "brilliant negative" and early exit from life. It takes no strain to grant that eloquent answers to the "negative" could dwell not just among the brilliant positives of somebody else's poetry, or in fireside advice from poets or other talky folk, but perhaps in living, and in recalling the lives of other wise people who have chosen to endure.

Yet "Cottage Street" needs closer scrutiny than this, for though such a reading might seem self-evident, it continues to be willfully or opportunistically resisted. Reviewing Wilbur's *New and Collected Poems* for the *Times Literary Supplement* in 1989, Ian Hamilton, Robert Lowell's biographer, thumbs back to this fifteen-year-old poem looking for leverage to push the whole Wilbur canon away from British readers and back into the cold North Atlantic. The opening third of Hamilton's essay is given over to drubbing "Cottage Street"—and ignoring the question of Edna Ward, the reading he works up seems both outlandish and self-serving:

> The poem ends, as so many genteel Wilbur poems try to, with a ringingly emotive punchline. Plath, he concludes, was "condemned to live" for a further ten years after their awkward tea-time meeting but was eventually allowed—after much "study"—"To state at last her brilliant negative/In poems free and helpless and unjust." Free, helpless, and unjust—the opposites, really, of what Wilbur would look or aim for in a poem. His taste from the beginning was for the shaped, the celebratory, the equable. Looking back on his meeting with Sylvia Plath, he is not simply re-

savouring some long-ago social discomfiture, nor does he greatly wish to perform a decent elegiac chore. There is a mechanical feel to those lines about a girl "immensely drowned"—in 1953, did Wilbur really think of Plath as doomed, or indeed think much of her at all? Is such distancing deliberate: does Wilbur mean us here to find him over-smooth, as maybe Plath did when she read him?

Of course with a real smoothie it is hard to tell, but the chances surely are that what Wilbur wants to measure in his poem is the distance between Sylvia Plath's kind of poetry and his own. For all his modesty, which seems genuine, he knows very well that the decline of his reputation since the mid-1960s has been in large part a consequence of Plath's posthumous appeal. "Unjust" is his last word on Plath's poetry; it could also be applied to the way in which his own glamour was eclipsed by hers.[10]

So Wilbur is actually grumbling about a dip in his own popularity, his eclipse by Plath in some important transnational opinion poll to which Hamilton is privy. Looking for help in what becomes a blitz against Wilbur as a "shallow" poet, Hamilton even quotes from a disparaging article Clive James wrote twenty years ago and neglects to mention that in a retrospective piece in *The New Statesman* James dramatically reversed himself about Wilbur six years later.[11] Having dwelt amid Robert Lowell for so long, Hamilton seems to have inhaled bits of his maestro's paranoia—that pumping or protecting one poet's reputation requires obliterating others, that poets and critics need to play games of "Who's First?" and that other people's essays and poems are actually minefields of professional jealousy.

Even so, one implicit idea in Hamilton's review is provocative in a useful way: by trying to read "Cottage Street" as a confessional poem in the Lowell manner, Hamilton assumes that Wilbur's poem might have something deeply personal and reflexive at the heart of it, might be a poem about truths and irrational compulsions rooted in private or family life. The poems of Lowell's *Life Studies* are about Lowell's father, mother, and close relations, none of them public figures; and the more we know about those people, the long decline of the Lowell family, and the trauma of growing up among them, the stronger and more poignant those poems become. If "Cottage Street" is indeed a Wilbur rarity, a confessional-style poem partly about one of the pre-eminent confessional poets, then should similar questions be asked? Should we know more about this Edna Ward, whom Richard Wilbur apparently sees in some sort of tension, in his own personal cosmos, with Sylvia Plath? When Richard Wilbur wrote recently about Edna

Ward, his emphasis fell not on the isolated figure, but upon a family, beloved places, a shared, improvised, courageous life, and a lost span of human time:

> She was brought up in Edwardsville, Illinois, and came of anti-slavery Virginia stock. A charming, gracious woman who loved to waltz and skate; also a woman of gumption and practical intelligence who studied law at a time when women didn't, and who when widowed and financially ruined (at the time of the Depression) developed a lot of business acumen. Her husband, Herbert Dickinson Ward, was a Congregational minister who had left the church and become a writer; for a while he was editor of the *Boston Post*. The Herbert Wards lived on Beacon hill, and made long stays abroad, especially in Italy, where my wife spent her earliest years. When Herbert brought his bride Edna home to the William Hayes Ward house in South Berwick, Maine, she remembered that at the first rather grave family dinner everyone was expected, in lieu of grace, to say some verse of the Bible in one of its languages; she was permitted to fall back on English, and said "Jesus wept," the shortest verse of all in the King James; she and her husband exchanging glances of covert amusement. She was not a literary or intellectual woman, but was intelligent and gay and a good hostess. In the early 50's she lived alone in a beautiful little house on Cottage Street in Wellesley, and we not far away in South Lincoln. She had many Wellesley friends, was devoted to tea, and we were often there at tea-time; there were a number of occasions on which the other guests were some middle-aged woman and her college-age daughter. I recall being asked to come to tea with Mrs. Plath and her talented, troubled daughter, but Charlee does not recall that we went; perhaps we did not; if so, my poem unconsciously blended a number of Cottage Street tea-times with my recollection of Sylvia Plath's pale, mute aspect when she interviewed me for *Mademoiselle*. Or it may be, as she just now conjectured, that on that day I went to Mrs. Ward's without her.[12]

Readers may recall that it was Edna Ward's father-in-law, William Hayes Ward, who first published Frost's poetry in the United States, and that Edna Ward therefore seems to belong also in an array of family connections to Richard Wilbur's mentor and good friend. And so, if one would try reading "Cottage Street" as confessional verse, Edna Ward might represent several related and very personal values: the solace of a family life, solace of an inexplicable and private sort which

Sylvia Plath apparently never found; a reserve, a resilience, and an unkillable curiosity about life, virtues which Wilbur is drawn to not only in his own family but in a great poet with whom they are associated; the will to resist bad fortune and adverse mores, and to meld adventure and bold nonconformity with grace and charm. Edna Ward isn't any more articulate or successful with Sylvia Plath than her son-in-law has been that afternoon: "frightened Mrs. Plath" has come with her daughter looking for somebody to recommend life; what they have received is tea with milk or lemon, and an hour or so of "genteel chat." And neither in her life nor in her words does Edna Ward seem to be offered here as a philosophical antidote to Plath's despair. Rather, these may be two ghosts who abide in the consciousness of one living poet— a large refusal, and a thoughtful, courageous, decorous, stubborn affirmation.

The last stanza contains most of the trouble:

Outliving Sylvia who, condemned to live,
Shall study for a decade, as she must,
To state at last her brilliant negative,
In poems free and helpless and unjust.

The bluntness at the end of "Cottage Street" is surprising, but since few poets writing in this language choose words more carefully than Wilbur, one must assume that "unjust" is what he means. As Hamilton senses, Wilbur's sympathy for the desperate young woman runs deep, but finally he states his stolid, unbrilliant positive, as *he* must, his faith in obscure yet fundamental possibilities in life. And literally to save his soul, perhaps, he turns away from a vision which is ontologically "unjust," meaning too certain in its hopelessness, as well as unfair. Though the word treads heavily, it seems as gentle and "just" an observation as anyone who believes, or even tries to, might make about someone who absolutely does not. Reasons, then, for the considerable risks of "Cottage Street": perhaps Richard Wilbur had to orient himself, privately and in public, under the considerable and troubling shadow which Sylvia Plath has cast over poets for twenty-five years. "Cottage Street" may continue to be hauled up as demonstrating Wilbur's "side" in some aesthetic or political controversy, or as suggesting some damning lightness in his own address to experience. But neither conclusion seems fair, and the effect of "Cottage Street" has apparently been to derail some people who might otherwise read Richard Wilbur with more sympathy and pleasure.

The "published poet in his happiness" became the official Public Poet in April of 1987, assuming the post of Laureate, a position which, for about two hundred years, has in itself threatened the repute of its British honorees, at least in the eyes of fellow artists. Ever since the ascension of Robert Southey to the English post, accepting such a job has been seen as tantamount to "selling out" to some established order which young poets, in never-ending romantic rebellion, are supposed to hate; and the occasional poems which laureates were to churn out for new railroad stations, birthdays, and other catastrophes in the Royal Family, only confirm the suspicion that art and integrity are compromised when the good poet takes the steady and glamorous job. And so, when the American Congress finally created a post of Poet Laureate, it did so with a splash of apologies and disclaimers: unlike poor Tennyson, poor John Masefield, our own official first poets would not have to churn out verse for christening the new waterworks, and few would have complained if Wilbur had avoided such involvements, as Robert Penn Warren did in the first years of the office.

The job of the American Poet Laureate is to bring public attention to poetry in general, and to American verse past and present; but when composer William Schuman approached Wilbur to join with him in something official and commemorative to mark the refurbishing of the Statue of Liberty on its centennial in 1987, Wilbur signed on. The challenge was a cantata, words for music, like the *Candide* project with Leonard Bernstein and Lillian Hellman—to be part of the big show in New York, the multimillion dollar Reagan–Iacocca–Sinatra main event, which would brim with Las Vegas glitz and corporate vulgarity. Nonetheless, it was a promising collaboration; Wilbur and Schuman had known each other long, and thanks to his work on *Candide,* Wilbur had solid experience in writing for music and singing voices and in getting along with the egos of other artists. And gaudy as it might have been, this was a genuine occasion, a national rededication of something everybody likes, a redefinition of sorts after Vietnam, Watergate, the "malaise" years, and a period of ugly materialism and self-interest. But celebrating the country, especially at some big ceremony, has not been something a major poet has done with a straight face since an aged and forgetful Robert Frost read "The Gift Outright" at Kennedy's inauguration almost thirty years ago—and Frost had written and published that poem many years before.

Wilbur has that poem in mind, evidently, in the opening lines of "On Freedom's Ground"; it expands on a tradition which Frost's brief poem exemplifies, of speaking about this country as a gift of which we become gradually more worthy. The language of the first section has a Robert Frost edge to it, the "bit speech" of New England: the meter echoes that of "The Gift Outright"; the diction is, like Frost's in "The

Gift," Yankee commonplace, and the attention, at the start, is on "the land," the natural fact, and not the nation that grew up here. But there is a move in a fresh direction right away: Frost's opening premise, that the land "was ours before we were the land's," is answered by the assertion that "before we came / To this calm bay," the land was essentially nobody's, belonged not even to time. Before the advent of the Europeans, "Freedom's Ground" was a place where freedom was not, a land run by the clockwork of seasons, the inevitabilities of numberless years—and so, according to familiar Wilburian metaphysics, it was the new imagination that transformed the landscape, made it a place alive with choice and opportunity.

One of Wilbur's favorite ideas about poetry makes a leap here, becomes for a second a matrix for American political and social history. Words for ceremonies are allowed such excess, provided they are not carried too far; and Part 2 of the cantata moves quickly in another direction, into a revised Concord Hymn in which, for once, the French get a little recognition for their efforts on behalf of our Continentals, and the Statue of Liberty's international pedigree seems historically right. These lines are simple, as hymn lines sometimes must be in order to give way to music, and one observes in this cantata that the rhetorical engines intermittently race and drop to an idle. As far as poetry goes, the action picks up considerably in Part 3, which proves to be Wilbur's best adaptation, for contemporary intentions and hearing, of the four-stress alliterative line he found in Old English and has experimented with for many years. This part is elegy, mournful memories of the all-but-forgotten American warrior, whose individual self is obliterated and whose cause has been compromised—perfect ore for an updated Anglo-Saxon dirge. But what distinguishes this, and makes it not only tolerable but musical, and moving, is its restraint, the uncharacteristic muting of the hard-drumming sounds of Old English alliterative verse: the effects have been moved out of the percussion section and are carried here, as it were, by the woodwinds. More is done with the alliteration of vowel sounds, and the hard consonantal noises are muted:

> Grieve for the ways in which we betrayed them,
> How we robbed their graves of a reason to die:
> The tribes pushed west, and the treaties broken,
> The image of God on the auction block,
> The immigrant scorned, and the striker beaten, . . .

Obviously this comes from the andante movement of the poem—which as a whole seems to mimic conventional sonata allegro form, with Part 4, "Come Dance," being the scherzo, and the last section, "Immigrants Still," recapitulating everything, weaving all together—the nature theme, the immigrant theme, the elegy, and the big one, the freedom theme. Therein lie the problems: first, that in the twenty-one short lines of this last part, the summation reads almost as a checklist and cannot stir and exfoliate as Whitman can at the close of "Crossing Brooklyn Ferry," the poem which this ending echoes; and second, that as an official, commemorative work on the Lincoln Center scale, this cantata must telegraph its gestures, must do pretty much what one expects it to do, and in the prescribed order. We open with an Aaron Copeland wilderness, fight the Revolution, mourn the dead and mourn our forgetting, discover or contrive excuses to dance and be happy, celebrate ethnic diversity, and ultimately declare that the American adventure is still beginning—a computer programmed to generate Fourth of July speeches might work in the same pathways. And that is the biggest problem, a reason why for more than a century poets and critics have cringed at the idea of laureateships. Public ceremonies can constrain: in one of his published speeches, Wilbur lightly concedes that these rituals "mean the same thing again and again," that ultimately there is no avoiding "saying what hundreds and thousands" of speakers in the same condition have said. Music constrains as well, as does the awesome sanctity of the Statue of Liberty as a national symbol, whose meaning to the American public might, in verse, be polished a bit, tampered with in small ways, but perhaps never transformed. It is dangerous out there. Walter Gropius's explanation for the ugly Pan American building in New York was that if he had not designed it himself, someone worse would have done the job; at this writing, I. M. Pei is still running a gauntlet of praise and outrage for his glass pyramid in the central court of the Louvre, and perhaps still overcoming the old catastrophe of the Hancock Building in Boston. There may be greater safety, for the artist, in avoiding "work" of a heavily public kind, out in the harshest spotlight. From safer zones, contempt can be mustered for those who try to enter the raree-show of official culture—and puzzlement as to why art does not seem to matter to that larger culture anymore.

Appearing in a section called "For Music" in the new collection, "On Native Grounds" presents itself in a book of poems, with no score attached, and no recording available yet in the shops. It comes, in other words, as a poem, workmanlike, yet perhaps a little drab. But does the fault lie in some measure elsewhere, in a dialogue *about* poetry which for most of this century has found no way to discuss verse heard, rather than overheard? As the great leaders of England died, Tennyson's elegies made a difference, to a large public if not to the Oxford dons; Kipling's "Recessional" matters a great deal as a cultural artifact, in expressing the mind of a certain time in Anglo-American civilization. Perhaps it is not the quality of public speech that brings the opprobrium, but rather the fact that such speech is attempted at all. With a composure that frustrates some critics, Wilbur does all sorts of things which run counter to accepted practice, whether that practice is truly bold and new, or as one sometimes suspects, a sanctioned "newness" whose fundamentals run back about seventy years. "He rhymes! He scans!" I once heard a young professor scream about Wilbur in a Carolina faculty lounge, as if these were conventions or heresies enough to dismiss his art. But if we are so inclined, we can do better than that, put together a long list of his transgressions against old and contemporary convention—as we might for any poet who has ventured, as Wilbur has, to keep poetry new and alive.

6. Wilbur as Translator

IN THE opening years of this century, the enterprise of translation evolved, under the brilliant guidance of Ezra Pound, from an almost anonymous craft into a recognized art of aesthetic and political consequence. While it might be argued that broad cultural forces which loosened the ties of other arts to civic duty—loosened, for example, ties of the graphic arts to photographic representation—helped translators reach unprecedented levels of freedom, there were other professed and unspoken reasons for this revolution, insofar as it pertained to poetry.[1] It seems fair to say that the translator's business, as Arnold described it in his 1860 lectures, was first and last an act of loyalty to the meaning, vitality, "nobility," and form of the original work, pretty much in that order: by the time Pound had done, having had his impact on Robert Lowell, Richard Howard, John Ashbery, Robert Bly, Galway Kinnell, and many other American poets, the sequence of obligations had shifted, and among newer priorities come the translating poet's personal response, often self-consciously idiosyncratic, to the original text, as well as his self-acknowledged need to make that text somehow the *translator's* poem, his own perception, and in some circumstances and ways, his personal story. Pound's translations of Old English poems, Provençal diatribes, and lyrics of Li Po are in a strict sense almost useless to the reader who wants to know, literally, what these antique poems have to say; but they say a great deal about Pound, about his mustering quarrel with tradition, his enthusiasm for the arcane, his rage against stale orders and canons, his desire for a "new" poetic relationship between past and present—and for a literary past which, with a little ingenious rereading, could help make a new present possible.[2]

Older and less militant schools of translation have persisted through and beyond the Pound era, continuing to do work which affirms that literature from other times and tongues can be rendered, more or less faithfully and decently, into modern English. Few objections have been lodged, for example, about Terence Kilmartin's amazing translations of Proust and Malraux, these meticulous, tonally astute, and (compared to Pound's work) self-effacing quests to bring difficult French moderns into our language as completely and perfectly as possible. And if readers still debate the virtues of Richmond Lattimore's *Iliad*, or John Ciardi's *Divine Comedy*, they do so on technical grounds, on matters of specific interpretation and felicity, not on the way two sensibilities, two artists of different epochs, clash or strike their bargain over a single work. One asks students to read Lattimore's *Iliad* to find something of Homer, not of Lattimore; yet one opens Lowell's *Oresteia* not so much to search for Aeschylus, as to seek dimensions of Robert Lowell. Why is this so? There are plenty of clues, out beyond the drama proper, to help us know, almost intuitively, which translation world we are entering: for example, Lowell's preeminence as a confessional poet, his well-documented efforts to offer himself to his country as a kind of Orestes, wrathful, guilt-driven, the last of a cursed and collapsing New England royal family. And for those who might know little of the poetry-and-celebrity complications of our time, there is the bulky evidence to the left and right of the book on the library shelf, the array of Aeschylus translations of the cautious, faithful type, by scholars and poets who, though perhaps lacking Lowell's imagination, linguistic gifts, and personal stake in the ancient drama, may have kept their Greek in better shape than Lowell had since his undergraduate days at Harvard and Kenyon. No, Lowell's move into classical tragedy has much to do with his presentation of himself, and with his own drama, which is to say, another genre altogether— the genre of poet as self-dramatizing performer. Pound's Bertrand de Born variations are about now, and about Pound: the translated text becomes the mask through which the translating artist may speak very much for himself.

Nonetheless, this was and is a treacherous craft, depending on matters of luck, intertextuality, and notoriety. Obviously a decision to translate aggressively can come to nothing if a poet of small distinction and following launches himself or herself at a text in something of the Poundian manner. Such an enterprise may require now an a priori sense of what or who lurks behind the mask of the appropriated text. Further, in reviewing quantities of modern translations, a reader has to be flexible, taking into account many exceptions to any general patterns. Even the most self-conscious of poet vaudevillians might translate, for example, poems by an old friend, whether or not they serve a purpose as a mask for the self; or catch a sensibility that matters to the translator not at all. By design or no, the translation of poetry can be a skill-sharpening exercise, or an act of almost perfect meaninglessness. What can one conclude about the labor of Francis Newman, brother to the great cardinal, who in the midst of a career which included the mastery of many languages and a graceless rendition of Homer—the failure of which triggered Arnold's essay—spent months translating Longfellow's *Hiawatha* into Latin? There it is on the shelf of the exhaustive collection, perhaps an early pathological indication of the modern scholarly mind. Conversely, if one found in, say, the papers of André Malraux, a French adaptation of *Pygmalion,* or in the Pound files a sheaf, from his furious middle age, of work with eighteenth-century light French verse, no satisfactory explanation might pop into mind. As we enter those peculiar worlds in which one strong writer, with a highly individualized persona, translates the work of somebody else, we must be aware of many possibilities, commonsensible and otherwise, about what has been brought about, what relationships are possible between the first author and the second—and between both of them and us, who must try to understand the blends of voices we hear, and what is signified in the blending.

Few poets since Pound have ranged as far as Richard Wilbur has in the art of translation; he has done roundly celebrated, and in some cases definitive, English versions of work in Old and modern French, in Russian, Old English, Latin, Spanish, Italian. He has made no published venture into classical Greek, which is remarkable, considering that neither his talent nor his education would seem to prevent his doing so. If generalizations can be made offhand about his taste, then perhaps this: that with the enormous exception of his work on Molière, he has been drawn to works which are out of the reach of most educated modern Americans, works that are short, unusual, oddly atmospheric, passionate, and highly resistant to good translation. He turns to works that are liable, given the current politics of canon formation, to drop catastrophically out of our collective sight, or never come to us at all with anything like their original power. The classical tragedies he does not engage, perhaps because they have tenders and mutilators enough; but back he comes repeatedly to Anglo-Saxon riddles and epics, to medieval devotional verse, to French symbolists, Russian emigrés, loyal home-staying Soviets. This seems more than a public works project to bring to an American audience the energies of poems which are not our own, and which are not worked up by somebody else in thick, sober college anthologies. Rather, it seems a way in which Wilbur engages with other realms in himself, other sensibilities of the sort which the latter-day formalist, the cautiously hopeful contemporary voice, is not thought able to assume. In some of these translations Wilbur seems to come completely out of himself, which is something more than a mark of skill at imitating someone else's temper. His success if often so absolute that what one sees is not merely, for instance, a "real" Verlaine, but another Richard Wilbur as well. I can think of no other plausible way to explain how excellent he commonly is at translating people who are, in their moods and imaginations, ostensibly so unlike himself.

Translation as homage, translation as performance, as ideological gesture, as personal or professional favor, as exercise, as noble correction of one culture's ear for the words of another—the act can have many implications, and in this fallen political-poetic world, where factions signify to each other in much that they do, it might be said that any poet's engagement with poems in other tongues has lost whatever innocence it might have had. Not all of this trouble should be laid at Pound's door; in Arnold's time, and in Pope's, facing up to Homer was apparently tantamount to fixing one's own claim on the sublime and the language's claim as a fit heir to the great tradition; in Shelley's age, to adapt into English from the classical myth, or from the Italian Renaissance, was to select allies in a war for human dignity, a stand against contemporary depravity and tyranny. And a great deal has been said about the motives which have cast shadows over translations of Scripture in the past dozen centuries. A translated text can moan round with many voices, choruses of implications. One can perhaps think of a *canon* of English translation, when poets feature them in decades of published work, and when poems play off against each other in significant ways. When the transformed words of an eminent South American nihilist share a short book, or a thin book segment, with those of a dissident Russian visionary, when the scene from Molière follows the Old English elegy, perhaps the translating poet is leaving his mark, his own clarifying sign to the world of how he engages with the literary past, the present, and the poet's role with regard to both.

But this ranges too far—and one should begin to make out Wilbur's life of translating by looking at single poems, simpler questions. What is indicated, for example, by his translating again a poem which nearly everyone knows, and which has been challenged by English poets for five hundred years? *Walking to Sleep* closes with three works by Villon, including the "Ballade des Temps Jadis"—one of the most familiar of French works to the Anglo-American ear. This ballade is actually four stanzas that come in the midst of *Le Grant Testament*. The antique French begins thus:

Dictes moy ou, n'en quel pays
Est Flora la belle Rommaine
Archipiada ne Thaïs

Qui fut sa cousine germaine
Echo parlant quant bruyt on maine
Dessus riviere ou sus estan
Qui beaulté ot trop plus qu'humaine?
Mais ou sont les neiges d'antan?[3]

In the course of his career, Wilbur has come back to Villon repeatedly, including him in all three major volumes of the past twenty-five
years, and showcasing three of Villon's poems at the end of the 1966
collection. Coming just after the long title poem of the book, a poem
which, as I have suggested, is structurally and thematically one of the
most open-ended works Wilbur has published, these ballades are vexing. Perhaps the idea is to present the poet, Wilbur himself, as reaffirming poetry as a careful and formal art—yet Villon, orderly as he is, is
hardly a poet *of* order, an artist of control and wit. The Villon personality has come down in legend as clear as the poems in the anthologies.
Villon is not popularly remembered as the first great French artificer,
but as the passionate scoundrel, the sensualist, the outlaw: the tight
French lines are crucibles for his high feeling, but they never for the
moment bottle it up. In a way Villon is the grandsire of all confessional-
ists, performing the act with unnerving candor, yet doing it also as a
display of genius, of poet engineering, of skill. In Villon there is both
poise and something like hysteria, a regulated refusal of the rules of the
world. Confining fire can make fire hotter: so much is clear to anyone
who has read through *Le Grant Testament*. But it is clear too that people
with a taste for such poetry will, by the time they get to Wilbur, know
some version of these poems already. What is better, or even margin-
ally significant, about another of Wilbur's late entries in very old
competitions? English translations of this fragment from *Le Grant
Testament,* with its well-known refrain "Ou sont les neiges d'antan?"
are usually apt at catching the all-is-vanity resignation in the original's
mood and at conveying that theme as a sort of dead end. To dwell on
this theme, as Villon seems to do, through several stanzas of versified
exempla, is to approach a species of Samuel Beckett silence. Though it
be for the Prince himself, Villon's *envoi* can muster no more than the
same shake of the head about time and the fate of passion.

But Wilbur's version comes up with more. Villon's speedy tour
through an array of bygone women, mythological, historical, religious, licentious, whatever, seems tinged with offhandedness, a certain bitter irreverence which, while not strongly evident in the original
French lines, is a presence throughout the long poem from which they
come. In other words, Wilbur translates aggressively here, bearing

well in mind who Villon is and the broader context of this extracted ballade. In his thirty-two years, Villon was arrested twice for theft, convicted of killing a priest, and sentenced to death for street violence, the sentence being later commuted to banishment. In neither history nor legend does he come down to us as someone with much reverence or sentimentality for the women and their lovers whom he name-drops in these lines. Any mode of love, spiritual or profane, ancient or very late, real or dreamed-up, is summarized in *Le Grant Testament* as only so much running around. It goes without saying that such spleen (if one can lurch ahead a few centuries to find a name for this mood) is not what Wilbur features in his own poems. The care he takes to create such a temper here, then, is a lesson in technique, but also perhaps a clue to some all-but-unspoken shadings in Wilbur's own consciousness. The liberties he takes with Villon are mild, by Poundian standards, yet they break from a contemporary mode that Dana Gioia lamented not long ago, in which "content" of the bulky, denotative sort, is rendered flatly into English with little regard for form or style, nor the nuances which build up *among* words.[4] For instance: in reference to Abélard's fate, Wilbur takes Villon's plain "chastre" (castrated) and renders it "shorn," a word joke referring to the amorous monk's sexuality as well as to his tonsure. Here is the stanza in question:

> Where too is learned Héloïse,
> For whom shorn Abélard was made
> A tonsured monk upon his knees?
> Such tribute his devotion paid.
> And where's that queen who, having played
> With Buridan, had him bagged and bound
> To swim the Seine thus ill-arrayed?
> *But where shall last year's snow be found?*

Nothing like the Abélard twist seems to occur in the original:

> Ou est la tres sage Helloïs
> Pour qui chastré fut et puis moyne
> Pierre Esbaillart a Saint Denis?
> Pour son amour ot cest essoyne
> Semblablement ou est la royne
> Qui commanda que Buridan
> Fust geté en ung sac en Saine?
> Mais ou sont les neiges d'antan?

"On his knees," which also translates nothing specific in Villon, is also edged with scorn: Abélard has not made some supreme sacrifice for love; he has been beaten, and he has put on his cassock in part as an acknowledgment of defeat.

Greater liberties are taken with Villon's short reference to Joan of Arc. Villon's words seem to have no sharp edges to them:

> La royne blanche comme lis
> Qui chantoit a voix de seraine
> Berte au grant pié, Bietris, Alis
> Haremburgis qui tint le Maine
> Et Jehanne la bonne Lorraine
> Qu'Englois brulerent a Rouan
> Ou sont ilz, ou, Vierge souvraine?
> Mais ou sont les neiges d'antan?

But Wilbur's words do:

> And Joan whom Burgundy betrayed
> And England burned, and Heaven crowned:
> Where are they, Mary, Sovereign Maid?

Joan moves through betrayal, martyrdom, and canonization faster than a fish through a cannery, and the aside about Burgundy's role in her fate is, from the perspective of fidelity to the original lines, gratuitous. But what is caught by Wilbur's embellishments is Villon's suspicion of nobles, of authority, established order—suspicions that hang over *Le Grant Testament* and that ought to be clear, somehow, in any important poem carved out of it. The breezy disrespect for royalty, history, and all high-serious enterprises is apparent also in Wilbur's handling of the fate of Buridan, a scholar who fell afoul of Jeanne de Navarre. The colloquialism and rough alliteration of

> And where's that queen who, having played
> With Buridan, had him bagged and bound
> To swim the Seine thus ill-arrayed?

is a good representation of Villon's sputtering French:

> Semblablement ou est la royne
> Qui commanda que Buridan
> Fust geté en ung sac en Saine?

But this is of interest more as craft than as artistic courage. More provocative, in a way, is what Wilbur does with lines which come just before the passage on Joan of Arc:

> La royne blanche comme lis
> Qui chantoit a voix de seraine

Berte au grant pié, Bietris, Alis
Haremburgis qui tint le Maine.

Bertha *au grand pied,* roughly Bigfoot Bertha, is the mother of
Charlemagne; the other two, Villon scholars affirm, are figures in a
Carolingian *chanson de geste.* Obviously Bertha's title is trouble for a
translator; but the women Villon pairs with her are so arcane now that
nobody but a French scholar—who would have no need of translations—would likely know who they are. Considering how often Wilbur resorts to endnotes to explain offbeat allusions in his own work, it
is curious, and perhaps telling, that he does not do so here. This is the
moment of Wilbur's boldest venture with Villon's poem, and perhaps
the best idea that he brings to it:

Queen Blanche the fair, whose voice could please
As does the siren's serenade,
Great Bertha, Beatrice, Alice—these,
And Arembourg whom Maine obeyed.

When "Berthe au grant pié" becomes Great Bertha, and Beatrice and
Alice are set with her without explanation, effects can build up which
carry the meaning of Villon, the sense and the consequence of what he
says, out of the confines of the fifteenth century. Each of these people,
unglossed, unlimited, can suggest the Bertha, the Beatrice, the Alice,
that a modern English-speaking audience can be expected to know—
and the impact is thereby greater. Bertha can be the timeless *femme
formidable,* the stereotype who gave her name to the great German gun
that hammered Paris in the First World War; perhaps the first Beatrice
one thinks of is Dante's, the slim child-woman whose ethereality could
not be more different; and our own Alice is Lewis Carroll's, a living girl
who put herself in the shade by dropping down a rabbit hole to a world
as unfindable as last year's snow. Such a reading may play fast and loose
with Villon's allusions, but in a sense Wilbur's changes are an act of
fidelity, if the idea is to catch the meaning of the original poem, its
emotional complexity, and the enduring human perceptions present
within it. Wilbur's translation is not concocted to fetter the poem or the
reader to forgotten details of the late Middle Ages, but rather to strike a
good bargain between Villon's antiquity and the timelessness of his
sentiment. In itself, it is not an aggressive reading of the original text,
yet it nurtures an aggressive reading of itself, a reading which infuses a
five-hundred-year-old poem with modern imaginative life.

Of the five Villon poems that Wilbur has translated and published
with his own work, none of them represents Villon's devotional

modes, his occasional spates of reconciliation with the world. No, the Villon whom Wilbur apparently values is the unregenerate soul, the progenitor, in a sense, of spleen as a legitimate spirit in modern lyric poetry. It is an undispellable grouchiness that Wilbur seems to like in Villon, and he translates that mood especially well. *The Mind-Reader* also includes Wilbur's translation of Villon's so-called "Ballade of Forgiveness," which comes off, in Wilbur's hands, as a deliciously failed attempt to be forgiving. The poem moves from soapbox sanctimony down into a tirade and a welter of bad memories, none of which François seems actually willing to forego. And in *The Whale* there is this quatrain of Villon's, which Wilbur refashioned around the same time he was at work on the poems in *Walking to Sleep:*

> France's I am; my lookout's glum.
> From Paris (near Pontoise) I come,
> And soon my neck, depending from
> A rope, will learn the weight of my bum.

Richard Wilbur's interest in François Villon may have as much to do with consciousness as with technique, for the Villon poems he favors and translates with such care are a fiercely precise poetry of emotional *im*balance, of moods unmediated, transitory perhaps, but ultimately unreconciled. Villon's presence in Wilbur's books is the sign of yet another "quarrel," but of that complex sort which Wilbur has perfected, in which a deep understanding of otherness transcends any indications of difference between this dark and unconsoled figure from the dawn of modern letters and the modern poet who returns to him again and again.

Onward to a much larger enterprise: Richard Wilbur has won fame for translating four Molière comedies, publishing his latest one, *The Learned Ladies,* in 1977; he is currently at work on *The School for Husbands.* If so much concentrated toil can signify something about Wilbur's interests, then one place to seek his motives might be the opening lines of Wilbur's 1970 introduction to *The School for Wives:*

> As Dorante says in the *Critique de L'École des femmes,* a comic monster need not lack all attractive qualities. Arnolphe, the hero of Molière's first great verse comedy, is a forty-two-year-old provincial bourgeois whom it is possible to like, up to a point, for his coarse heartiness and his generosity with money. He is, however, a madman, and his alienation is of a harmful and unlovable kind. *What ails him is a deep general insecurity,* which has somehow been focused into a specific terror of being cuckolded. . . .

Arnolphe, then, is one of Molière's coercers of life. Like
Tartuffe, he proposes to manipulate the world for his own ends,
and the play is one long joke about the futility of selfish calculation. (Emphasis mine)[5]

There is no end of good reasons for deep, general insecurity; but it is an
odd turn to see Arnolphe introduced, and even Tartuffe introduced, as
men who do what they do because of some profound alienation, rather
than out of foolishness or malignant hypocrisy. Following this line of
thinking, can it be said then that each of the Molière plays which
Wilbur has translated, with such an investment of time and care, is
about harmful, unlovable alienation—and a need to mind the distinctions between that sort and some other kind? The roots and the finer
points of hypocrisy are not subjects to which the literary world seems
to pay much heed at the moment: as some wisdom seems to go, one is
either alienated or one is not, and if not, one is either a saint, a madman,
or a fool. In doing the translator's job, Wilbur is also engaged in the
poet's job of honoring distinctions which one's own times might be
disinclined to value. If the modern public wants to read *Tartuffe* as a
satire about a religious hypocrite, then perhaps the public is wrong. As
Wilbur reads the play, the center of attention is Orgon, and his problem
sounds eerily modern, an idolatry resulting from a collapse of faith in
himself, and of his intuitive trust in the goodness of a life not regulated
in ideological ways. From Wilbur's introductory note:

> We gather from the maid Dorine that Orgon has until lately
> seemed a good and sensible man, but the Orgon whom we meet in
> Act I, Scene 4 has become a fool. What has happened to him? It
> appears that he, like many another middle-aged man, has been
> alarmed by a sense of failing powers and failing authority, and that
> he has compensated by adopting an extreme religious severity.[6]

Wilbur interprets Orgon as an idolater—like Poe, like Baudelaire,
like the Undead or the Mechanist, yet also like the idiotically optimistic
Pangloss, whose song from *Candide,* Wilbur's comic opera of Voltaire's
tale, is published by itself in *Advice to a Prophet.* And like these others,
Orgon reduces life to some kind of thesis, catches himself in the trap of
his own too-certain judgments and expectations. The disordered souls
in Wilbur's world are usually so because they have lost power—not
precisely the power to hope, but the power to see that there are other
ways of seeing, and that the mind can move nimbly among these other
ways and lose neither its sustaining hope nor its identity. Based on what
has been said previously in this book with regard to Wilbur's thinking,

such a judgment is no surprise, predicated as it is on much evidence beyond the translations themselves. Remarkable facts about them fly in that wider orbit: first, that these celebrations of formal verse drama, all scanned and rhymed and eminently composed in the midst of the disheveled sixties, are really celebrations of an *informality of mind,* giving the lie to assumptions that verse formality and the oppression of thought have any connection to each other. The dramas are about -isms, about single-mindedness with regard to everything from social foibles to divine will—and by extension, with regard to drama itself. Wilbur's introduction to *The Misanthrope,* the earliest of these translations, reads the play as resisting both pat social critique and pat indictment of the critic himself; he holds that the rhymed alexandrines allow Molière to make his getaway from narrowness in theme, tone, and form, and that a faithful translation of the work ought to do likewise:

> The constant of rhythm and rhyme was needed, in the translation as in the original, for bridging great gaps between high comedy and farce, lofty diction and ordinary talk, deep character and shallow. Again, while prose might preserve the thematic structure of the play, other "musical" elements would be lost, in particular the frequently-intricate arrangements of balancing half-lines, lines, couplets, quatrains, and sestets. There is no question that words, when dancing within such patterns, are not their prosaic selves, but have a wholly different mood and meaning.[7]

But a second notable constant in Wilbur's twenty-year involvement in Molière's plays is that Wilbur likes Molière's madmen, that he finds them sympathetic, even charming. Alceste he calls both a moral giant and an "unconscious fraud"; a man of playacting and self-aggrandizing, and at the same time a "victim, like all around him, of the moral enervation of his times." Orgon he deems a victim as well, who was once a man of love and common sense, but now, at the play's opening, is a man of "vicious fatuity"; Arnolphe he describes as an essentially generous man who out of sheer dread has fallen into coercing life. And translating Molière, therefore, has been for Wilbur another way of understanding otherness, speaking fiercely in other voices of his culture, other voices of his own generation. The best commentaries to date on Wilbur's work with these plays are by Raymond Oliver and John Simon, both of whom praise Wilbur's fine ear and the chances he takes with language, and find him superior to flat-footed literal translations and freewheeling "imitations" of the same originals.[8] But the success of a passage like the following, the famous lament by Arnolphe when his plans for a foolproof marriage and life

have come to grief, depends on more than a skilled ear and a way with
words:

> The evil star that's hounding me to death
> Gives me no time in which to catch my breath!
> Must I, again and again, be forced to see
> My measures foiled through their complicity?
> Shall I, at my ripe age, be duped, forsooth,
> By a green girl and by a harebrained youth?
> For twenty years I've sagely contemplated
> The woeful lives of men unwisely mated,
> And analyzed with care the slips whereby
> The best-planned marriages have gone awry;
> Thus schooled by others' failures, I felt that I'd
> Be able, when I chose to take a bride,
> To ward off all mischance, and be protected
> From griefs to which so many are subjected.
> I took, to that end, all the shrewd and wise
> Precautions which experience could devise;
> Yet, as if fate had made the stern decision
> That no man living should escape derision,
> I find, for all my pondering of this
> Great matter, all my keen analysis,
> The twenty years and more which I have spent
> In planning to escape this embarrassment
> So many husbands suffer from today,
> That I'm as badly victimized as they.   (4.7)

Compare this to other English translations of *The School for Wives*,
in and out of print, and one will not find as rich a blend of ridiculous-
ness with pathos in this voice of Arnolphe undone. Perhaps we all
coerce life, one way or another—poetry being one of the ways—and to
recognize a bond with one "fellow" madman is to escape, at least for a
time, from both the trap of madness and the blind alley of too much
normality. Thus it is that, over and over, Wilbur's best energies and
instincts shine out strongest in the words of the abnormal mind, the
mind that is not his own, yet not really alien either. Orgon, from
Wilbur's *Tartuffe*, says:

> I gave him gifts, but in his humbleness
> He'd beg me every time to give him less.
> "Oh, that's too much," he'd cry, "too much by twice!
> I don't deserve it. The half, Sir, would suffice."

And when I wouldn't take it back, he'd share
Half of it with the poor, right then and there.
At length, Heaven prompted me to take him in
To dwell with us, and free our souls from sin.
He guides our lives, and to protect my honor
Stays by my wife, and keeps an eye upon her;
He tells me whom she sees, and all she does,
And seems more jealous than I ever was!
And how austere he is! Why, he can detect
A mortal sin where you would least suspect;
In smallest trifles, he's extremely strict.
Last week, his conscience was severely pricked
Because, while praying, he had caught a flea
And killed it, so he felt, too wrathfully. (1.5)

Something of a reason, then, for Molière as Wilbur's classic and long-term undertaking as a translator: the completion of one's own voice, in ways that poetry in that voice's own manner might not allow. But how to explain the recent work with Racine? Wilbur has not run out of Molière, after all, and the turn to obdurate classical tragedy makes little sense as either a venture into a new and, for our culture, a needed psychological territory, or an instructive or aesthetic boon for an English-speaking mass audience. Wilbur's preface to his *Andromache* treats the play, and his own labors with it, as a mild blow against cultural habits:

> It is frequently said that Racine is untranslatable, and that he is in any case not for export. . . . The fact is that Racine's theater is not ours, and that it is usually described by us in terms of its exclusions. The *Times* recently quoted an art critic as saying that "in Racine, nobody sneezes; the disorder of everyday life is outlawed by classic tradition." True enough. Racine's drama is sparing of physical action; there is no dueling or dying onstage, no crowd movement, certainly no sneezing; there is but a single set, and what takes place on it, however dreadful, is contained by a courtly decorum; the characters speak—sometimes at length, and often in conventional dialogues between principal and confidant—within the artifice of rhyming verse. All this is so remote from our contemporary stage that "adaptation" could not possibly bring it near. Our best hope, I think, is to see whether a maximum fidelity, in text and performance, might not adapt us to *it*.[9]

Even so, what has a modern public to gain from such adapting? In jumping from Molière's verse drama to Racine's, Wilbur denies himself one of his great advantages, his unsurpassed skill at resonant wordplay, that linguistic spectacle which makes a reading of the Molière translations an experience in the melded wit of two artists. In *Andromache* Wilbur has to play the language straighter, has to roll through five acts of high-intensity, grand-style rhetoric unrelieved by any touch of wit, or Wilbur's own flourishes, whether comic, metaphysical, or profound. It should be clear that Wilbur is no pedant, and that as a translator he has not wasted his time in ponderous exercises; and so this slow-moving, monochromatic tragedy, virtually unknown on Anglo-American stages of this century, is a mystery worth musing about, as a clue to where Wilbur has been heading of late, as both a translator and as a poet who customarily speaks through all that he does in verse.

Racine's play is all of a mood, but not all of a voice. And some of the voices in Wilbur's version of the drama are hard to listen to. As the spurned lover, Pyrrhus in the opening act takes leave of his unhappy, widowed captive, who through no design of her own, finds herself reeling at the center of a five-act nightmare, a universe of betrayal and love gone afoul. Here Pyrrhus seems to vault, with no intermediate steps, from one sort of rage to another:

> So be it, Madam; I must accommodate you:
> I must forget, or rather, I must hate you.
> My passion's grown too fiery, too intense,
> Ever to end in mere indifference.
> Think well. Unless my heart can from this date
> Love with abandon, it must fiercely hate.
> In my just rage I'll give more cause to mourn:
> The child shall answer for the mother's scorn;
> Greece asks for him, and I am in no mood
> Forever to protect ingratitude.   (1.4)

This, from devious, amorous, warlike Pyrrhus, who torments Hector's helpless widow every time he enters—this rings a bit hollow, and one wants to know why. Racine's Pyrrhus, as Wilbur reads him, is a king who loves like a moonstruck politician, waffling about breaking his marriage pledge to Hermione, and failing to win in her place the grief-stricken Andromache, this Trojan prisoner who, through no will of her own, has swung his affections her way. In other words, this speech, and the love it describes, is unwholesome, false: Pyrrhus is using his fine words to dissemble, and to deceive himself in the process, a duplicity which seems clear as well, yet perhaps less pronounced, in the language of Racine's text:

Hé bien, Madame, hé bien, il faut vous obéir.
Il faut vous oublier, ou plutôt vous haïr.
Oui, mes voeux ont trop loin poussé leur violence,
Pour ne plus s'arrêter que dans l'indifférence.
Songez-y bien. Il faut désormais que mon coeur,
S'il n'aime avec transport, haïsse avec fureur.
Je n'épargnerai rien dans ma juste colère.
Le fils me répondra des mépris de la mère,
La Grèce le demande, et je ne prétends pas
Mettre toujours ma gloire à sauver des ingrats.

There are false-ringing lines, cumbersome rhymes, in Wilbur's *An-dromache*. Most of them belong to Pyrrhus and Hermione, who try to mix passion, wrath, and political dealings in slick, perverse, and ultimately lethal ways. On the point of marrying Andromache by force, Pyrrhus is slain by Orestes, at Hermione's bidding—Hermione never knowing and rarely asking herself whether love or hate is her own truest motivation. And with Pyrrhus dead, she scorns and vilifies Orestes, who by the final scene has gone mad with anguish.

Wilbur has an advantage over Racine, and he uses it. English has two great word streams within it, the Romanic which belonged to Racine, and the Anglo-Saxon, which can be turned to for sudden contrasts, clarity, strength. If Pyrrhus and Hermione sound in the translation like depraved diplomats, people so long in courtly maneuvers that they have forgotten where they have laid the truth, then Orestes sounds at times like a lovesick Briton, as crazed, perhaps, as these others, but at least consistent, and in accord with himself. If the play, or rather Wilbur's version of it, is in a sense about the ways that orderly and formal language can overlay emotional chaos, then his Orestes is there to embody plainer speaking which does not disguise the turmoil within:

> *I* was deceived, I fear.
> Dear friend, don't chide a wretch who holds you dear.
> When have I hid from you my heart's desires?
> You saw my passion's birth, its earliest fires.
> . . . .
> You saw my grief, and since have witnessed me
> Dragging my chain of woes from sea to sea.
> Against my will you followed everywhere
> Your sad Orestes, pitying my despair,
> And daily saved me, daily calmed the surge
> Of some quick rage or self-destroying urge.
> At last, reflecting how Hermione

Had turned her wiles toward Pyrrhus, scorning me,
My vengeful heart resolved, as you recall,
To blot her from my memory, once for all.
. . . .
In that delusive calm I came to Greece,
And found its kings and princes all assembled
To cope with some great threat at which they trembled.
I joined them, sure that war and things of state
Would fill my thought with cares of greater weight;
That, roused once more to action, I would find
Love's final traces banished from my mind.
But look, my friend, how fate has made me run
Into the very snare I sought to shun.   (1.1)

Compare this to Racine's language, which seems to contrast Orestes to Pyrrhus nowhere as markedly:

> Je me trompais moi-même.
> Ami, n'accable point un malheureux qui t'aime.
> T'ai-je jamais caché mon coeur et mes désirs?
> Tu vis naître ma flamme et mes premiers soupirs.
> . . . .
> Je te vis à regret en cet état funeste,
> Prêt à suivre partout le déplorable Oreste,
> Toujours de ma fureur interrompre le cours,
> Et de moi-même enfin me sauver tous les jours.
> Mais, quand je me souvins, que parmi tant d'alarmes,
> Hermione à Pyrrhus prodiguait tous ses charmes,
> Tu sais de quel courroux mon coeur alors épris
> Voulut, en l'oubliant, punir tous ses mépris.
> . . . .
> En ce calme trompeur j'arrivai dans la Grèce;
> Et je trouvai d'abord ses princes rassemblés,
> Qu'un péril assez grand semblait avoir troublés.
> J'y courus. Je pensai que la guerre et la gloire
> De soins plus importants rempliraient ma mémoire;
> Que mes sens reprenant leur première vigueur,
> L'amour achèverait de sortir de mon coeur.
> Mais admire avec moi le sort, dont la poursuite
> Me fait courir alors au piège que j'évite.

Wilbur's escapes from literal translation will be self-evident—as, perhaps, will the fact that a more faithful rendition of this speech could, for a modern audience, result in something absurd, Orestes as lovesick psychiatrist, analytic to the end about the passions which, he declares, still rule his soul. The moment of gratitude to Pylades seems to work better—again, for a modern audience—in Wilbur's version than in Racine's: lines six through nine of the translated passage lack the unwieldy self-pity which a more faithful treatment of the original language would carry with it. Wilbur has recognized the archaisms and lost connotations ("ma flamme," "mes ennuis," which here means deep suffering, not boredom or discomfort), but more than that, he has introduced a lean directness into Orestes' voice, an economy which one does not hear in the roundabout syntax of the original, which regularly delays the subject to the end of the verse. The result of the change is a tone which more befits a guileless man in love, not admirable by any means, but not despicable either. This is passion that one might believe, respect, and understand in contrast to the poisonous emotionalism of Pyrrhus and Hermione. I have written before about risks that Wilbur has taken over the course of a long career; it seems right to say that *Andromache* constitutes a bold experiment for Wilbur as a translator. Linguistically, the project meant hemming himself in; tonally, he is cut off from that range of feeling and that play of wit which are so much a part of his own sensibility and best work, and of Molière's. And thematically too, this play is perilous. For it seems possible, from both the preface and the translated text, that Wilbur regards the work as being about something threatening to himself and to his art: the confounding and the loss of the self in the formalities of speech, the entanglements of words, the consequences of language. These passionate people speak ritualistically to each other, to themselves, about what they feel and what sense they make of the world; and the more they talk, the closer they come to confusion, to unconscionable deceit, to murder, madness, and self-destruction. What goes on here could be unnerving for a poet: the possibility that provides a central idea for Wilbur's translation of this play—that passionate intensity and rhetoric make deadly combinations. The paradox of *Andromache* (again, as it comes through in Wilbur's version) is that it is an obsessively classical, bottled-up drama about failures of form, failures of the word, failures of the culture, and the furious ambiguities of the human heart, which no measure of culture or language can keep clear or bottled up for very long. And so out of the characters' quarrels with each other, Wilbur makes rhetoric; out of the quarrels with themselves, poetry. In any case, that seems to be the method, a governing idea behind this translation. *Andromache* is, in a way, another risk, a venture in Jean Racine's company into the timeless doubtfulness of the poetic enterprise.

Another anxiety that seems inherent in the *Andromache* translation is one we have looked at previously. Virtually unknown and perhaps unknowable to any substantial American or English audience, Racine is close to being one of those Etruscan poets whose clear vision and perfect fashionings have, as Wilbur says in his short poem about them, vanished from sight like footprints in the snow. And so in a sense Wilbur is playing curator, cleaning and refurbishing an artifact that few people may ever look at closely, giving the play the best treatment it has had in English in nearly four hundred years. This is a blow against oblivion for well-made verse, even though any impact has to be archival, academic, slight. Racine's ceremonies of hysteria, his self-trumpeting unities and symmetries, cannot be refreshed even by a fine English version, without a revolution in our own taste. For the student of drama this careful translating will matter, as much, perhaps, as it should for readers who understand why and how poets look into an abyss, and how the abyss looks into them.

In 1986, Richard Wilbur published a translation of *Phèdre,* Racine's last tragedy, commonly regarded as his masterwork. The complexity of its characterization, and the difficult emotional chemistry which pervades the drama, make it Racine's ultimate challenge for a modern English-speaking translation, especially one which would represent the formality of the rhymed French verse and its importance to an understanding of the original text. But there is another presence to be reckoned with. In 1960, in the midst of the turmoil which spawned two great collections, *Life Studies* and *For the Union Dead,* and the controversial collection of *Imitations* of European poems and poets, Robert Lowell was at work on a translation of this same play,[10] and a comparison of these two texts, Wilbur's and Lowell's, reveals much, not only about the differences in the way these poets define the translator's art, but in the way they define the modern self. To regard Wilbur's translation as a quarrel with Lowell's ghost, or as the graceful correction of some mistake of the middle generation, seems to me to belittle the importance of both books and overlook documents which, taken together, speak eloquently about the human and artistic problems which that generation has borne in mind.

Robert Lowell prefaces his translation with a flat disclaimer:

Racine's plays are generally and correctly thought to be untranslatable. His syllabic alexandrines do not and cannot exist in English. We cannot reproduce his language, which is refined by the literary artifice of his contemporaries, and given a subtle realism and grandeur by the spoken idiom of Louis the Fourteenth's court. Behind each line is a for us lost knowledge of actors and actresses, the stage and the moment. Other qualities remain: the great conception, the tireless plotting, and perhaps the genius for rhetoric and versification that alone proves that the conception and plotting are honest. Matisse says somewhere that a reproduction requires as much talent for color as the original painting. I have been tormented by the fraudulence of my own heavy touch.(P. 7)

Though this preface includes no manifesto on the dominion of the present over the past, the translator over the original text, there are good grounds for reading Lowell's *Phaedra* as one reads some of his other translations and "imitations"—as acts of conquest for deeply personal reasons. I have commented before on Lowell's will to read the national history, and substantial artifacts from the Western literary heritage, as representations of his own family's history and crises; his *Oresteia* and the verse dramas in *The Old Glory* seem to me cases in point, dramatizations not of Aeschylus, Hawthorne, and Melville, but of crises in the life of modern America and Robert Lowell, crises involving faith, the dark side of the national history, the gathering storm about race in the United States. Why then Robert Lowell's plunge into Racine?

Looking into Lowell's translation, one can find a number of reasons to regard it as a failure, although Benjamin Britten thought so highly of it as to adapt it for a cantata. There are lines throughout which, in context or out of it, seem undeliverable by human beings, or preposterous. In the opening scene, Hippolytus' tutor Theramenes, an even-tempered and logical foil for the Prince in Racine's play, cross-examines his student on his wish to flee the court and the presence of his stepmother. On hearing that Hippolytus fears Aricia, an Athenian princess, there is a mild exclamation of disbelief:

> Quoi! vous-même, Seigneur, la persécutez-vous?
> Jamais l'aimable soeur des cruels Pallantides
> Trempa-t-elle aux complots de ses frères perfides?
> Et devez-vous haïr ses innocents appas?

> What? Do you persecute her as well, My lord? The good-natured daughter of Pallas never took part in the treasons of her perfidious brothers. Must you hate her innocent grace?

This is Lowell's translation and expansion of the same four lines:

> Prince, Prince, forgive my laughter. Must you fly
> Beyond the limits of the world and die,
> Floating in flotsam, friendless, far from help,

And clubbed to death by Tartars in the kelp?
Why arm the shrinking violet with a knife?
Do you hate Aricia, and fear for your life,
Prince?   (P. 13)

The echo of "The Seafarer," or rather Pound's imitation of it, seems a
gratuitous aside in a play which has nothing to do with seafaring or
being lonely; these Tartars in the kelp, conjured from nowhere, might
suggest a sandwich in a Boston deli, and the line following seems both
trite and impossible as a metaphor. Problem passages like these abound
in Lowell's text. The moment in Act 2, Scene 3, in which Hippolytus
ends his confession of his love for Aricia:

Moi-même pour tout fruit de mes soins superflus,
Maintenant je me cherche, et ne me trouve plus.
Mon arc, mes javelots, mon char, tout m'importune.
Je ne me souviens plus des leçons de Neptune.
Mes seuls gémissements font retentir les bois,
Et mes coursiers oisifs ont oublié ma voix.
    Peut-être le récit d'un amour si sauvage
Vous fait en m'écoutant rougir de votre ouvrage.
D'un coeur qui s'offre à vous quel farouche entretien!
Quel étrange captif pour un si beau lien!
Mais l'offrande à vos yeux en doit être plus chère.
Songez que je vous parle une langue étrangère,
Et ne rejetez pas des voeux mal exprimés,
Qu'Hippolyte sans vous n'aurait jamais formés.

And I, for all my fruitless pains, now I seek my former self, and
cannot find myself anymore. My bow, my spears, my chariot, all
weary me. I've forgotten what Neptune has taught me. My lam-
entations echo in the woods, and my stabled horses have forgotten
my voice. Perhaps the tale of such an uncouth passion makes you
blush in hearing what you've done. What a wild way to offer you
my heart! What a strange captive for so lovely a chain! But my
tribute to you therefore ranks higher. You see that I speak to you in
a strange new tongue; do not spurn these poorly-chosen words of
love, which Hippolytus could not speak without your help.

becomes this, in Lowell's *Phaedra:*

I have no courage for the Spartan exercise
that trained my hand and steeled my energies.
Where are my horses? I forget their names.

My triumphs with my chariot at the games
no longer give me strength to mount a horse.
The ocean drives me shuddering from its shores.
Does such a savage conquest make you blush?
My boorish gestures, headlong cries that rush
at you like formless monsters from the sea?
Ah, Princess, hear me! Your serenity
must pardon the distortions of a weak
and new-born lover, forced by you to speak
love's foreign language, words that snarl and yelp . . .
I never could have spoken without your help.   (P. 37)

Beyond the problems which Lowell's lines create for the ear, there may be a flat mistake here in the handling of the line about Neptune, whom Hippolytus is thinking about as the patron of horsemanship, not master of the sea. And since the Prince was prepared, a few minutes before, to sail off to kelp and Tartars, he is clearly not set shuddering by the sight of the ocean. The line in Lowell's play makes poor sense—but there may be a point to that failure and to many of the excesses for which his translation can be faulted. Robert Lowell seems to want a different play to translate from the one Jean Racine wrote, or rather to release in Racine's characters possibilities which Racine interdicted. Lowell eliminates Racine's 1677 preface completely, and it is not difficult to guess why. From the opening paragraph one reads:

> En effet, Phèdre n'est ni tout à fait coupable, ni tout à fait inno-
> cente; elle est engagée, par sa destinée et par la colère des Dieux,
> dans une passion illégitime, dont elle a horreur toute la première.
> Elle fait tous ses efforts pour la surmonter, elle aime mieux se
> laisser mourir que de la déclarer à personne; et lorsqu'elle est forcée
> de la découvrir, elle en parle avec une confusion qui fait bien voir
> que son crime est plutôt une punition des Dieux qu'un mouve-
> ment de sa volonté.

Wilbur translates the passage as follows:

> Phaedra is, in fact, neither wholly guilty nor wholly innocent. She
> is ensnared, through her destiny and through the wrath of the
> Gods, in an illegitimate passion by which she is the very first to be
> horrified. She does everything she can to overcome it. She had
> rather let herself die than make it known to anyone. And when she
> is forced to reveal it, she speaks of it with a shame which makes it
> quite clear that her crime is a divine punishment rather than the
> product of her own will. (*Phaedra*, p. 3)

These lines, which Wilbur heeds and Lowell apparently rejects, seem to me crucial in understanding the different path these translations take. In a tale of a noble family undone by passion, the attention can fall on the passion itself, the ravages of the madness, its usurpation and *definition* of the self—or it can fall instead on *resistance* to the madness, the futile struggle of the self to be something other than unbridled passion, than insanity. In the latter case, the self is implicitly defined as something potentially different from the forces that overwhelm it, even if those forces come from within. For Racine, the madness of *Phaedra* is externally inflicted, by the gods, by fate. Wilbur respects that distinction throughout his version of the play, and not as the mere good student keeping faith with the testament of the long-gone master, and correcting in the process a bad job by a famous contemporary and good friend. For Robert Lowell, madness was an indelible part of selfhood; for Wilbur, it is a companion, and the difference is vital. In Lowell's translation, as in so much of his best poetry, human beings do not contemplate their own madness, or capacity for madness, with any measure of detachment: they dive headlong into it, and shatter themselves in its depths. But Wilbur's Phaedra and his Hippolytus have not been mad always, and when they speak, phantoms of royal blood and habit linger in their words, as do phantoms of noble and rational selves. Passion overwhelms them, but it does not *replace* them. Here is Wilbur's version of the speech by Hippolytus which closes Act 2, Scene 2—the speech referred to a moment ago:

> What use to struggle? I am not as before:
> I seek myself, and find myself no more.
> My bow, my javelins and my chariot pall;
> What Neptune taught me once, I can't recall;
> My idle steeds forget the voice they've known,
> And the woods echo to my plaints alone.
> You blush, perhaps, for so uncouth a love
> As you have caused, and which I tell you of.
> What a rude offer of my heart I make!
> How strange a captive does your beauty take!
> Yet that should make my offering seem more rich.
> Remember, it's an unknown tongue in which
> I speak; don't scorn these words, so poorly turned,
> Which, but for you, my lips had never learned.   (P. 39)

In one sense, Lowell's translation of these lines may be a shade closer to Racine's than are Wilbur's. Racine's Hippolyte has struggled against love and has failed; Lowell emphasizes that failure, to the point of making it a physical defeat, offering us a Hippolytus who seems devastated, drained of his blood, skill and energy. Wilbur's Prince, however, seems a prince still, a man bewildered by passion, who has consciously decided that there is no point in resisting further, who like Hamlet has lost his delight in old pursuits, but is neither weak nor base as a result. The speech is of passion, but the language is measured, and in the resistance between passion and word is the poetry—and the identity of the character.

Phaedra is similarly intensified, realized, as a presence in the play, by the hard confinements of language. This is a passage from her speech in Act 4, Scene 6, which Wilbur in his introduction calls the "ultimate expansion of the play's scope, an expansion rendered all the greater by its Christian overtones" (p. xv). Phaedra here is in a profound and complex Calvinist turmoil, affirming that the cravings which have undone her have come from without, yet dreading an ultimate reckoning for her moral condition and her crimes. At the moment of plotting Aricia's destruction, she observes herself with horror:

> Que fais-je? Où ma raison se va-t-elle égarer?
> Moi jalouse! Et Thésée est celui que j'implore!
> Mon époux est vivant, et moi je brûle encore!
> Pour qui? Quel est le coeur où prétendent mes voeux?
> Chaque mot sur mon front fait dresser mes cheveux.
> Mes crimes désormais ont comblé la mesure.
> Je respire à la fois l'inceste et l'imposture.
> Mes homicides mains promptes à me venger
> Dans le sang innocent brûlent de se plonger.
> Misérable! Et je vis? Et je soutiens la vue
> De ce sacré Soleil dont je suis descendue?
> J'ai pour aïeul le Père et le Maître des Dieux;
> Le Ciel, tout l'Univers est plein de mes aïeux.
> Où me cacher? Fuyons dans la nuit infernale.
> Mais que dis-je? Mon père y tient l'urne fatale.
> Le sort, dit-on, l'a mise en ses sévères mains.
> Minos juge aux Enfers tous les pâles humains.
> Ah! combien frémira son ombre épouvantée,
> Lorsqu'il verra sa fille à ses yeux présentée,
> Contrainte d'avouer tant de forfaits divers,
> Et des crimes peut-être inconnus aux Enfers!

This is especially difficult material. The succession of verses end-stopped with exclamations, the spate of rhetorical questions, the potentially awkward description, by Phaedra, of the symptoms of her own terror—there are many opportunities for a translation to go painfully astray. It should be said that Robert Lowell rises to the challenge. His translation of this speech, into strong and convincing terror in the English tongue, is arguably the best poetry in his version of the play. Repetitious language and an occasional clumsy construction can make psychological sense here, given the unprecedented emotional height that the protagonist is reaching:

> What am I saying? Have I lost my mind?
> I am jealous, and call my husband! Bind
> me, gag me; I am frothing with desire.
> My husband is alive, and I'm on fire!
> For whom? Hippolytus. When I have said
> his name, blood fills my eyes, my heart stops dead.
> Imposture, incest, murder! I have passed
> the limits of damnation; now at last,
> my lover's lifeblood is my single good.
> Nothing else cools my murderous thirst for blood.
> Yet I live on! I live, looked down upon
> by my progenitor, the sacred sun,
> by Zeus, by Europa, by the universe
> of gods and stars, my ancestor. They curse
> their daughter. Let me die. In the great night
> Of Hades, I'll find shelter from their sight.
> What am I saying? I've no place to turn:
> Minos, my father, holds the judge's urn.
> The gods have placed damnation in his hands,
> the shades in Hades follow his commands.
> Will he not shake and curse his fatal star
> that brings his daughter trembling to his bar?
> His child by Pasiphaë forced to tell
> a thousand sins unclassified in hell?   (Pp. 72–73)

Wilbur's treatment of the same lines is:

> I'll what? Has my poor reason grown so dim?
> I, jealous! And it's with Theseus I would plead!
> My husband lives, and still my passions feed
> On whom? Toward whom do all my wishes tend?
> At every word, my hair stands up on end.
> The measure of my crimes is now replete.
> I foul the air with incest and deceit.

My murderous hands are itching to be stained
With innocent blood, that vengeance be obtained.
Wretch that I am, how can I live, how face
The sacred Sun, great elder of my race?
My grandsire was, of all the Gods, most high;
My forebears fill the world, and all the sky.
Where can I hide? For Hades' night I yearn.
No, there my father holds the dreadful urn
Entrusted to his hands by Fate, it's said:
There Minos judges all the ashen dead.
Ah, how his shade will tremble with surprise
To see his daughter brought before his eyes—
Forced to confess a throng of sins, to tell
Of crimes perhaps unheard of yet in Hell! (P. 83)

Like Lowell's, Wilbur's language is clear and largely of Anglo-Saxon derivation; but Wilbur's syntax is complex here, featuring periodic constructions and prepositional phrases which intrude to slow and steady the pace and maintain the impression that Phaedra, for all her torment, has not slipped over the precipice into pure hysteria. Even at this moment, myth for Phaedra remains myth: the ordering of Hell is still unsure, as it is in Racine's original lines, and the sins she suffers from, while terrible, are not legion, not the "thousand" into which Lowell's crumbling Phaedra expands them. For Racine, for Wilbur, a mad queen is still a queen. Wilbur does not miss the opportunity which Racine offers to link Phaedra with other "distracted" monarchs in the Western literary tradition, specifically to Lady Macbeth, troubling to the end over her own bloodstained hands; yet what is remarkable about Wilbur's translations of these great monologues is that they seem intense, modern, and noble all at the same time. The fiercest storm is the storm almost confined; the self that matters is the locus of conflict, of tension; and if there is surrender, then it must never be complete. The conversation between two major American poets about this antique and rarely staged French tragedy has much to do with identity as we struggle to define it now, about the affirmations which language achieves, in the very act of probing the turmoil of the self.

An earlier chapter in this book suggested that Wilbur's periodic quarrel with Edgar Allan Poe has involved a great deal of excellent work on Poe's behalf, including a popular edition of the poems and a succession of ground-breaking critical essays, all of which demonstrate a sympathy which commentators on this supposedly adversarial relationship often miss. But that deep-running sympathy with otherness shows itself as well in his translations of Poe's self-proclaimed heirs, the French symbolists. Wilbur has done much with Baudelaire, whose worship of Poe and whose own imaginative extremism are familiar enough; and it is to Poe's diction that Wilbur often turns, to find the right analogue for language in Baudelaire's poems. And so these translations of Wilbur's have a strangely backwards arrangement behind them: to translate Poe's great admirer, Wilbur has to sound like Poe himself. Here is the opening of Wilbur's translation of "L'Invitation au Voyage":

> My child, my sister,
> dream
> How sweet all things would seem
> Were we in that kind land to live together,
> And there love slow and long,
> There love and die among
> Those scenes that image you, that sumptuous weather.
> Drowned suns that glimmer there
> Through cloud-disheveled air
> Move me with such a mystery as appears
> Within those other skies
> Of your treacherous eyes
> When I behold them shining through their tears.
> There, there is nothing else but grace and measure,
> Richness, quietness, and pleasure.

As one of Baudelaire's most familiar poems, "L'Invitation au Voyage," a cadenza of dreamy otherworldliness, comes in the middle of *Things of This World;* it is bracketed in the sequence by "Looking into History" and "Digging for China," both of them poems about the need to look for the richest wonders in the daylight of one's actual and immediate surroundings. It is "Digging for China" that seems to cast an intertextual shade on the Baudelaire, and to wear well the colorations that "L'Invitation au Voyage" bestows in return. "Digging for China" is about one portentous moment of dizziness, whose significance lies in the fact that it takes place both in and out of the world; but Wilbur's own poems are not tracts, and his translations of French symbolists are not there as straw men to be rebutted or corrected. Just as "L'Invitation Au Voyage" colors *Things of This World,* Gérard de Nerval's "Antéros," a short dramatic monologue that is close kin to the speech of Poe's world refusers, turns up in the midst of *Advice to a Prophet,* just after the courtly angst of "Ballade for the Duke of Orléans" and just before "To Ishtar," a poem about forcing one's own imagination back to work, celebrating nature and love in drab late winter. The position of these translations seems to matter: the abject dream, the devil's implacable fury at the basic shape of reality—these extremes of feeling, these refusals of "this world" work not as other voices and little proofs of one poet's range as a mimic, but rather as dissonant strains in the music of one consciousness; not spells recovered from, but realms of feeling which must be accommodated, and spoken, if only by remaking the poem of someone else. One can obviously make too much of the physical position of a translated poem in a poet's book—everything has to go somewhere. But as the resort to Villon, at the end of *Walking to Sleep,* makes musical sense—returns to something cold and clear and passionate after the crepuscular uncertainties of the title poem—the bracketing of Wilbur's symbolists, his various Poe voices, suggests a movement into and then away from that mode of consciousness, and offers some accounting for the verve with which he gives those voices an English tongue.

Baudelaire's "Correspondences" is about a possibility that threatens much that Wilbur seems to hope for, the chance that whatever order flickers in the surfaces of experience could be order born of malice. "All hangs together if you take it hard," he smirks in another place, when beset by professional nihilists in the Vietnam years; but for Baudelaire he outdoes himself, in making that hanging together disturbingly plausible and dead serious. Here is the opening of "Correspondances," in a 1953 translation Wilbur published in *The Whale:*

> Nature is a temple whose living colonnades
> Breathe forth a mystic speech in fitful sighs;
> Man wanders among symbols in those glades
> Where all things watch him with familiar eyes.
>
> Like dwindling echoes gathered far away
> Into a deep and thronging unison
> Huge as the night or as the light of day,
> All scents and sounds and colors meet as one.

This is not merely good wordsmithing; it suggests the comprehension of an opposite personality. Wilbur gives no hint of regarding opposition of any sort as simple; in fact he has written and illustrated an amusing children's book on the subject.[11] Something of our adversaries we recognize in ourselves; in various ways we become what we behold—none of these psychological or literary commonplaces are lost on Wilbur, and there are reasons to contend that these translations, all that we have looked at so far, constitute a quarrel with Ezra Pound to match his controversy with Poe. In light of Wilbur's achievement, some freewheeling "imitation" can seem self-indulgent, simplistic, faithless, and meticulous literalism can seem hollow, spiritless. Wilbur's translations make a case that an artist with enough talent can be true to a text, to art, and to the self at the same time; but beyond that, they give the lie to an assumption that very different poetic sensibilities cannot know or enter one another, cannot lay claim to an alien mind as part of themselves. These translations do not sound alike: the translated voices of Villon, Molière, Racine, Nerval, Baudelaire, Brodsky, Voznesensky, Ponge, Yevtushenko, Akhmatova, all have their own character, and none of them is much like Wilbur on his own. Yet all this poetry comes of one shape-shifting mind, and speaks as a chorus for a change in the way poets are looked at, as entities to be narrowly defined, turned inside out in a couple of essays, arranged neatly with one another in a convenient history of the time.

A review of Wilbur's enthusiasms for other voices, for verse forms and personalities different from himself, needs to consider his abiding delight in working with medieval Latin and Old English. His experiments with poems of the Middle Ages constitute an array of translations running back to the beginning of his career, demonstrating an enthusiasm equaling what he has shown for French lyric poets of the past two centuries. It is a time, rather than a language, which seems to fascinate him; he has never engaged, as far as I can tell, with a Latin work from the golden age of Roman poetry, nor anything from classical Greek; but the taste for medieval works carries him far and wide, from riddles to epics, bestiary poems, freewheeling imitations—including a few ventures into that absolutely free adaptation that Pound made possible. It is too simple to say that Wilbur seems drawn to this material because it represents a simpler time, that these translations are a nostalgic sojourn in an age of faith. Rather, the appeal of these poems, Latin and Old English alike, is their celebration of clarity, directness, and above all force, an energy which is the nature and pleasure of Wilbur's modern renderings. These are poems of rough-cut stone: the beauty is in the main strength that shows in their construction, not in elegance of shape or subtlety of design. They have the appeal of old Celtic crosses or heavy, stubborn ruins, shadowing a little the modern poetic landscape. It is not their inherent faith or despair, but instead their fiercely willed convictions, or their sheer strangeness, that make them provocative and significant in Wilbur's collections.

One might rightly begin with the simplest ones first, the mere riddles Wilbur likes to bring over from the near-absolute obscurity of Aldhelm, or Syphosius, or the Exeter Book. Only a few hardy graduate students wander now in such places, and few of them come back with profundities from the riddles. Here is an Exeter Book translation, thirty years old, that shows up in *The Whale:*

> I saw in a corner   something swelling,
> Rearing, rising,   and raising its cover.
> A lovely lady,   a lord's daughter,
> Buried her hands   in that boneless body,
> Then covered with a cloth   the puffed-up creature.

In his 1987 *New Poems,* Wilbur went back to Symphosius, to play as he had a quarter-century before in *Advice to a Prophet.* In the center of this latest and strongly elegiac collection, there are eight more of these:

> Earth gave me body; strong through fire am I;
> Earth bore me, but my home is ever on high;
> Though moisture drenches me, I soon am dry.

> I come when good and ready, and I glut
> Men's eyes with myriad forms and phantoms. But
> None goes to me unless his eyes are shut.

The answers are a loaf of bread, a roof tile, and sleep; the answer to the poet's career-long delight in translating such riddles is more complex. In chapter 5 I looked briefly at Wilbur's interest in riddling itself, and at how he finds in riddle ways of freshening language, the imagination, and the natural world. These antique riddles he translates are then perhaps small ways of reaffirming timeless centers of poetry, principles that stay the same no matter what shifts in faith or aesthetics might rock or overthrow the culture. If riddles can make the familiar world new and interesting again, then very old ones, successfully respoken, bond old poets to new ones in the basic business of seeing and speaking, and enact at least a momentary escape from the oppressions of context and religion and politics and ponderous, intervening tradition. In a gentle way, Wilbur claims ancestry for himself in these riddles, shows certain habits of his own echoing in old verse, verse from times long before the quarrels broke out, and before the scholastic obsession with sorting everything into ages, movements, coteries. These riddles lighten Wilbur's books somewhat, and for the moment dismiss certain expectations.

More imposing and consequential as presences in these books are the Middle English bestiary poems. Wilbur has shown a long interest in the bestiary, doing an edition of it early in his career, and working up translations himself of some of the most intractable poems, preferring odder beasts from both the medieval Christian and the modern perspective. His 1985 collection *The Whale* is named for one of these, which might suggest something of the pleasure or the consequence that he finds in these ventures. Now the medieval idea of whales is a good deal different from our own. First of all, the marine biology which this whale fable piously reports is preposterous: this moralizing poem is based on the notion that a whale is a fish, which it is not, eating other fish, which it does not; that it lives on the bottom of the sea; and that sailors in trouble are given to mistaking whales for islands, landing on them, camping out. The truth to be extracted from such nonsense is that the whale is a text in which to read the ways of Satan, whose false assurances drown the souls of many life-voyagers.

This is charming foolishness, yet more perhaps than that. When T. H. White drew upon the various Latin, Old English, and French bestiaries to make his own collection, *The Book of Beasts,* the object was patently fun, a holiday in the superstitions of the medieval mind, a look into Arthur's kingdom, a tour of the world when it was flat. Wilbur's beast stories have a different feel to them. Choosing as he does the wilder ones, this whale, the mermaid, and the pelican myth of the bird feeding its young with the blood of its own breast, and doing up the moral lessons in deadpan earnest, Wilbur raises a paradox which is nicely caught in a few lines from his "The Siren" translation, words that come just before the "Signification":

Surely this monster,
Half fish and half woman,   Must harbor some meaning.

Can it indeed? Can patently false representations of the natural world harbor any signification except a lie? These poems are among the oddest in our heritage, bad science conjoined to wisdom; or to put it another way, poems in which, in perfect opposition to Wordsworth's, truth is perceived but worldly experience is entirely created. And Wilbur's sonorous high-serious tone, which runs through all these beast poems, has strange effects: mock solemnity in the exposition, sobering urgency in the moralizing. These poems can make one a little heady, complicating assumptions that the universe we accept and the truth we ascribe to have easy connections to one another.

Most of Wilbur's beast poems and beast translations were first collected in an elegant, miscellaneous book of 1955, edited by Wilbur and illustrated by Alexander Calder: *A Bestiary*[12] assembles all sorts of Western pronouncements, running back to Pliny and up to Veblen and Wilbur himself, on the nature of beasts and their "meaning"; and the overall effect is like that of Melville's "Extracts"—a pleasurable disorientation, a recognition not only that we have diverse company on this planet, but that most of our long thinking about these neighbors is a mix of scientific error, whimsy, piety, and truth stumbled upon rather than worked out. Such a look at the animals is a look at ourselves, at how the wisdom of a culture accumulates in a leisurely, shifting, backtracking, almost geological kind of way, rather than by linearity and sure method; at how trusting either to reason alone, or to faith alone, or to cool, agnostic science alone, is in some longer run not as trusty a method as an improvised balance among all three, and finally not the way that we as a culture have done most of our best work in making sense of the world. *A Bestiary* has no introduction, no explanatory note, except Wilbur's poem "Beasts," which as an epigraph includes these lines:

> Far from thicket and pad-fall, suitors of excellence
> Sigh and turn from their work to construe again the painful
> Beauty of heaven, the lucid moon
> And the risen hunter,
>
> Making such dreams for men
> As will break their hearts as always.

Having lost the intuitive sense that animals have of their own place in reality, the human race must look with envy at the beast-world they have left behind, where even violence and death affirm a kind of harmony, and where all α ϡ not suffer with pondering what they are. The moraine of material that is the rest of the book, and Calder's breezy illustrations, try to take one again back to wonder, to a condition of mind in which one happily gives up on all methods for understanding nature. One finds one's way by a suitably skeptical modern path, to a mood which medieval bestiaries, as works of faith, can adduce: a peaceful, simple acceptance of nature's bigness, of its reach beyond any conception of it, and of the possibility that its intentions are similarly beyond our grasp, no matter how one tries to pull them in.

That is the effect of Wilbur's version of Philippe de Thaun's "The Pelican," which appears both in *A Bestiary* and in *Things of This World:* Wilbur's ringing, earnest diction makes the poem work both as a curio of strong faith and faulty bird-watching, and as a modern work with some pathos in it, laboring as it does to find some heartening signification out of bizarre reports about what these birds do. The emphasis which Wilbur gives to the flat declaratives and the admonitions which close Thaun's "The Pelican" outstrips the original, and nurtures a complex response from a contemporary reader. It goes almost without saying that the more a poem insists on something, the less likely it is that the reader will believe it: this has been standard procedure in the psychological warfare of poetry at least since the Victorians, and Wilbur certainly knows that the stridency of this poem can put an audience off, at least on the narrow issue of believing what it hears. But forced away thus from the poem, the reader must, as it were, tread water: if we believe not this meaning, then what answer shall we make to Thaun, to ourselves, about creatures as strange as pelicans, about the whole natural world? The poem coaxes one toward a soft version of Blake's tiger problem, for if one does not accept some proffered, antique, explanation of the nature and purpose of things, then at some point one must find or mug up a narrative of one's own. True or false as reports about them might be, pelicans are a puzzle; and the contemplation of quaint old lies, hard-made and demanding ones, forces one to recognize one's own uncertainty about the truth. If Wilbur is manifestly impatient with anything about contemporary discourse, it is glibness, a too-quick trust to received ideas and thirdhand iconoclasms, and a consequent loss of sustaining, humanizing uncertainty about all sorts of matters which, finally, are anything but settled about our condition. Insofar as we improvise with every power and resource we have, we are human; and these poems which squawk and splash are meant to push us, in a sense, off of the false island of the whale's back, out into deep water where we must float, exert our strength, and concentrate our attention on the mysterious epistemological business always at hand.

To move backward among Wilbur's array of translations to his Old English work is, I think, to move out of such cerebral business and into an experience of mood, but also into some remarkable experimentation with form. The Old English alliterative two-stress half-line has drawn attention from a number of this century's most important poets, Auden and Pound among them, because of its amazing resonations and aura of high and dark seriousness—but the luck of the moderns and postmoderns with Anglo-Saxon verse-making has been mixed at best. If one goes full tilt into such driving and structured utterance, one runs a sizable risk of sounding silly. Auden's "Doom is dark and deeper than any sea-dingle" is a case which comes quickly to the mind of anyone who has tried to teach that poem to American students, as might these lines from Pound's freewheeling yet lumpy translation of "The Seafarer":

> Not any protector
> May make merry man faring needy.
> This he little believes, who aye in winsome life
> Abides 'mid burghers some heavy business,
> Wealthy and wine-flushed, how I weary oft

Must bide above brine.
Neareth nightshade, snoweth from north,
Frost froze the land, hail fell on earth then,
Corn of the coldest. Nathless there knocketh now
The heart's thought that I on high streams
The salt-wavy tumult traverse alone.[13]

The problem is more than alliterative overkill; it has to do with too close a fidelity to cadence, and a failure to recognize that for the last few hundred years the Anglo-American ear has grown used to variations and colorings in set rhythms, and to a blending of the Anglo-Saxon and the French roots of the language into a richer discourse. What Wilbur has recognized is that to translate Old English effectively, for a modern reader, does not mean taking a pledge to eschew half of the words in our dictionary, just as good translations of *The Aeneid* or *The Divine Comedy* have not meant that one must have Latinate noise in every English line.

In other words, Wilbur knows when to stop, knows how to keep a poem alive by not giving in to some unspoken translator's dogma. Here are the climactic lines of "Beowulf's Death Wound"—lines 2688 through 2693 of the first English poem—an excerpt which Wilbur published as a separate poem in *The Whale:*

Then for a third time,   thirsty for carnage,
the fatal firedrake   and folk-despoiler,
raging and battle-grim,   rushed at the ruler,
forcing him backward;   the fire-hot fangs then
breached his gullet;   Beowulf's breast
was wet with his lifeblood;   it welled out in waves.

While plenty of these words are fittingly Anglo-Saxon, some of the ones which stand out in this passage, varying the pace and markedly altering the sound, are Romanic, or lucky hybrids of the two strains. *Carnage* comes straight from the French, and the effect is patently darker and more formal, both on the ear and on the mind, than *slaughter, murder,* or other English-rooted alternatives which turn up in other available translations of these lines. Beowulf's death impends, and this is a moment for sobriety. "Despoiler" coming likewise from Old French, is almost a euphemism here for "killer" or something like: to despoil is, strictly speaking, to take away, which is an oddly soft way of saying what this dragon does. Again, the choice needs to be understood as a way of keeping this poem within tonal bounds, of creating a modern poem, reasonably and atmospherically faithful to the original, rather than a freak of speech rationalized by some strict-construction

194

linguistic theory. At the very moment of the wounding, Wilbur turns to "gullet," another French word and a diminutive at that, to represent the West Saxon *heals;* he therefore comes up with an Anglo-Saxon sound by a kind of cheating—but that does not matter. What results is verse that conserves the most important qualities of the original—its dignity and its air of tragedy—and a poem which works as a poem rather than as an artifact, yet which does no violence to the sense of the Old English lines.

Wilbur has liked the Anglo-Saxon tradition well enough to try poems entirely of his own in this mode, and a look at them, in a chapter on translation, can broaden an understanding of what appeal he has found in Old English verse. "Junk" and "The Lilacs" are the two lyrics he has published in alliterative half-lines, and though the subjects are not at all antique—ax handles in a neighbor's garbage, lilacs in a Middletown garden—the themes, like the mechanics of the poems, are straight from the English Middle Ages: the matrix of darkness and ruin in which beauty fleetingly lives; mortality's everpresent mark on the natural world; the need for stoic courage, both to be and to value being.

"The Lilacs," which is about the astounding outburst of heady blossoms from dead-looking, winter-ravaged bushes, evades any pat resurrection motif and chooses, again in the Anglo-Saxon way, to look at spring's exuberance as a cryptic indication about death itself:

> These lacquered leaves
> > where the light paddles
> And the big blooms
> > buzzing among them
> Have kept their counsel,
> > conveying nothing
> Of their mortal message,
> > unless one should measure
> The depth and dumbness
> > of death's kingdom
> By the pure power
> > of this perfume.

The only problem with the poem is that, beyond its metrical and alliterative experiment, it is not very interesting. Wilbur does not try any kennings in "The Lilacs," and the metaphors he puts in their place are sparse, oblique, conventional: the lilacs in late winter look like walking wounded; they heal in the "hospital quiet" of spring.

Similarly, "Junk" seems more a catalogue than an imagist poem, rising to modest metaphoric heights only when the speaker rages for a moment about the way things are often made nowadays:

And the men who make them
>   for a little money,
Bartering pride
>   like the bought boxer
Who pulls his punches,
>   or the paid-off jockey
Who in the home stretch
>   holds in his horse.
Yet the things themselves
>   in thoughtless honor
Have kept composure,
>   like captives who would not
Talk under torture.

Readers who know a range of Wilbur's work might find such lines dry, and perhaps, in the fabric of the books in which they appear, they play some role in balancing or counteracting the richness of Wilbur's more characteristic speech. My purpose is to explain plausibly, rather than to justify or excuse, and with that end in mind I suggest one way more of looking at these imitations. True to the Anglo-Saxon spirit, they are about a bare-bones condition of the soul, something stubborn down below faith, below anything that modern folk signify by the word "courage." They are poems about an unreasoning, indwelling hardness which is part of being alive, and which bespeaks nothing but the opaque mysteries of mortality. They are poems, in other words, about the way that natural things, and the human spirit with them, continue along on sheer nerve when any fancier reason has failed; and more, that this continuance is itself natural, in some raw and strict sense, something that one can affirm about life when one is of a mind to affirm nothing else. Reasonably, then, if not quite successfully, these are unadorned poems representing some somber, simple condition of mind that precedes and perhaps subtends everything else. The shades they cast over the range of Wilbur's poems may be slight, but it goes without saying that in certain landscapes a dark patch here and there can make all the difference in the world. Poetry for Richard Wilbur is an entirely natural act of the mind, which need not depend on erudition, nor tradition, nor even upon belief—beyond, that is, the basic but not simple belief that life, death, joy, sorrow, and the spoken word have deep relationships to one another. Wilbur's Old English translations and Anglo-Saxon imitations are ways of presenting that belief as a cornerstone for poetry—his own, and everyone else's in the English tradition.

7. The Figure a Poet Makes

Now, Wilbur, you're good, but you must stop
publishing in *The New Yorker*.
—Wallace Stevens, 1951

A FEW HILLS away from the William Cullen Bryant homestead, Richard and Charlotte Ward Wilbur have built a house on a sunlit spread of rolling country in the austere township of Cummington, Massachusetts, which in its heyday, a hundred years ago, claimed a population of a thousand, but now holds only about half that many. Down a winding side road, near a dairy farm, on acreage which looks convincingly like outback New England, the Wilbur place is not concealed, and to read the outdoor poems in his last three books of poetry is to have a good sense of its setting. Botanists describe the flora around Cummington as transitional, for winter-tough evergreens of farther north mingle here with broadleaf trees common to mid-Atlantic Appalachia, or the Connecticut countryside Wilbur knows from his twenty years as professor at Wesleyan. Though the town lies about twenty miles from Northampton, and the famous "Five College" area which attracts tourists and weekenders, as yet there are no condominiums out in Cummington, no boutiques, pricey cafes, or other signs of rural Disneyfication. A few years ago a resort was built nearby, with lots of fieldstone chimneys and hot tubs, but the project has failed, and the slick brochures now tell lies. Many of the locals still farm, tend orchards, find blue-collar work in the neighborhood; for the past thirty years, a few writers and academics have lived back in these hills, valuing the landscape, the low rents, and the authenticity. Country that has an air of keeping quietly busy and getting by: something of the rough, unmastered New England which Bryant and Frost valued seems here to be still alive.

But Bryant's reputation has slid far from what it once was, and though his rambling, well-tended house—white clapboard with big windows, green shutters, and fine views across the valley—has been open for years as a shrine, it attracts a trickle of visitors, fewer than other poet places in this state, the Emily Dickinson house in midvillage Amherst, or Longfellow's expansive yellow mansion near Harvard Yard. In the middle of the last century, Bryant reigned in New York as a presiding elder of American letters, and while his poetry broke trail for Longfellow and even for Dickinson, in the reshufflings of the American canon he has become something of an out-of-the-way poet, commemorated—sometimes patronized—by an occasional essay or a few pages in a thick anthology; and by this backwoods house, a place to be enjoyed by those who like prowling the empty quarter of the state, or who trouble with poems and poets out of fashion. Cummington is a site for a little reflection, about the peculiar practice of passing judgment on a poet's achievement, or foretelling the scope and longevity of someone's place in an unstable American canon.

Built about twenty years ago, the Wilbur house is an intelligently modern hillside ranch, calling no attention to itself as it makes smart use of a southern exposure and a sizable stand of trees; in a suburb the style of the place, with expanses of glass, large wood deck, and swimming pool, would not be remarkable. Nonetheless, if Richard Wilbur's reputation holds and builds, this home of his might make a respectable landmark, if only for the poet's tower.

The old fantasy of the perfect study apparently has not vanished from the world, but has rather been driven—sometimes literally—underground. In relaxed moods, friends admit to dreaming of lairs on the order of Disraeli's mahogany paradise at Hughenden Manor, Ruskin's long, bright room above Coniston Water, or Emerson's square and dignified chamber—which in our time has been harvested like a saint's relic, chopped out of its proper house and reconstructed down the street at the Antiquarian Society. With few exceptions, such perfect hideouts seem memorials to Victorian affluence and craftsmanship, or world-defying accomplishments by a handful of indomitable early moderns. Writers I have talked to seem resigned to the contemporary fate of the cramped office, the narrow den in the city apartment, a corner of the family room, or a dry spot in the basement, convenient to the water heater and the cat box. Stylish schemes to escape from such traps, and work instead in antique and splendid style, are quixotic adventures that one can admire. What Wilbur has contrived for a study at Cummington seems inspired simplicity: two precut wooden silos, set up one inside the other on a block foundation, with the space between the walls packed with insulation and cut for large windows. On the top, a broad skylight and a chimney for the Franklin stove—and the result is a big, freestanding, round, fir-lined room, high and

bright and easily thirty feet across, with a spiral staircase and lots of
bookshelves and writerly mess lining the walls. Down in the foundation story, there is room for some of the bric-a-brac which accumulates
when a family with wandering children lives in the hills.

Whether or not Wilbur intends this weathering tower, or the
whole homestead, as some kind of statement, in an age when houses,
automobiles, and off-the-rack clothing are analyzed with such high
seriousness as modes of speech, is not sure at all. But Richard Wilbur
knows the dramatized connections, in this century, between poets and
strange buildings in outlying places, what they might signify about the
rebuilding of a self in middle age, or the embrace or resistance of
tradition, the hand hewing of one's own identity out beyond the taste
and reach of the mob. Gestures of that sort can backfire: Robinson
Jeffers's California castle seems now like an absurd marker for the
barren misanthropy of his later life. Yet one cannot imagine saying
dismissive things about, for example, Thoor Ballylee, the tower house
which seems so central to understanding Yeats, and which has been
valued a long time as a poem in stone, as eloquent perhaps as any word
poem in the Complete Edition. The mood of Wilbur's gray silo seems
much lighter than these, and its meaning—again, should there be any
at all—is much less pretentious. There are as yet no poems drawing
attention to it, and if its symbolic bloodlines include a certain Irish
tower, they might also include the windowed turret atop the Dickinson house, where one intense woman preferred to go quietly, not to
dramatize her isolation, but to be alone for a while in the buzz of
middle-class life. Bemusedly aware of its past, a building, like a poem,
may speak quietly of composure or independence. If a house can
signify, it can mean that life, literate and historically conscious and
perhaps scalded a bit by experience, can be lived, can sometimes be
taken in hand; and perhaps that family, fidelity to self, to others, and to
the virtues of a little order and a bit of planning still count for something, though they might be sparsely represented in poetry about
modern experience and how we must inhabit it.

But having paused on the road to the Wilbur place, it is time to
move away: Wilbur's personal life has not been my subject, and it shall
not become so now. From Wilbur himself, and from people who know
him well, one can gather enough indications that his life has been more
complex and difficult than the reserved demeanor of some of his poems
might imply. My reasons for veering so far toward him, in one final
chapter about poetry, are merely these: that in the past few years,
Wilbur's poems have begun to address more steadily problems of aging
and his own peculiar condition of being a survivor who, by genius or

default, finds himself left now as a spokesman of sorts for a vanishing, notorious, passionate generation. Further, a meditation on the poetry of one artist cannot avoid some species of rendezvous with the persona which these poems, and life in the public eye, have ultimately made. From a decent remove, what then can be said of *this* artist, this self, which a long array of words and deeds imply?

In our time, happily or not, poems lead toward the poet. The poetics of personality may trace back to Byron, whose self-dramatizations mingled verse and life in ways that the culture apparently has neither outdone nor outgrown. But the contemporary "poet-game," as it has been called, may be fueled by more than public appetite for notorious personalities. Well before Byron, poetry was on its road to becoming a species of tragic drama; not just an "overheard" record of the private life of the self, but an extended agon, the enemies being mortality, madness, the oblivion into which utterance, thought, and hard-won wisdom must disappear. And because those foes usually win, such dramas have informed the canon and career of poets at least since the early Romantics. Many of the major crises in the art since then—the "damnation" of the French symbolists, the domestic vastations of Eliot, the ideological pageants of Pound, the Beats, confessionals, and so on, have reinforced in critical response expectations that perhaps were laid out first by John Stuart Mill, our first skilled "overhearer"—that poets most worth the reading are poets who, somewhere along the line, have had a proper nervous breakdown or some other harrowing experience from which the truest and best poetry, intense and personal, can spill.[1] The artist himself may be the dramaturge, seeking to manipulate such a show of self-presentation, in verse and beyond it: Nerval, Pound, and Yeats are obvious and spectacular instances. Or the public may go looking for the poet, or in a sense invent one to complement what it may find on the printed page, as has been the case for Stevens, Williams as the busy city doctor, or Sylvia Plath in the twenty years after her death. It is harder to know what to say about Frost, the persona of the rough, charming New Englander whom America "found" in the forties and fifties, but whose jealous, dangerous, self-promoting side was widely known only later, with the publication of a great biography[2]—or Robert Lowell, whose showmanship and drive to build his reputation as a premier sufferer of his generation were jumbled by bouts of real, certifiable madness.[3] Who is in charge—persona, poet, or public—and by how much, will vary with the artist in question; the point is that reading a poet can become, sooner or later (again, for better or worse), part of the act of reading the poetry, and that poets who have spent careers writing in this age have known that this is true even now, when the latest act in the tragic drama has to do with a decay of faith in poetic language itself.

Thanks to ground-breaking books on the subject, critics have learned to speak of "sequence" in considering poetry forged by a single hand over a stretch of time, for sequence is a way into the drama, a process of failed quests, of incomplete visions and revisions, or struggles to apprehend the truth of one's own condition.[4] Because one virtue of sequence is incompleteness, the managed inadequacy of utterance along the way, Wilbur's canon, on the surface, does not seem amenable to that kind of reading, and the issue should not be forced; if there is tragedy inherent in both the poetry and the living, it may lie another way, perhaps avoiding a path which has been described as a great mode for our time. One way to think about this question is to recognize what luck and artistic temperament have made of Richard Wilbur: not only the man who has managed to succeed professionally, but also one of a few talented poets of his generation who has actually endured, and who is called on now by circumstance to speak of survival and the shape of lives, careers, and a passing era. The end of the last poem in one of Robert Lowell's last books—"my eyes have seen what my hand did"—could stand as his last words as an artist, and they can be irksome because they suggest final recognitions which in the verse might not come clear. Lowell died suddenly at the age of sixty, on the verge of growing old, or as American poet lives go, on the verge of full maturity and the possibility of some culminating performance. Lowell was gone so soon, as were Wright, Roethke, Sexton, Hugo, Olson, O'Hara, and so many others, that a generation or two of poets seems in danger of extinction without making its mark deep, without anyone good left to finish its difficult conversation with itself.

Perhaps, then, there is an opportunity, or a special necessity, for a distinguished survivor: to speak in elegy, or be "gaseous and great" for more people than oneself. But the poems which make the needed response in Wilbur's 1987 collection seem eerily modest, as they venture into such reflections on age, on being settled, "finished," complete. Four new poems enter these subjects; two of them, an elegy for W. H. Auden and a satire on an aged philanthropist, displace the conversation a bit; two others, "The Ride" and "Leaving," are direct in subdued ways. "The Ride" is another of Wilbur's small palace insurrections, another wise and troubled extension of a Frost conceit; seeming to pick up where "Stopping by Woods" leaves off, it finishes out a life-journey through the snow and cold, the miles traveled in a faith that living and imagining are, in spite of all, promises darkly worth keeping. Though the speaker rides his horse now, and there is no sleigh, these spare lines recall the famous Frost scene and perhaps the Frost voice, though occasional bursts of rhetorical flourish break away from Yankee simplicity:

> I rode with magic ease
> At a quick, unstumbling trot
> Through shattering vacancies
> On into what was not,
>
> Till the weave of the storm grew thin,
> With a threading of cedar-smoke,
> And the ice-blind pane of an inn
> Shimmered, and I awoke.

To wake from this ride dream is to lose touch with the unconscious, and also to lose faith in it, in the intuitions which can keep the self going, giving what clearance there can be for a life of wakeful imagining. The eight-line question which closes "The Ride" is not late-hour nostalgia for dreams one cannot go back to and finish. Should one "think" too certainly that "there was no horse at all," then everything comes to grief—dream, poem, *all* the poems, life. One believes in the dream horse because one must, and this poem is the acknowledgment, the nurture, the blanket and stall one can offer to the imaginative side of the self. Much of this may sound familiar, but not the echo of finality here, the elegiac mood, the address to such imaginative rides as something possibly over, and irretrievable. This is not Wilbur's "Ben Bulben," a poet's farewell to his art; "The Ride" seems too unassuming for that. But there is no mistaking the backward glance, or a sense of ordeals and victories now done with, yet perpetually in doubt.

This poem seems to work as part of a set, not only with "Leaving" but also with the Auden elegy, with a burst of angst called "Lying," an edgily reflexive satire called "The Finished Man," and perhaps the best poem in the new collection, "All That Is," which I discussed in an earlier chapter. Over each of these poems hang shadows, solid, even burdensome, of the older man who senses with mingled comfort and regret that most of the work is already done in making a self, that one is eventually—now, in this case—blessed and besaddled with identity, voice, and vision. A poem as modest as "The Ride," "Leaving" is a sketch of static existence as a late stage of civilized, successful life, a *golfo placido* of "finished" men and women whose struggles and successes have brought them to the comfortable confinement of self. The conceit in the poem has to do with statuary: in the twilight, human guests at a subdued garden party, as they take leave from their hosts, resemble the stone figures which can be made out along the borders of the scene. Again there is odd simplicity in the style here, another leave taken from fine flourishes; the lines read like a seventeenth-century valediction, something by Carew or Herbert:

We saw now, loitering there
Knee-deep in night,
How even the wheeling children
Moved in a rite

Or masque, or long charade
Where we, like these,
Had blundered into grand
Identities,

Filling our selves as sculpture
Fills the stone.
We had not played so surely,
Had we known.

In these last verses lurk difficult questions: would it really have made a difference, to have "known" before this, how life leads toward a too-solid establishment of self? Is it plausible that such people as these, artists, scholars, famous wits, and other industrious "dignities," would have played their lives out differently in order to evade (if in fact one could) such closing days of well-fed, wistful regret? What is interesting, in other words, about the speaker's parting judgment of his own life, and the amber-dipped grand identity that he and the others have blundered into, is the empty civility of what he can say, finally, in the face of this truth. These curt "would-have, should-have" suppositions closing the poem make no more sense than the pleasantries he must deal in as a party guest. The formal judgment of the shape of one's own life—at this late hour, with the self "Knee-deep in night"—might be just another formality, one more sign of the finished shapeliness to which the self must come.

To miss a strain of resignation here is to miss what seems most honest in the tone of "Leaving." The poem's central paradox is that the identity one builds or wins in the outward world will ultimately run inward to the core, so far inward that elegies for lost freedom will themselves be cramped by civility and form. But there is yet another step to take in describing the tone and sense of all this: the best lines in the poem come just before the conventional close. "Filling our selves as sculpture / Fills the stone" is an arresting *reversal* of convention, and a recognition signaling that down underneath the stone of accumulated identity, a poet is very much alive. The perception itself is paradoxical: sculptors as long ago as Michelangelo may have thought of their art as taking stone away to reveal the figure, but the art itself—one might think of those unfinished slave figures, bursting out of the rock and seeming to concentrate its substance, its possibilities—makes this off-hand-sounding simile worth the remembrance. The fleeting image provides some of that "clearance" by which one can continue to dream, to read, and to be.

Other poems in this set are valedictions in one way or another, and when they are manifestly about somebody else, they show an under-current of reflexivity; even the satire has a nether edge to it. The sixteen-line "For W. H. Auden," who died in 1973, did not appear in *The Mind-Reader* until two years later, and the delay of the poem's publication for four years more deepens somewhat the air of poise[5]—which is the quality of both Auden and his verse which this poem lauds. In fact almost nothing more about Auden is mentioned in the elegy than this; the man and his differences from Wilbur in belief, temperament, prosody, sexuality, are nowhere made visible, except in a shadowy way, the resemblance of these loose unrhymed pentameters to some of Auden's best work before the Second World War. Three stanzas pass before the poem directly addresses its announced subject: such reluctance to "go home," as it were, takes one back to the attenu-ated farewells of "Leaving," but also forward, to an uneasy glimpse at the calyx of careers and reputations. Auden is not here, in his own elegy—just as Auden is not "there," as more than a passing voice, in a scattering of poems in the anthologies, poems to which fewer and fewer readers can affix an identity, a life story, a face, all of which have figured in our century's dialogue with him. Most of "For W. H. Auden" is a calling-up of lost moments and lost people, split seconds in which others have become clear in the mind, then receded into a fabric of recollections that mean something only in fleeting moments of special awareness, like the lilacs in "The Mill" or the nearly forgotten convoys of "In Limbo." According to the musings of this forestalled elegy, what may be remembered best of Auden is this, that he "sus-tained the civil tongue / In a scattering time"—and it takes no leap of inference to see that similar, simple words might be cut for Richard Wilbur too. The nameless remembered folk of the previous lines are people who by will or default move against the grain of time and human busyness, or who find themselves perilously out of place, like these Indians or the German prisoner of war. Auden, by like reckon-ing, was a poet out of place, working against a tide, which having taken the man, now begins to erode the memory. Through that "common door"—a suitably commonplace metaphor—pass all men and women, and the greater part of any poet's work and career.

Richard Wilbur has thought long about the long view. His whole canon—poetry and criticism alike—can attest to that. He seeks still to understand what time is and does and for perspectives which reach beyond the panic of the immediate; and if we come to his work from the myopia of recent quarrels about movements and reputations, it is worth a moment to consider other perspectives. A few months ago, in the course of thinking over some questions that underlie this chapter, questions about poets and schools and the turmoil of our literary scene, I had a chance to wander for a couple of gray days, with a tiny car and a treacherous guidebook, over the countryside traversed by the Albert-Bapaume highway—the two-lane blacktop which once was the spinal cord of the Battle of the Somme. I saw only what every visitor sees, those hundreds of scattered Commonwealth cemeteries, and the defiant monuments to armies decimated in a vast catastrophe which my students can no longer name. The care with which these graves are still tended is haunting in itself: the roses are trimmed, the grasses nurtured, everything kept just so; and in most of these places (all, I suppose, except for the Sepoy regiments and the Chinese Labour Corps) there is the tall Excalibur cross, with its vow that the names of these men "endureth for evermore."

When I came home, having wondered where the dead were of Leipzig, Valmy, Waterloo, and thinking of how the dialogue about literary movements rattles along on with no sense of proportion or of its own responsibilities to a culture with a great deal else on its mind, I found my shrink-wrapped new copy of *Critical Inquiry* in the mailbox. On the cover was an amazing chart, like an insane football play, showing the scramble of aesthetic -isms in the first three decades of this century, before and after the Great War: how they begat, merged, and rebounded away from each other. There were more than thirty little boxes and arrows, running down the page like raindrops on a windshield; the lead article was a critique of someone else's critique of this diagram.[6] Literary historicism is not hard to parody; but in surveying the intellectual and artistic life of this fast-closing century, our best scholars may not be able to indulge themselves for much longer. One impending obligation is to define, in broad, basic ways, what was most characteristic of longer stretches in American letters, and to speak accurately and efficiently to that fraction of an intelligent public who will value such matters at all. Some of the best commentators we have now—Carruth, Pritchard, Vendler—seem already to take that circumstance for granted, and avoid school-partisan argumentation in their discussion of modern and postmodern verse.[7] Richard Wilbur seems to have accepted that reality long since, as witnessed by his refusal to say much in and about the aesthetic warfare in his own times. But in trying to speak sensibly about *him,* about the figure he has cut in such an era as this, one must make a stab at describing the landscape of postwar poetry, in those fundamental shapes and colors from which literary histories will eventually have to be made.

Clues about our situation, the big-scale truths beneath the surfaces, are perhaps everywhere. One which dwells in my own mind turns up in a letter from Theodore Roethke to Robert Lowell, a note now in the Lowell Papers at the Houghton Library. This note was written from a psychiatric ward at Swedish Hospital in Seattle, where Roethke had been confined for a while in the wake of a crack-up; the scrawl is wild, the prose manic, obscene. But in the grip of madness, what Roethke wants from Lowell emerges clearly. It is a petition: Roethke wants Lowell to wangle him a job teaching on the faculty at Harvard.[8]

There are reasons why a retrospective of our time, from a literary-historical standpoint, may need to reckon with one stubborn fact of social, economic, and artistic life: that since the Second World War, American poets have been in large numbers absorbed into an enormous, unprecedented college-and-university empire, and that in some ways poetry has felt the effects of that migration. As a generalization, this does violence, but no more than others about art in the Cold War era; there may be truth enough in such a premise to give it some staying power. If a century and a half of New England puritan life, with its factions and upheavals, can now be condensed, without much scholastic protest, into five-page summaries in our doorstopper anthologies or short chapters in our sanctioned literary histories, if the English Victorians can be "boiled down" every term to a few hours of overview, even in the graduate seminars, then one can imagine how the postwar scene in poetry, with its many transient confederations, might be summed up in educated minds a few decades from now. If my proffered caricature will not serve, other and perhaps worse ones might stand in for it. Happily or not, many of our poets have been brought in from the wild like the California condors; they have been banded, nurtured, and loosed in the pleasant, peculiar habitat of American colleges, with tolerable coffee to drink, reasonably civil and smart young people to work with, genial career academics with whom to commiserate and talk things over. The American poet is to be found readily on campus, as an academic employee with a secure job; his friends and much of his public are likely to be professors and students. Some poets in such circumstances, or critics in their stead, may protest such a sketch of the artistic life as it is commonly lived, but one can protest only with a certain risk of absurdity, of playing what Irving Howe has called "the guerrilla on tenure," the *enragé* who cannot quite acknowledge the mild ways of everyday academic life.

Such circumstances may indeed be affecting poetry itself, perhaps mattering a good deal more than, say, the British East India Company figures in our reading of those romantics who sometimes found employment there. For instance, like rivers in American cities, the ordinary flow of ideas can apparently be altered or reversed, by this coming of the artist into academe. Earlier in this century, language and literature scholars customarily collected their ideas from artists and imaginative writers: George Eliot and D. H. Lawrence seem to have made F. R. Leavis possible; first a Wordsworth and a Frost, then a Trilling to read them. Lately, however, it seems that the linguistic theorist can be the one who comes first, or the postphenomenologist, or the latest treatise about defamiliarization—the poetry gets written downstream. A recent manifestation of this transformed relationship, the self-styled L-A-N-G-U-A-G-E poets, seems hard to explain except as an effect of the infection of poets with academic pathogens, and the growth or decay of some poetry into scholasticized discourse, fashioned to fit dissertations rather than the other way round.[9]

If this is in some ways an academic age in American poetry, then Richard Wilbur has cheerfully, frequently, and honestly presented himself to this world as an academic citizen. There was the Amherst success to begin with, and after the war the postgraduate fellowship and the faculty position at Harvard; there were the Guggenheims and the Prix de Rome, and for years after all that, Wilbur held what Roethke, trapped in that ward in Seattle, regarded as the ultimate job for a poet in the late fifties, the chair in poetry at Wesleyan. In his spare time Wilbur has been president of the American Academy of Arts and Letters; in 1977 he came to Smith College, where he taught for ten years; he is now active as an emeritus professor of poetry. He has edited, read for university presses, corresponded with professorial critics, read from the college lecterns, given keynote addresses at their ceremonies. And as the second Poet Laureate of the United States, Wilbur was ever the gracious, enthusiastic, available public man. There is no pretending that he has defied mainstream America as one of our Jeremiahs. But from that longer and perhaps distorted perspective, which might seem more strange? The American postwar poet as self-aware citizen and professional? Or the poet as Caliban with an annuity, an assigned parking space, dental insurance, and a corner office in Old Main? One way or another, if personality will continue to figure in the reading, enjoyment, and valuation of the verse of our time, then better attention should perhaps be paid to Wilbur's uncommon public guise, in an age which has not lacked for masquerade.

Wilbur does seem to like presenting himself as one of the last, loyal guardians of a civil tongue in a scattering time, and the latest collection plays that theme heavily: an afternoon's thoughts on a calculation in the writings of Bede, thoughts on a wife primping herself in a new dress, on a still life by Andrew Wyeth (who has played something of the same complex, peculiar, old-guard-innovator role in American painting that Wilbur has in verse); and there is this hyperdomestic companion piece to "Leaving" called "Lying"—which also begins at a party and drifts away into a serene reverie, literary, botanical, metaphysical, professorial. There are short Stevensesque lines in the opening half of "Lying," recalling Stevens as chaos connoisseur, or Wilde as the saturnine expert on the decay of fine art:

> You may enjoy a chill of severance, . . .
> . . . .
> . . . In the strict sense, of course,
> We invent nothing, merely bearing witness
> . . . .
> Clothed with its usual thunder, and the stones
> Beginning now to tug their shadows in
> And track the air with glitter.

Even the handsomest perceptions in this opening have an armchair feel to them, for the voice here is like that of a gaseous-great personage holding forth, coyly cynical about the business of speaking out about these party situations that call for cleverness and half lies, misdemeanors against truth. If the tone is abrasively genial, ironic in barren ways, it gets worse before getting better: there may be too much self-assurance in the offhand-sounding suggestion about the self as a latter-day, low-tech aeolian harp. For a moment, Coleridge seems to conjoin with W. C. Williams here; but such party wit cannot be trumped up into reconciliations of the Romantic seer with the antiromantic poet of things as they are, with no winds of inspiration blowing that world and imagination into new shapes:

> We invent nothing, merely bearing witness
> To what each morning brings again to light:
> Gold crosses, cornices, astonishment
> Of panes, the turbine-vent which natural law
> Spins on the grill-end of the diner's roof,
> Then grass and grackles.

This garrulous, hop-and-skip poem making seems odd in the Wilbur canon; the closest thing to it is the voice of the mind-reader, the burned-out Italian fortune-teller and professional liar that Wilbur enacts in the 1975 collection. But there is no "lui parla" disclaimer at the head of "Lying," no Other to bear the blame for this unease. The speaker—this poet, every poet?—is a species of liar, in whose tones one can sometimes hear, as now, a groping for solid ground, for a truth whose whereabouts, amid the civil distortions, he has forgotten; and a valid, self-consoling excuse for the lies in all fictive music. The speaker has been flailing about, and going under; around line thirty-four, he strikes the firm bottom he needs, and the tone of "Lying" changes, takes on steadiness and a conviction that the awkward party is over, and that the work of rebuilding is under way. Like a true modern, he rebounds off Nothing, yet the philosophical turning point of "Lying," apropos of nothing, is handsome in its economy and simplicity: "What is it, after all, but something missed?" While the parenthetical "after all" sweeps away many years of passionate, complex conversation about what Nothing is and is not, this dismissive affirmation has not the same glib ring to it as what went before. The difference has something to do with the quality of the imagining, the concrete universal, as it were, which represents this idea of nothing as "something missed":

> It is the water of a dried-up well
> Gone to assail the cliffs of Labrador.

From here on, the rhetoric of "Lying" rises, has Tennysonian if not Miltonic colorations and shows more patience and confidence about its own imagery. For the rationale, as yet unannounced, has been intuited: *likening,* as a species of lying, is what makes reality real, what makes a "thing most itself," as the speaker observes a bit farther on. Ontological conundrum, modern semiotic commonplace—it does not matter what status this idea of the world is assigned, what body of thought it is catalogued with; at the heart of the poem is a nonideological assertion of the connectedness of experience, either made or found out by the lies of the imagination. That is classic Wilbur; what is interesting here is the array of selves now given license to meditate about this: the sober academic, the observant naturalist, the poet gently replying to friends and contemporaries. The reinterpretation of Milton's Satan, which takes only the next ten lines, is fresh, provocative: as the "arch-negator" Satan is like one of Wilbur's mechanists, a creature whose purely "intellectual sight" unmakes the "given world"—given meaning objectively present, given meaning divinely bestowed. Seeing and making conflate in the lines following these, and they whirl around each other; "Lying" will not be drawn into accepting suspicious formulas for the composition of the universe and for the imagination's exact role within it. When Satan leaves the world, it blooms and ramifies again, which might suggest some a priori richness and form; but no more of that, for the poem shifts to catbirds on the mock orange in the yard, chopped onions in the kitchen, tarps flapping in the wind out in the barnyard—ordinary experiences of a summer's day in a place like Cummington, small things not missed, but rather seen closely, and likened:

> And in the barnyard near the sawdust-pile
> Some great thing is tormented. Either it is
> A tarp torn loose and in the groaning wind
> Now puffed, now flattened, or a hip-shot beast
> Which tries again, and once again, to rise.

A case in point: the object is most itself when the right simile is found for it. The imagination makes reality more real by finding or mugging up those connections. Right then, after this small cadenza, "Lying" seems to respond to another poem, one of the anthologized standards about life as we know it now, in its unadorned, unconnected, raw truth. The question of "Lying" is partly rhetorical, but also sober and genuine: "What, though for pain there is no other word, / Finds pleasure in the cruellest simile?" builds from the premise that human nature can *never* stop likening, that the poetic act of lying and half-right referring is essential to our being and the world's—but beyond that, there is no saying what that compulsion is or how, psychologically or even metaphysically, it works. In like manner, poems keep talking to poems; and this one is perhaps Wilbur's best and most forthright answer to Randall Jarrell's eloquent, abject refusal to lie to himself or anyone else about experience, those lines from "90 North" that I quoted in chapter 2 and quote again, as a splendid utterance of the difficult creed of the postmodern condition:

> I see at last that all the knowledge
>
> I wrung from the darkness—that the darkness flung me—
> Is worthless as ignorance: nothing comes from nothing,
> The darkness from the darkness. Pain comes from the darkness
> And we call it wisdom. It is pain.

Things are only what they are—except that this recognition comes to a speaker out of the symbolic dream of a failed Arctic trek, and that this supreme negation that "nothing comes from nothing" comes from a play, and that the speaker in the play turns out to be fatally wrong about what comes from nothing. In other words, even in the most perfect darkness there is no escape from likening, from the connections and the truth quest of the imagination; and with a quiet insistence, "Lying" here voices what "90 North" cannot say straight out. The imaginative motion hereafter in Wilbur's poem is a laureate's sweep, kept from being too magisterial by the firmly vernacular voice in which the poem's grandest likenings are sketched. The big finish involves Homer, Genesis, Milton, and the Song of Roland, "great lies told with the eyes half-shut / That have the truth in view," and what links them in these last twenty lines is this theme about the ways of the poet, the human compulsion to name and reorganize the world as part of the process of knowing it better.

Chiron is presented as someone like the figure that this particular poet would make:

> Who, with sage head, wild heart, and planted hoof
> Instructed brute Achilles in the lyre.

While the play of "lyre" against the "truth" two lines before is fine Wilbur panache, the pose and the constituent parts, as it were, of this centaur are what count most: wisdom, wildness, courage—not quite the classic triad that, in Plato's reckoning, makes for the ideal public citizen, but still an idea of the self as three forces in a kind of mix, or at least a stubborn and stable quarrel. The "truth in view" in this detail mustered from the *Iliad* has to do with the temperament of the right sort of liar. The mention of Eden, just after, follows a favorite pattern in Wilbur's poems: for thirty years he has used Eden to mythologize some lost condition of unity between the word, the named thing, and its primordial wonder, and the allusion here seems to hew to that line. But here is that word "scattering" again, from the Auden elegy; it refers now to the Fall, and more, to a million-year babel of lost connections between language and what Wilbur calls in "Alatus" (the previous poem in the collection) "the hid pulse of things." All this, as a warm-up to the biggest lie that "Lying" remembers, the inflation, over centuries, of one sordid raid on a Moorish baggage train, into the preeminent French *chanson de geste,* the hero tale of Roland, without which the lore of the European Middle Ages would be much diminished.

But the loveliness of the old poem aside, what truth is viewed or served by such violence against historical fact? What counts in the *chanson,* as remembered in "Lying," is Roland's "blood," his faith—not his warlike prowess, not even his historical existence—and what he has been faithful to is faith itself, that refusal of negation which "galled the arch-negator" and keeps the world "dove-tailed," handsomely co-herent, thanks to some dark cooperation between divinity and the imagination. Again the ontology is cautious, even coy, heedful of the phenomenological minefields that spread out around contemporary thought about such things. And again the language of Christian re-demption is self-evident here, for Roland dies full of religious fervor, faithful unto death to the king and to the dove that represents the Holy Spirit—if we are indeed to believe this legend woven out of lies and forgotten facts. But though the salvation suggested in this language, in this ending, stays as uncertain as the truth of Roland, the poem itself is dove-tailed like the fine woodwork in a Queen Anne highboy: Ro-land's devil melds with Milton's, and this interconnecting wordplay hearkens back to the catbird in the neighbor's bushes twenty lines before, and to the catbird's balancing act with his tail twenty lines before that, and back to the grackle lie which set all this going, and which turns up again as an echo in the "beaked ladle" at the party where the lie is told. Everything works fiercely together, faithful unto death to that theme—but more than that, faithful to Wilbur's way. Out of a meditation's bourgeois beginnings in grackles and dead parties, a grand yet unpretentious recognition grows, and the epic, the religious, the skeptical, and the mundane imagination make a kind of peace. Such a poem might seem, to some readers, measured and mature to a point of excess, but that judgment will have more to do with the temperament of readers than with aesthetics, or politics, or other wellheads of mod-ern critical discourse. This poet is who he is; and alone in his time or not, as an aging centaur-chevalier he means to plant his hoof and wind his horn.

Yet such a geste, displaced, modernized, mollified though it is, requires its antiphon, for Wilbur seems to take it on faith that in human experience nothing, and certainly not the self, is ever sufficiently de-scribed. Another companion poem to "Lying" in this latest collec-tion—playing off against what Lowell, in a late book, called the "ma-chismo of senility"—is "A Finished Man," which both is and is not about the Other, somebody else of about Wilbur's age and station in life. A poem much like this one in his canon is quite old: "In The Smoking Car," which dates from the fifties, is an ambitious young artist's cold satire on the self-pitying mentality of the modern failure. But that mentality is known from the inside, well imagined, just as the complacency and the entrenched resentments of this "finished man" are understood. The last poem but one in the new set, "A Finished Man," seems not so much satire as elegy, for a consciousness that has lost its flex, its capacity for change. "Finished" here means everything it can—completed, perfected, dead: the old distinguished guest has finished his career, finished his quest for riches, and begun to give them up again. He is a perfect triumphant materialist, wanting perfection of another sort, and from the perspective of the speaker this fellow is finished, beyond hope, set deep in his psychological ways.

Wilbur himself has collected plenty of honorary degrees, sat on many a dais next to such great givers—but what are his credentials for describing how they tick? This is condescension—unless there be a reflexive undertone here, something that hints that this macerated Other is known and knowable because he is not unlike a side of the self. I think such reflexivity is implicit in the detail with which this mind is furnished, the clarity of the old pain:

> It was himself whom he could not forgive;
> Yet it has been a comfort to outlive
> That woman, stunned by his appalling gaffe,
> Who with a napkin half-suppressed a laugh,
>
> Or that grey colleague, surely gone by now,
> Who, turning toward the window, raised his brow,
> Embarrassed to have caught him in a lie.

We are inside a specific mind, but perhaps not yet inside a very good poem. As far as language goes, this seems ordinary, and the justification, that it represents well the pedestrian patterns of this "finished" soul, may be one of those arguments that looks good primarily on paper. Wilbur has not written about such drab, unhappy people for about twenty years—the last instances before this are "Playboy" and "The Mechanist"—so why is this here, set between such classic Wilbur poems as "All That Is" and "Hamlen Brook," both of which leave familiar human banality behind and zoom off to look at miraculous trout, lambent gods, the trickeries of time, and the unslakeable human spirit?

While I have been trying to avoid commentary which forgives or rationalizes every rattle in Wilbur's work, I wish I could account better for this dose of the sad mundane—unless it helps to complete some sensibility that takes shape over the whole run of these poems, as "Playboy" and "The Mechanist" bring *Walking to Sleep* out of reveries and down to earth, as "A Fire-Truck" does the same work in *Advice to a Prophet,* as "McCarran Act" does for *Things of This World,* and back to "Potato" in *The Beautiful Changes*—brief voyages into ordinary perceptions, vanities, rancor, sloughs of mind that this poet, as a complete sensibility, dares to speak of and share. Our age does not need poetry to mirror its own commonplace and unresponsive moods; but as Lowell,

Berryman, Bly, Ashbery, and others have been lauded for the completeness of range and the balance of the sensibilities they present in their collections, so should we recognize a way these poems might interact, the small, grey, unheroic ones giving breadth, balance, validity to ones that soar—and make it possible to believe in a human sensibility, a self encompassing them all.

A self: the idea may seem a little out of place in a time whose dominant critical theorists often fulminate against such notions. When Wilbur is discussed, he is sometimes mentioned uncomfortably, as a survivor of the awkwardly named Middle Generation, with Lowell, Jarrell, Bishop, Snodgrass, whose idea of the individual and the poetic act cannot quite be reconciled with that of truer postmoderns—John Ashbery perhaps chief among them—but who nonetheless casts a shadow, attracting talented admirers like Dana Gioia, Wendy Cope, Brad Leithauser, and others who seem to persist in believing in an immanence of self and signification in poems and the world. Like many of his departed contemporaries, Wilbur is a performer; he can put on a Wilbur show, the phases of the personality matching the magic of revelation, affirming, in voice and observation, that the self and the reality we experience are not quite as fictitious or indeterminate as a Wittgenstein-Foucault-Lacan line of reasoning might exhort the world to decide.

When Wilbur overplays the role of Professor Wilbur, bemused armchair elucidator of overlooked symmetries, mild-mannered judge of aesthetic and epistemological lemming runs, he can seem magisterial, stuffy, dated in his intellectual habits, especially if one does not read through the book and hear other Wilburs who are given voice. But whether or not his canon operates by some principle of sequence, the poems must be allowed to work together. For example, "Icarium Mare," in the latest collection, seems by itself an extreme case of the Professor Wilbur mode. There are few subjects more bombarded by verse in this century than the fall of Icarus: and anthologies now sometimes publish Icarus poems in packs and sets, including good ones by Spender, Auden, Williams, Edward Field, Robert Phillips. Wilbur's entry into the game does not seem to speak from a privileged location, on scene in the Aegean: it is hard to place this voice anywhere, except perhaps at a podium in Memorial Hall. In fact the opening stanza—

> We have heard of the undimmed air
> Of the True Earth above us, and how here,
>   Shut in our sea-like atmosphere,
> We grope like muddled fish. . . .

—seems to compress and refine an ungainly metaphor that William James featured in one of his more famous Boston lectures.[10] But much as Wilbur may improve James, he cannot make this True Earth or Icarus' disaster more than a construct, a place to begin some happy intellection. Icarus is posited—and then in the same neighborhood (as the poem, still in its armchair, tours the Cyclades for other big historical doings) it finds Aristarchus and St. John the Divine. And so things begin to fit together: Icarus' waxen wings prefigure the geographer's flight of understanding about the earth's orbit and the sequestered saint's great visions which became the Book of Revelation. We have been through this before; the only bit of craft which stands out is the way the allusion to "John's bejeweled inward view" leads to the inspired image of "The saint's geodic skull"—another of those astonishing moments in which an old, old subject, divine inspiration, is refreshed by some close scrutiny of natural fact. Not too many lay people, and I suspect few poets, have looked hard at a geode, considered the rounded, dull, exceptionally skull-like exterior shape, and then cracked it open to find dazzling crystal formations hid within. That moment is worth the price of admission to "Icarium Mare"; it is Wilbur at his artistic best in the midst of an otherwise academic poem, which ends up with another exposition of a familiar Wilbur idea of poetry and the human condition—again, from some unlocatable dais, a how-to lesson about keeping our "proper range" in imagining and understanding the world:

> Aspiring, with this lesser globe of sight,
> To gather tokens of the light
> Not in the bullion, but in the loose change.

The trouble for "Icarium Mare" is that the loose change is not here, among these grand reorderings and the hypothetical Aegean sunshine. It is concentrated elsewhere in the "New Poems," in a half-dozen short, brilliant observations of the natural world, poems which modestly yet firmly *refuse* closure, keep the mystery of man unsolved, the philosophical axioms of the moment at bay, experience curious and new. For forty years Wilbur has persisted in being a nature poet; no one else of his generation except Ammons looks as intensely at the details of reality as Wilbur does, or affirms, as he does, the humility and the open-endedness of looking. In these poems dwells an antiphon to Professor Wilbur; in them the strongest enthusiasms and the special intelligence and presence of the poet come clear.

Some of these poems are small in scope, sketches and short, close looks, sometimes reminiscent of other poets, but usually something new in intensity, focus, and style. "Wyeth's Milk Cans" is one of these; it has a clarity, a directness, a boldness of its own, yet it also melds voices from Frost and Williams and Pound, though such a melding might not seem imaginable. In his published interviews, Wilbur has not spoken about Wyeth, but a look at the work of both artists leads one to suspect that sympathy between them runs deep. Enjoying now much the same sort of reputation as Wilbur—a wide, admiring audience of intelligent people, but an awkward respect or an uneasy silence from academic students of the contemporary, who do not know how to classify him—Wyeth is comparably stubborn in his interest in the natural mundane, in his faith that life as seen still has eloquence left in it, that the moods and mysteries of what we perceive are neither simple nor redundant. Buckets and cans abound in Wyeth's paintings,[11] either in the foreground or in small corner details: they seem to represent what Faulkner calls the "doing" that moves "terribly along the earth," the ugly and wonderful brutalities and heroics of ordinary living. The haikulike compression of Wilbur's short poem reflects the simplicity of Wyeth's very still life, two milk cans in the foreground, a barren, frozen landscape stretching out behind them into the distance. Wilbur gets the scene summarized in three short lines, and then drops his vorticist bomb:

> What if these two bells tolled?
> They'd make the bark-splintering
> Music of pure cold.

The splintering bark is right, from both a natural and a literary perspective. On reading these lines, it is hard not to think of Pound's "wet, black bough," the parent stock of quick American apparitions, but here chilled down to zero. If this is recognizable as the sort of landscape that troubles Frost and inspires Williams, then why the Pound? These are empty tins on an empty scene, poised between revelation and nothingness; they will *not* toll; they are not bells, except to the fancy, and fancy cannot be trusted. Is this then a vorticist insight, or a Williams-style look at ordinary things that signify nothing beyond themselves, or something else from an unclaimed zone of experience between them? It is that uneasy, haunted ontological position that can vex people who look long into such a Wyeth scene, that Wilbur manages to catch in less than thirty words; there are none of the laureate's lessons here, only the unsettling, uncertain ring of the loose change.

A little time spent on truly unfamiliar ground, in the camp of the contemporary scientist and technologist, can raise in the intellectual tourist a concern—that in affirming the dead end of observation, the tedious mystery of phenomenal experience, one can lose connection to a cultural and (strictly speaking) philosophical movement which may now be making the real difference—if not to the humanities at the moment, then to the civilization to which the humanities sometimes are heard to condescend, and which, in a species of elegant revenge, has allowed much of the discourse about art to molt into a tolerated quaintness, into frill. While the visiting lecturer in the humanities, sketching in "the modern condition" for his uninitiated audience, may raid Einstein or Heisenberg or theories of relativity, entropy, and paratacticity as scientific grounding for a historically inevitable poetics of indeterminacy, the working scientific mind often seems to accommodate itself gracefully to measures of uncertainty in the natural universe—because the physicist, the biologist, the astronomer, neither insensitive nor brittle, is not always undone by a collapse of handsome theories and perfect universal principles. One might visit the lab across the street to test this assertion, or look at some of the oddly buoyant commentaries on the human condition by practicing scientists who also write, and who still try to make connections.[12] If things are true most of the time, if the world as perceived behaves, pretty reliably, by discernible laws, then an interest in old and new particulars opens up wonders, keeps nature new. To the scientist, the world can yet seem interesting, charged with possibility, including possibilities of truth, of value: curiosity is not always balked because Kant's model of reality or Hegel's model of history no longer rolls without a wobble.

Richard Wilbur recalls a visit to his house by a prominent abstract artist and good friend; taking a walk in the woods and listening politely for a while to Wilbur's details about this and that wild bush and bloom, the guest interrupted him with finality: "To me, this is all a smear of green."[13] The postmodern woods can indeed seem a smear of undifferentiated and dismal green; those are the woods that seem to flicker in and out of view at times in the middle distance of Ashbery's poems, or Levertov's, or Rich's. But a philosophical reluctance to look at such details as Wilbur wearied his guest with, a reluctance to believe in the continued value of such looking, remains out of keeping not only with scientific praxis, but with diurnal human experience, the fabric of identity. Yet it is in science that contemporary humanists, when pressed to it, often ground excuses for looking no more. A deep rift between the scientific consciousness—which is perhaps to say the genuine contemporary self—and the scholastic humanist mind may lie in this, in their different curiosity about and faith in the details of the world we wander through, a willingness, on the part of the mind beyond the seminar, to live with continued interest in the available universe, the one knowable through the five senses and describable, more or less adequately, in the English language.

In other words, what might be truly "out of joint" now among the arts is a sense of proportion: their understanding or intuitive sense of the relation of ideas to identity. Whether or not John Ashbery's brilliant proponents are, by some ideological argument, wrong-headed or right, really is not the issue,[14] for it is hard to imagine that the postmodern sensibility, as it is now represented and discussed, will be a point of arrest in thinking about experience, inquiry into the imagination, its power and prospects. The intellectual life of the West has never been more involved with particulars, with the mysteries of the specific detail; and to my mind the most important and culturally appropriate quality of Richard Wilbur's poetry is not that it refreshes this or that tradition, but that it sees. To regard external experience as a smear of green is to be intellectually and imaginatively restricted, and sooner or later a poetics which assents to such confinement will cease to give nourishment, will cease to hold value for the culture or the contemporary self—if such poetics have not begun to lose their force already. Whether or not a larger world will eventually turn to Wilbur's poetry is a prophecy nobody can make. But his vision does seem to express not only much about Western cultural history, but about where we are and where we may be going—a vision neither of Jerusalem nor of The Void, but of the world as it manifoldly and fascinatingly is, with shifts and colorations and particulars to refresh, rejuvenate, and even, perhaps, convince. The minute particulars of the world and of language are where the fun is, and the mysteries which a few years of sequestered philosophical discourse have not begun to drive from the taste of human beings.

From several perspectives, "Shad-Time" could make the grade as a postmodern poem; eddying around not just a play on words but a sort of pun in the cycles of nature, it twirls the mind, raises uncomfortable questions about what the self discovers and what it conjures, about the inherent poverty and excess of the world as found, about the "blank" we may really be looking at, and the compulsions of the mind in the face of voids. Like the moving water it emulates, "Shad-Time" melds two natural events, the spawning of the shad in eastern rivers, and the blooming of the shadblow, or serviceberry tree, in the woodlands along the bank. The opening stanza gives no hint as to which will be the subject, fish or tree; in the first four short, rime-royal lines all is colorlessness and motion, to set up, in symbolist fashion, the "burst" of white and red in the second quatrain and the jump to an image of the landscape of the mind. The image is not of revelation: the head is "vacant," and the "spitting fuse" of the dream may just be random fireworks of synaptic nonsense. The pace of the poem is swift; the only subjects looked at for more than a flash are the "white racemes," the blossom clusters of the serviceberry, and they command only a moment before the poem dives again into the most classical of metaphors, rejuvenated by wordplay and oblique exposition:

> Or as the Thracian strings,
> Descending past the bedrock's muted staves,
>   Picked out the signatures of things
>   Even in death's own caves.

The attention here is on Orpheus' music, not on the death-defying artist; the sound of the lyre echoes from the black rock around him as he descends to the underworld, making music, or finding it, there in bowels of the great vacancy. "Signatures" is yet another perfect Wilbur word choice, the musical signature of Orpheus' song and stay against confusion, and perhaps the language of things in themselves, "picked out," which is to say sounded or extracted, seen or dreamed beneath the surfaces of the experienced world. And "staves" works handily with the other puns, suggesting here the supporting ribs of the cave as well as some musical order that lurks even in the blank of bedrock. But what has happened to the supposed subject of all this, the shad and the shadblow, both of which have been outclassed and obscured by these pyrotechnics? The drama of the poem is taking shape, and it is a drama constantly at the heart of such self-conscious, defiantly crafted poetry. The contest is between the natural thing in motion, in itself, and the imaginative impulse to cast it, Orpheate it, lock it up in the muted staves of a poem. Wilbur has long known the price of artifice; and "Shad-Time" ponders that price. The fourth stanza wrests the poem out of Hellenistic reveries and back into the cold spring day, back to a Williams or a Wyeth world where things have to be looked at first, and perhaps last and always, as they are:

> Shadblow; in farthest air
> Toss three unsettled birds; where naked ledge
>   Buckles the surge is a green glare
>   Of moss at the water's edge;
>
>   And in this eddy here
> A russet disc of maple-pollen spins.
>   With such brave poverties the year
>   Unstoppably begins.

"Shadblow"—not a word more about it. The tree is there, and with a sort of determined indeterminacy these two stanzas blur their way around the rest of the moving landscape. It is not like Wilbur to let birds be only "birds," rather than gulls or grackles or something specific; but birds are uncertain in the uncertainty of "farthest" air. And where, relative to the shadblow, this naked ledge is that buckles the surge, is not sure either, or just where the "here" is that holds the spinning maple-pollen—though they must be close by to be seen so surely. The poem will not stop for such reflection; it is quick, clear observation now, charged with that peculiar satisfying discomfort people recognize who have been out near a cold rushing stream, early in the day and the year. This is cold music to match the chime of Wyeth's milk cans, and "brave poverties" could apply to much of the best of Wyeth's work too, the hard, unsentimental gaze at a world stripped of the blossom, the warmth, all the confounding loveliness. Who is being brave? The compliment spins like the maple-pollen, affixing itself neither to the scene, nor to the seer; no romantic consolations, no existential self-congratulations either. It is cold, and there is no time for such postures by streamside. Wilbur's place-poems rarely forget where they are, and this is a case in point, a wilderness poem that does not forget the wilderness. "Brave poverties" is not mannered ambiguity, a hedge on the epistemological bet. It is a vague thought, an idea in an early-season stage, a suspicion, such as might occur to a mind improvising its way through daily experience, rather than reflecting in the warm, ritualized tranquillity of the reading room, where but a fraction of mental life goes on, and only part of a belief system takes shape.

The drama of "Shad-Time" has other dimensions which parallel and extend the one I mentioned before, the conflict between nature in itself and the artifice of the imagination. This is also a poem about two kinds of thinking which claim dominion over the self, different sides of the consciousness: not ego and id, nor even wakeful and hypnagogic levels of thought, but rather the mind in the high arts of formality— Western-style reasoning and poem making—versus the mind wakeful but off-duty, on its own, thinking neither referentially nor for the ages, but point-to-point, in and for a particular time and place. This other "mind" is therefore as real and as impoverished as the landscape it shivers through, and its "bravery" might well be as stupid or word-lessly sublime as human-scale bravery can be. Can one concede that this, happily or not, is a way we often are—more often, perhaps, than we are the composed, bodyless, mandarin reader-people presumed in much verse and commentary now? But concessions really do not have to be made; acknowledged or not, the self moves as unstoppably as the river, improvising, as Lowell liked to say, out on the razor's edge.

The final three stanzas of "Shad-Time" are one long splashing sentence; the world and the season are on the move, and we can look or play blind as we see fit. There are eddies of fine artistry afloat on this stream, but the cadence and the sense of the lines imply that artistry, in and of itself, does not matter, unless it be part of something bigger, some larger, changeful, multisurfaced consciousness. The interrupted drama moves to its resolution, or rather two of them: the Orpheus music conceit, the poetic tradition business, comes back in some word-play, on "Concert" in line twenty-three, in the "Scored" boulder, striated and musically composed, out in the spray—and in the Shake-spearean use of "numbers" two lines later. But this pastoral symphony does not lunge from the text. It is a barely heard and perhaps imagined melody in the "great fields of emptiness," the "abyss" of ordinary experience which refuses to yield and make sense. Orphic verse mak-ing, the impulse to charm and organize hell, is neither extolled nor expelled, because that desire and that tradition are part of *us;* once more the real question for the contemporary mind has to do with propor-tion. What are we doing when, in spite of everything, we dream, or feel the power of ancient ways of dreaming? "Shad-Time" makes no answer. The final stanza returns to dubious motion, the "scattered roe" in line thirty referring suddenly to the other sort of shad, which caused confusion at the start:

> Though cloudily astrew
> As rivers soon shall be with scattered roe,
> Instant by instant chooses to
> Affirm itself and flow.

Lowell ended one of his early poems in a curiously similar way, leaving behind kindred questions. Adapted from a famous troubled letter by Jonathan Edwards about the suicide of a kinsman, "After the Surprising Conversions" closes thus:

> September twenty-second, Sir, the bough
> Cracks with the unpicked apples, and at dawn
> The small-mouth bass breaks water, gorged with spawn.

To anyone aware of nature's profligate cycles, both of these images, of roe and spawn in the water, totter truly on a razor's edge, for they speak of bounty, of renewal—and of appalling waste, the seasonal slaughter of innocents. To try to make sense of it all, in some obdurate, all-weather way, as Edwards tried, is to end up as "cloudily astrew" as the "pure numbers" heard or fancied on a good morning at the river's edge; to dismiss all meaning and, as it were, affirm the abyss, is to do no better—this seems to be the mild rejoinder of "Shad-Time" to the feverish epistemological games of the modern West. Experience remains a "swarm of shadows" from which there is no trusty recourse, Platonic or otherwise; what one can "affirm" is only what one can and does affirm intuitively, out beyond the grip of ideology, that "Instant by instant," experience seems to affirm itself, to make a kind of music and a species of sense. If such thinking, here or elsewhere in Wilbur's poetry, is anything special, any sort of intellectual or artistic breakthrough, it has to do with rediscovering a human actuality and conferring dignity upon imaginative, intellectual, and moral experience as an ongoing, disheveled, changeful totality—not the fine or terrible moment treasured, the insight fixed and affirmed through all weather, but rather the experience *of* experience, sheer temporality, flux, and the genuine, unscholastic indeterminacy of being alive. This is how pastoral poetry has grown since Frost, how it keeps profoundest relevance to the human condition.

Several times in every decade, academic books are published which try to map out a Periodic Table of the Poets, arranging and accounting for every one of them who has written consequential verse since 1945. It is an amusing if dubious game, a favorite of people who like to have things in place: add an extra neutron of angst, and Snodgrass yields a Berryman isotope; stir in some deep-image doctrine, tinker with the politics or the continental influence, and define the philosophical and artistic status of almost anyone.[15] Such orderly highscience histories of contemporary poetry can rarely avoid a problem with Richard Wilbur: one of the latest such books discusses him for six lines in two hundred pages, labeling him repeatedly a "late modernist," an "elitist," a "specialist"—as if the American common reader could curl up now in his Barcalounger with "accessible" plain folk like Ashbery, Merrill, Lieberman, Levertov, Merwin.[16] The experienced reader may not care about this practice of model making, namecalling, and scorekeeping—but what worries is the possibility that all this amounts to more fiddling while Arcady burns or is sold off in chunks for another shopping mall.

A tour through the literary reviews suggests that American poetry might be in one of those dry seasons that Jarrell used to mourn; but the long-term climate may be worse than that, with the genre as we know and value it withering under a hot wind of videos and sound bytes, CDs, DATs, and FAX machines, arrogant, disputatious teaching and repulsive scholastic discourse. The major booksellers in the United

States, even in the college towns, commonly stock only a handful of titles by living poets, and it seems that a mass of supposedly educated people, scarred by freshman English or some frustrating afternoons with *The New Yorker,* regard the enterprise as a trivial or exclusionary game. Poetry will surely "survive." Tragedy survived in the hands of Seneca; a few brawny Celts still refine the art of heaving telephone poles, and somewhere devoted, sequestered artisans keep a few connoisseurs supplied with inlaid snuffboxes. The American writers' workshops are not in danger of shutting down. The question is whether poetry as an art will continue to be a living and consequential enterprise, will regain some dimensions and meaning for a culture which once valued it a good deal more.

As the second American Poet Laureate, Richard Wilbur took to the job with good-humored seriousness, kept himself constantly busy in the cause of verse and in reopening a conversation between American poets and at least some sizable fraction of the intelligent American public. Reading and talking, he has been featured on the Public Broadcasting Service specials on American poetry; he has turned up on commercial network newscasts. He has presided at elegant and vulgar festivities in New York, Washington, and elsewhere around the country and at small, fierce commemorations; on national tours, he continues to read his own work and that of others, poets living and dead, in his famous round baritone—reading with range and humor, not intoning in the inexplicable fashion of some of his peers. This past year, as Moscow thawed in a Glasnost springtime, the American State Department sent over the poetry team of John Ashbery and Richard Wilbur— a pairing which, though it might make some American critics gasp, delighted the Russian audiences no end—and the two friends spoke and read before packed houses at Moscow University, the Mayakovsky Museum, and the American Embassy. On stage, in conversation, in prose, Wilbur reliably extends welcome, seems always there for *poetry,* not poetry of one time or temperament or stripe.

The age of seventy is coming on Richard Wilbur soon; he needs no lecture from anyone on the monstrosities, the dislocations, the cultural impoverishment of the century he has read and known firsthand. Because his idea of culture seems to come in part out of Ruskin—in "Poetry and Happiness" he calls it "the humane unity of a whole people"—he wants much from his culture and the age. Like all such idealists he is much disappointed, and his pain reechoes through forty years of his verse. But the cause, to speak not merely for the self but for *us,* remains constant, and the hope that, as with the puppets in the poem he wrote long ago, sharing each other's lack might in itself provide some of the humane unity we need. Few poets in our time have done more to fight the deadly involution of the humanities, or to keep alive and full the conversation between the world as experienced, the culture as read and invented, and the evasive, intractable, infuriating, magnificent self, which refuses, as it must, all reductions of the world, of its range, its pain, its music, and its hope.

Notes

1. Wilbur's current reputation, and the possible reasons for it, are considered in some detail in the last chapter of this book. But from one of the influential "doorstopper" anthologies—a major force in the formulation and perpetuation of the canon—this evaluation of Wilbur, as a comparatively bland, "genial" Old-World artisan, is fairly typical:

> Wilbur's poetry has continued to attract readers who see the continuity of American poetry with the formal verse of the English past. The rougher line of American verse, from Emerson through Whitman to Ashbery, insists on discontinuity, rupture, and spontaneity, whereas the Europeanized tradition exemplified by Stevens, Frost, Merrill, and Wilbur values continuity, gradualism, and musicality. . . .
>
> . . . Though Wilbur's use of stanzaic structures and regular meters reflects his attachment to poetic tradition, his genial, understated American voice has naturalized older English forms into new indigenous ones. His intricately musical meditative writing continues, in a secular vein, the reflective verse of such seventeenth-century religious poets as George Herbert and Thomas Traherne.
>
> —McQuade et al., *The Harper American Literature*, 2 vols. (New York: Harpers, 1987) 2:2354–55.

2. The last sustained study of Wilbur's work, Donald Hill's *Richard Wilbur* (New York: Twayne, 1967), stops with Wilbur's 1961 collection *Advice to a Prophet* and mentions "The Mill" in a single sentence. Since then, I can find no criticism published in books or periodicals that has substantively treated the poem. With the notable exception of Wendy Salinger's collection of essays by various critics, *Richard Wilbur's Creation* (Ann Arbor: University of Michigan Press, 1983), commentary on Wilbur has been fairly scarce for the last twenty years; a bibliography of the most useful material can be found at the end of this volume.

3. Wilbur's major books of poetry (excluding chapbooks and a short volume of uncollected translations) have been brought together in *New and Collected Poems* (New York: Harcourt Brace Jovanovich, 1988). "The Mill" was

originally published in *Nimbus* in 1955 and collected in *Things of This World*. John P. Field's *Richard Wilbur: A Bibliographical Checklist* (Kent, Ohio: Kent State University Press, 1971) is still an invaluable source for the sequence of Wilbur's publishing, from his undergraduate days at Amherst through *Walking to Sleep*. A new and exhaustive bibliography of Wilbur's work is now underway, and is listed in the bibliography of this book.

4. *Complete Poems of Robert Frost* (New York: Holt, Rinehart and Winston, 1962), p. 276. All the Frost poems cited in this book are drawn from this edition.

5. One of the first writers to speak about Wilbur's interest in Poe was Paul Cummins, in his monograph *Richard Wilbur: A Critical Essay* (Grand Rapids, Mich.: Eerdmans, 1971). John P. Farrell's essay, "The Beautiful Changes in Richard Wilbur's Poetry," *Contemporary Literature* 12 (1971):74–87, gives a good lesson in how to interpret the connection intelligently, and keep recognitions about it in proportion. Salinger's collection brings together much of the good periodical commentary on Wilbur through 1982.

6. The most important poetry reviewer, appearing in several different journals in the same season, was Randall Jarrell, who during the war years wrote for *The Nation, Partisan Review, New Republic, Southern Review, Kenyon Review,* and elsewhere. A *Partisan Review* piece from the winter of 1945, an overview which first deflates Marianne Moore, then extols Jarrell's former Kenyon roommate, Robert Lowell, gives an idea of what he was calling for in "the next first-rate poet":

> Since Pharaoh's bits were pushed into the jaws of the kings, these dyings . . . have happened, by the hundreds of millions; they were all wasted. They [these deaths] taught us to kill others and to die ourselves, but never how to live. Who is "taught to live" by cruelty, suffering, stupidity, and the occupational disease of soldiers, death? The moral equivalent of war! Peace, our peace, is the moral equivalent of war. . . . Miss Moore's seeing what she sees, and only now, betrays an extraordinary but common lack of facts, or imagination, or *something*. But how honest and lovable—how genuinely careless about herself and caring about the rest of the world—Miss Moore seems in this poem, compared to most of our poets, who are blinder to the war than they ever were to the peace, who call the war "this great slapstick," and who write (while everyone applauds) that *they* are not going to be foolish enough to be "war poets." How could they be? The real war poets are always war poets, peace or any time.
> —Reprinted in *Kipling, Auden, and Co.* (New York: Farrar, Straus and Giroux, 1980), p. 129.

7. In the wake of the 1960s, Wilbur was occasionally bristly on the subject of confessional or conspicuously egocentric verse. He told a *Crazy Horse* interviewer:

> I should say that the world is ultimately good and every art an expression of hope and joy. But forced enthusiasm and an exclusive sunniness can put

both of those propositions in doubt. What art needs to do, as Milton said, is to reflect how all things "Rising or falling still advance His praise," and in the process to make a full acknowledgment of fallen-ness, doubt and death. Not all art, of course, will accomplish these things on the scale of the Sistine Chapel; there is nothing wrong with modesty and homeliness. But there is something wrong with poems which lack all redeeming gaiety—and there may be gaiety in art which confronts the most desperate things. I do not enjoy poems which are mean, glum, artless and querulous. Isn't it odd that our American society, the most cosseted in human history, is now given over to petulance and dreary complaint, like the huge sad lady of Auden's "The Duet"? Grousing is not the mood of any art which is doing its job.
—"An Interview with Richard Wilbur," *Crazy Horse,* no. 15 (Fall 1974): 37–44.

8. Hall, "The New Poetry: Notes on the Past Fifteen Years in America," in *New World Writing, Seventh Mentor Edition* (New York: Mentor, 1955), pp. 231–47.

9. Robert Dale Parker's *The Unbeliever* (Urbana: University of Illinois Press, 1988) is the first detailed discussion of Bishop to consider her as a poet of profound internal conflict, as woman, poet, uneasy visitor to contemporary experience. Cary Nelson's discussion of Merwin in *Our Last First Poets* (Urbana: University of Illinois Press, 1981) regards Merwin's long journey from linguistic opulence to austerity as a drama representing the failure of language, and of the individual consciousness, as a stay against modern confusion.

10. As *kayak*'s designated manifesto writer in the late sixties, Bly offered this commentary on behalf of editor George Hitchcock and against Wilbur and other poets whose work they apparently needed for straw men, adversaries to define *kayak's* own position:

Unlike the *Kenyon Review,* which everyone for years has been hoping would kick off soon, *kayak* would be missed very much if it developed a leak and sank. George offers some kind of nourishment. Every hand of course is sometimes open, sometimes closed. As a fist, *kayak* is raised against stuff like this, crystallized flower formations from the jolly intellectual dandies:

Mind in its purest play is like some bat
That beats about in caverns all alone,
Contriving by a kind of senseless wit
Not to conclude against a wall of stone.   (Wilbur)

But *kayak* is also against the high-pitched bat-like cry of the anal Puritan mandarin:

That I cannot take
and that she will not

not give, but will not
have it taken.   (Sorrentino)

This trapped, small-boned, apologetic, feverish, glassy, intellectualist
fluttering is just what George hates. He has tried to provide a place where
poems that escape from that glassy box can come. If you turn into a fish,
he has a muddy pond, with lots of foliage.
—*kayak* 12 (1967): 46–47.

Wilbur's versified rejoinder, which appeared in the next issue, is quoted and
discussed in chapter 5 of this study. *kayak* sprang its fatal leak and sank about
fifteen years ago; an overhauled *Kenyon Review,* at last report, remains afloat
and well.

11. Interview with Richard and Charlotte Ward Wilbur, Cummington,
Massachusetts, May 1982.

12. James Breslin's history of the early days of postmodern poetry, *From
Modern to Contemporary* (Chicago: University of Chicago Press, 1984), counts
Wilbur among the "New Rear Guard," who in the late forties put up resistance
not only to postmodern innovations, but to modernism as well. Breslin seems
to treat the 1947 poetry conference at Bard College as a kind of Fashoda Crisis,
where the battle lines of a coming struggle were drawn and fixed. Wilbur and
Williams were cordial for years after, until Williams's death in 1963. Critics
fond of warring-camp models of postwar poetry should recognize that personal relations among these poets over the past forty years have not followed
ideological rules. A rich, anecdotal history has yet to be written about the help
that these supposed adversaries have offered one other, professionally and
personally, in the decades since the last World War.

13. Wilbur's thoughtful and combative essay, "The Bottles Become New,
Too," began life as a speech at the Bard conference. The essay is a spirited but
unvenomous reply to Williams, who was in a messianic mood about traditional verse forms and their dubious value to new poets. There is no question
that Wilbur dissented from Williams's line of thinking about prosody, and
about the metaphysical possibilities in experience—and that he continues to
disagree. Nor is there any doubt that the two men found their disagreement
healthy and enjoyable. But the essay is an early one, and it needs to be read in
the context of Wilbur's other prose. Later years found Wilbur writing sensitive
appreciations of Whitman, Housman, Dickinson, Shakespeare, Nims, Moore,
Lowell, Bynner, Poe of course, and others; and as a reader for university
presses he has championed the cause of poets who obviously do not see the art
as he does. In short, such catholicity of taste shows itself in Wilbur's prose and
other work since the late fifties, so that readers should be suspicious of references to the 1947 essay as a reliable guide to the man, his vision, and his work.

2. WORDS

1. Herbert Leibowitz, rev. of *The Mind-Reader, New York Times Book
Review,* 13 June 1976, p. 10.

2. Calvin Bedient's commentary on *The Mind-Reader* takes up a few
sentences in a review of several contemporary poets in *New Republic,* 5 June

1976, p. 21. The reviews were not uniformly cool, of course: Anthony Hecht was far more sympathetic to the book in his review "The Motions of the Mind," *Times Literary Supplement,* 20 May 1977, p. 602, reprinted in Salinger:

> This delight in nimbleness, this lively sense of coordinated and practiced skill is, first of all, a clear extension of the dexterity the verse itself performs. If it were no more than this it might be suspected for an exercise in that self-approval which, like one of the poet's fountains, patters "its own applause." But it is more. For again and again in Wilbur's poems this admirable grace or strength of body is a sign of our symbol for the inward motions of the mind or condition of the soul.

What is puzzling is the perceptible rift between Wilbur's work and the tastes of younger poets and academics in the 1970s, and the apparent confusion that has followed about what to say of his achievement.

    3. Wilbur has talked about his early life in several interviews: a good place to begin, in assembling the story, is Richard Calhoun's biographical essay in *The Dictionary of Literary Biography* (1977) 5:247–50, or with the interview with Peter Stitt, Ellessa Clay High, and Helen Ellison, *Paris Review* 72 (Winter 1977): 68–105. Some of the lore in the following pages comes from my own conversations with Wilbur, cited earlier.

    4. "An Interview with Richard Wilbur," *Crazy Horse,* no. 15 (Fall 1974): 38–39. Reprinted by permission of Philip Dacey, interviewer.

    5. See Kunitz, ed., *Twentieth Century Authors,* First Supplement (New York: H. W. Wilson, 1955), pp. 1079–80.

    6. The 1947 Bard College conference on poetry drew Wilbur, Williams, Elizabeth Bishop, Louise Bogan, Jean Garrigue, Robert Lowell, Loren Mac-Iver, Lloyd Frankenburg, and Richard Eberhart. David Kalstone's *Becoming a Poet* includes Elizabeth Bishop's recollection of some of the discussions that weekend:

> all the POETS were dragged up front around a table and you know *made points* and dragged in dynamos and for some reason the rhythm of milking a cow seemed to figure quite a lot, too—amounting in all to no more than each one's elucidating his own style but all very well received & everyone kept on saying it was the best thing that ever happened at Bard. Those present were Richard Wilbur, Eberhart, Cal, Lloyd, Jean Garrigue, Williams and Miss B., me, & a wild man from California in a bright red shirt and yellow braces named Rexroth who did his best to start a fight with everyone and considered us all effete and snobbish easterners. He never quit succeeded and finally had to prove his mettle or his reality or something by taking three of the prettiest undergraduates off for an evening in the cemetery.

David Kalstone, *Becoming a Poet,* ed. with a preface by Robert Hemenway, afterword by James Merrill (New York: Farrar, Straus and Giroux, 1989), p. 145. For a more sober evaluation of the meeting's significance, see Breslin, *From Modern to Contemporary,* pp. 23–52.

7. In Peter Brazeau, *Parts of a World: Wallace Stevens Remembered* (New York: Random House, 1983), p. 168.

8. See my interview cited above.

9. Robert Frank and Stephen Mitchell, "Richard Wilbur: An Interview," *Amherst Literary Magazine* 10. 2 (Summer 1964), reprinted in *Conversations with Richard Wilbur*, ed. William Butts (Jackson: University Press of Mississippi, 1990), pp. 19–20. A similar account is included in Wilbur's 1977 interview for *Paris Review*, also reprinted in Butts.

10. Wilbur gave his "Poetry and Happiness" speech at a 1966 symposium on the arts at the College of Wooster in Wooster, Ohio. It appears in Wilbur, *Responses, Prose Pieces: 1953–1976* (New York: Harcourt Brace Jovanovich, 1976), pp. 91–114. Quoted material is on p. 107.

11. Hill talks about wordplay in *Richard Wilbur*, pp. 167–74; Cummins mentions it briefly in *Richard Wilbur: A Critical Essay*, p. 7.

12. Wilbur, "Poetry and the Landscape," in *The New Landscape in Art and Science*, ed. Gyorgy Kepes (Chicago: Paul Theobald, 1956), p. 86.

13. "Round About a Poem of Housman's," originally a lecture given at a poetry festival at Johns Hopkins in 1961, appeared in *The Moment of Poetry*, ed. Don Cameron Allen (Baltimore: Johns Hopkins, 1962) pp. 73–98. Reprinted in Allen's *A Celebration of Poets* (Baltimore: Johns Hopkins, 1967), pp. 177–202. Also reprinted in *Responses*, pp. 16–38. Cited material appears on pp. 16–17.

14. David Dillon, "The Image and the Object: An Interview with Richard Wilbur," *Southwest Review* 58 (Summer, 1973): 247.

15. Ibid., p. 242.

3. QUARRELING WITH POE

"For Dudley," an elegy for Wilbur's longtime friend Dudley Fitts, was first published in *Hudson Review* 21 (Winter 1968–69): 645. It appears in *Walking to Sleep*, p. 23.

1. *Poe: Complete Poems*, with an introduction and notes by the general editor, The Laurel Poetry Series (New York: Dell, 1959), pp. 7–39.

2. "The House of Poe," *Anniversary Lectures: 1959* (Washington: Library of Congress, 1959), pp. 21–38. This influential piece does not appear in *Responses*, perhaps because that collection contains three other essays by Wilbur on Poe.

3. "The Poe Mystery Case," *New York Review of Books*, 13 July 1967, pp. 16, 25–28. Reprinted in *Responses*.

4. *The Narrative of Arthur Gordon Pym*, ed. with an introduction by Richard Wilbur, illust. Gerry Hoover (Boston: Godine, 1973). The introduction is reprinted in *Responses*.

5. "On My Own Work," *Shenendoah* 17. 1 (1966): 66. Reprinted in *Responses*.

6. Kalstone, *Becoming a Poet*, pp. ix–x.

7. Elizabeth Bishop, *The Complete Poems* (New York: Farrar, Straus and Giroux, 1969), p. 17.

8. Introduction to *Poe: Complete Poems*, pp. 38–39.

9. "The House of Poe," pp. 24–25.

10. *Poe: Complete Poems*, p. 25.

11. "The House of Poe," p. 119.

12. *Poe: Complete Poems*, p. 17.

13. See for example Hill, *Richard Wilbur*, p. 107.

14. *Poe: Complete Poems*, p. 11.

15. Wilbur, "Poetry and the Landscape," p. 86.

16. *Poe: Complete Poems*, p. 30.

17. It is worth noting that Merlin himself passes out of reality through a version of the vortex: lured by a voice like "dark diving water" he enters a "deep unsoundable swell" which spells the end of his imagination and of his magical arts. But it seems to the reader a smooth and unharrowing journey; those whirlpools and abysses into which Wilbur drops himself, and us with him, are likewise plunges which we can manage without terror and reconcile with continued imaginative existence: a hole drilled in the living room floorboards ("A Hole in the Floor"), a pit dug by an eager child in a New Jersey farmyard ("Digging for China"), the drop of a leaf into the falls of a pool ("Piazza di Spagna, Early Morning").

4. LONGER POEMS

1. Commentary on "Walking to Sleep" is not extensive; Mary Kinzie's "The Cheshire Smile: On Richard Wilbur," *American Poetry Review* 6 (May–June 1977): 17–20, was not collected in Salinger, but is worth the hunt. Kinzie considers four of Wilbur's toughest poems, including "Walking to Sleep" and "The Fourth of July," and searches for the anti-Wilbur, the side of him that resists order and sunlight and yearns for Poe-like escape from the real. Wilbur's art for Kinzie is a record of a soul in deep conflict with itself. Kinzie's essay obviously shares some of my own perspectives. Ejner J. Jensen's "Encounters with Experience: The Poems of Richard Wilbur," *New England Review* 2 (Summer 1980): 594–613, treats several of the poems in *Walking to Sleep,* including the title poem, as ventures into the "very homes of dread," and sees Wilbur as almost alone in his time, as a figure of imaginative courage:

> In most of Western Literature, rational man is viewed approvingly and his triumphs celebrated. More recently, particularly in poets who reject modern society, the higher value attaches to instinctual man, to man in nature. In a way, each of these answers is false; certainly they are both too easy. The more daring vision is the one that maintains the paradox and confronts it with full awareness of its extremes.

2. Anthony Hecht, "Behold the Lilies of the Field," *The Hard Hours* (New York: Atheneum, 1967), pp. 10–12.

3. And the echo of Whitman here—of Section 11 of "Song of Myself," in which twenty-eight young men "bathe by the shore," and a young woman watches in secret ecstasy—seems comic as well, in its contrast to Borrow's unshakable piety.

4. These are the closing lines of Robert Lowell's great, bitter elegy, "For the Union Dead."

5. These lines are from *Moby-Dick,* chapter 7, "The Chapel."

6. Arthur Symons, *The Symbolist Movement in Literature* (New York: Dutton, 1958), pp. 93–94.

7. *Randall Jarrell: The Complete Poems* (New York: Farrar, Straus and Giroux, 1969), p. 113.

8. Hill says of "Castles and Distances": "The interest with which we follow the argument of this poem is a witness to the boldness and discrimination of Wilbur's mind; the confidence we feel in the ultimate coherence of the pattern is a proof of the skill with which he keeps his intellectual and linguistic balance as he develops the argument through its several phases and applications" (Hill, *Richard Wilbur,* p. 68). Hill offers a detailed, schematic reading of the poem on pages 68–70.

9. One swipe at MacLeish's idea of poetry as "public speech" comes at the end of Jarrell's essay "Changes of Attitude and Rhetoric in Auden's Poetry," *Poetry and the Age* (New York: Farrar, Straus, 1971), p. 150. MacLeish and Auden take a drubbing throughout Jarrell's four books of criticism, as Jarrell worked to clear the way for new voices—but the attempts to bury MacLeish, for taking, during the war, the role of public poet, seem especially rough-handed. See for example the attack on MacLeish's *The Fall of the City, Sewanee Review* (Spring 1943), reprinted in *Kipling, Auden, and Co.,* pp. 101–11.

10. From "Looking-Glass Insects," in *Through the Looking Glass: The Annotated Alice,* intro. and notes by Martin Gardner (New York: New American Library, 1974), pp. 225–26.

5. CHANCES

1. The painter I am referring to is Ronnie Cutrone, a "postpop" artist who worked with Andy Warhol—who of course amassed a fortune with this sort of gesture twenty-five years ago. For a lively, bewildered discussion of the avant-garde in art, its corporate entanglements, and the blurred distinctions between high art and kitsch, see Christopher Reed, "Off the Wall and Onto the Couch: Sofa Art and the Avant Garde Analyzed," *Smithsonian Studies in American Art* 2.1 (Winter 1988):32–43.

2. The definitive biography of St. John Chrysostom for our time is *John Chrysostom and His Time* by Dom Chrysostomus Baur, O.S.B., 2 vols. (London: Sands and Co., 1959). Volume one concentrates on Antioch and the saint's youth and schooling. Baur is lively on the subject of the depravities of the town and province, but implicates his protagonist not at all.

3. "Five Riddles from Symphosius" appears in the last unnumbered pages of the chapbook *Advice from the Muse,* illust. Timothy Engelland (Deerfield, Mass.: The Deerfield Press/The Gallery Press, 1981).

4. "The Persistence of Riddles," *Yale Review* 78. 3 (Winter 1989): 347.

5. *Ibid.,* p. 334.

6. See note 9 in chapter 1 of this study.

7. "A Postcard for Bob Bly" appears in *kayak* 13 (January 1968): 15. This was not a good-bye note between poet and "campy magazine," however, and again one should resist the temptation to regard such exchanges as estrangements. Wilbur's translation of Villon's "A Ballade to End With" was featured in *kayak* later that year.

8. Anne Stevenson, *Bitter Fame: A Life of Sylvia Plath* (Boston: Houghton Mifflin, 1989), offers the best account to date (pp. 34–68) of Plath's Smith years, her early publishing, and her 1953 suicide attempt and subsequent psychiatric treatment.

9. I am also indebted to Robert B. Shaw, one of the current judges of the Glascock Competition, for details about the history of the prize.

10. Ian Hamilton, "A Talent of the Shallows," *Times Literary Supplement*, 15–21 September 1989, pp. 999–1000.

11. Clive James's negative review of Wilbur is "When the Gloves are Off," *Review* (London), no. 26 (summer 1971): 35–44. His change of mind is to be found in "As a Matter of Tact," *The New Statesman*, 17 June 1977, pp. 815–16.

12. Letter to BFM, 21 July 1990.

6. WILBUR AS TRANSLATOR

1. While there are, at this writing, few wide-ranging commentaries about the poetics of translation and how they may have changed since 1900, there are a number of narrower, provocative commentaries and exchanges of ideas on the subject. One good place to begin is with the *Poetics Today* special issue on translation (2.4 [1981]); the articles in this issue tend to be technical but diverse, and sensitive to the transformed ethics of such work. For strong opposition to the Poundian strategies described in note 2, one might consult George Steiner's essay, "Two Translations," in his *Language and Silence* (New York: Atheneum, 1967). Focusing on the Robert Lowell translation of Racine's *Phèdre*, Steiner attacks the post-Pound ethics of "free" translation:

> I yield to no one in my admiration of Lowell's poetry or in my awareness of his stature as a poet. I rejoice in the rhetorical flourish and pace of his *Phaedra*. As an exercise in verse drama it is often brilliant. . . . But I submit that *Phaedra* has an unsteady and capricious bearing on the matter of Racine. Far too often, it strives against the grain of Racine's style and against the conventions of feeling on which the miraculous concision of that style depends. . . .
>
> . . . In short: what Lowell has produced is a variation on the theme of *Phaedra,* in the manner of Seneca and the Elizabethan classicists. To link this version with Racine implies a certain abeyance of modesty. But modesty is the very essence of translation. The greater the poet, the more loyal should be his servitude to the original.

2. In *The Pound Era* (Berkeley: University of California Press, 1971), Hugh Kenner's important chapter, "Words Set Free," subsumes the practice of translation into Pound's grand and overall attempt to redefine the artist's

relationship to both language and the accumulated past. Kenner's introduction to *The Translations of Ezra Pound* (London: Faber and Faber, 1970) comes from a more straightforward period in his own writing; Kenner praises, perhaps a bit defensively, some of Pound's more controversial translations (for example *The Seafarer*) for their "boldness and resource to make a new form, similar in effect to that of the original" (p. 9). From this defense for Pound's strategy:

> He doesn't chafe at restrictions unusual to his lyric practice. A good translation seems like a miracle because one who can read the original can, so to speak, see the poem before the poet writes it, and marvel at the success of its wrestle to subdue his own language to the vision; but Pound has always written as if to meet a test of this kind, in a spirit of utter fidelity to his material, whether a document or an intuition. He has told of working six months to fix a complex instantaneous emotion in fourteen words. Translation is indeed for Pound somewhat easier than what is called 'original composition'; those six months were spent less on finding the words than in bringing the emotion into focus, and a text to be translated, once grasped, doesn't wobble. The technical difficulty is comparable, but the emotional discipline, if no less exacting, less exhausting. . . .
>
> It is because so many Poundian principles meet in the translator's act that the best of his translations exist in three ways, as windows into new worlds, as acts of homage, and as personae of Pound's. (P. 10)

> If he doesn't translate the words, the translator remains faithful to the original poet's sequence of images, to his rhythms or the effect produced by his rhythms, or to his tone. Insofar as he is faithful, he does homage to his predecessor's knowledge of his job, his success in securing from point to point the precise images and gestures to embody a vision which is neither his property nor that of the translator. Pedantry consists in supposing that the importance of a moment of thought or feeling lies in the notation somebody else found for it. The Poundian homage consists in taking an earlier poet as guide to secret places of the imagination. (P. 12)

3. *The Poems of François Villon*, trans. with an introduction and notes, Galway Kinnell (Hanover: University Press of New England, 1982), pp. 46–48. Kinnell's unrhymed, unembellished, and (by Poundian standards) pedantic translations make an interesting foil for both Wilbur and Pound.

4. The article by Gioia, somewhat snidely called "The Successful Career of Robert Bly," *Hudson Review* 40.2 (Summer 1987): 207–23, includes a brutal attack on Bly as a translator, and on the effect that Bly has had on the practice in the past twenty years:

> By propagating this minimal kind of translation Bly has done immense damage to American poetry. Translating quickly and superficially, he not only misrepresented the work of many great poets, he also distorted some of the basic standards of poetic excellence. His slapdash method ignored both the obvious formal qualities of the originals (like rhyme and meter)

and, more crucially, those subtler organizing principles such as diction, tone, rhythm, and texture which frequently gave the poems their intensity. Concentrating almost entirely on syntax and imagery, Bly reduced the complex originals into abstract visual blueprints. In his hands, dramatically different poets . . . not only all sounded alike, they all sounded like Robert Bly, and even then not like Bly at his best. But as if that weren't bad enough, Bly consistently held up these diminished versions as models of poetic excellence worthy of emulation. In promoting his new poetics . . . he set standards so low that he helped create a school of mediocrities largely ignorant of the pre-modern poetry in English and familiar with foreign poetry only through oversimplified translations. (P. 214)

5. Wilbur, introduction to his translation of Molière, *The School for Wives* (New York: Harcourt Brace Jovanovich, 1971), p. ix.

6. Wilbur, introduction to his translation of Molière, *Tartuffe* (New York: Harcourt Brace Jovanovich, 1963), p. viii.

7. Molière, *The Misanthrope and Tartuffe*, trans. with an introduction by Richard Wilbur (New York: Harcourt, Brace and World, 1965) p. 9.

8. Raymond Oliver's "Verse Translations and Richard Wilbur," *Southern Review*, n.s., 11 (Spring 1975): 318–30 (reprinted in Salinger) begins by taking little for granted and builds a case for the virtues of translation over "imitation," arguing that the latter shows a lack of understanding for formal devices and deprives readers of "all but the most limited, self-centered relations with other cultures and the past." Oliver compares Wilbur's rendering of Valéry's "Hélène" to Robert Lowell's treatment of the same poem and finds Wilbur's superior on all counts. The other major discussion to date of Wilbur's translations is John Simon's 1976 essay, "Translation or Adaptation," in *From Parnassus: Essays in Honor of Jacques Barzun,* ed. Dora Weiner and W. R. Keylor (New York: Harper and Row, 1976), pp. 147–57. Simon compares Wilbur's *Tartuffe* to Tony Harrison's freewheeling rendition of the same play. Again, by all of Simon's criteria for success, Wilbur wins hands down.

9. *Andromache,* trans. with an introduction by Richard Wilbur (New York: Harcourt Brace Jovanovich, 1982), p. xiii.

10. *Phaedra,* a trans. Robert Lowell (New York: Farrar, Straus and Cudahy, 1961).

11. One of Wilbur's two children's books is *Opposites* (New York: Harcourt Brace Jovanovich, 1973), a batch of clever short poems considering problems like "What is the opposite of soup?"—and finding good answers. But as cleverness is not ever sufficient, even in fun, *Opposites* ends with this two-liner:

What is the opposite of opposite?
That one's too difficult for me. I quit.

12. *A Bestiary,* compiled by Richard Wilbur, illust. Alexander Calder (New York: Spiral Press, for Pantheon, 1955).

13. Pound's translation of "The Seafarer" appears in the Kenner collection cited above.

7. THE FIGURE A POET MAKES

Epigraph cited in Brazeau, *Parts of A World*, p. 197.

1. Mill's famous distinction between poetry and eloquence, that "eloquence is *heard,* poetry is *overheard*" (p. 348), is found in his essay "Thoughts on Poetry and Its Varieties"—and the early date of this commentary (1833), explains the insistent tone and the rather absolute distinctions of a young utilitarian, needing perhaps to justify his own late-arrived enthusiasm for poetry, and to define not only the genre but its major personalities. Having diagnosed them as beings "so constituted, that emotions are the links of association by which their ideas, both sensuous and spiritual, are connected together," and as creatures of enormous feeling, Mill goes on to lament the case of Wordsworth—whose poems had helped Mill recover from psychological collapse in his twenty-third year:

> Wordsworth's poetry is never bounding, never ebullient; has little even of the appearance of spontaneousness: the well is never so full that it overflows. There is an air of calm deliberateness about all he writes, which is not characteristic of the poetic temperament: his poetry seems one thing, himself another; he seems to be poetical because he wills to be so, not because he cannot help it: did he will to dismiss poetry, he need never again, it might almost seem, have a poetical thought. He seems never *possessed* by any feeling; no emotion seems ever so strong as to have entire sway, for the time being, over the current of his thoughts. (Pp. 358–59)

Readers may recognize parallels between the language and assumptions in this indictment and a paragraph quoted at the opening of chapter 2 of this study. The craft of reviewing in the postmodern era may not be entirely cleansed of Victorian tastes for displays, genuine or otherwise, of raw and furious sentiment. Mill, *Autobiography and Literary Essays,* ed. John M. Robson and Jack Stillinger, Vol. 1 of *Collected Works of John Stuart Mill* (Toronto: University of Toronto Press, 1981).

2. Thompson and Winnick's accounts of Frost's public and private jealousy make for uncomfortable reading throughout the last third of their biography, but it cannot be said that the general conception of Frost as the sweet-natured American country bard has much altered in the national imagination; for example, the latest *Harper American Literature,* one of the major gateways for students into American letters, talks of Frost's early sufferings, his education and long apprenticeship; it summarizes his personal life as a "Gothic chronicle of disasters," and allows the poetry to suggest the kindly and stoic personality the public prefers to recall. Lawrance Thompson and R. H. Winnick, *Robert Frost: A Biography* (New York, 1982); McQuade et al., *Harper American Literature* 2:1501–03.

3. Ian Hamilton's *Robert Lowell: A Biography* (New York: Random House,

1982 is not as disconcerting as Thompson and Winnick's book, because of Lowell's willingness to portray his psychological problems in poems through-out his career. The poet's periodic obsession with Hitler, however, and his extended paranoid episode at Yaddo do show us an aggressive and dangerous side of the man which is not apparent in the verse. See for example chapter 10, pp. 138–63, on Lowell's troubles over the course of 1949, and chapter 13, pp. 209–15, on Lowell's Hitler fixations in 1954.

4. Subtitled "The Genius of Modern Poetry," M. L. Rosenthal and Sally M. Gall's *The Modern Poetic Sequence* (New York: Oxford, 1983) argues for the philosophical and aesthetic appropriateness of a "grouping of mainly lyric poems and passages, rarely uniform in pattern, which tend to interact as an organic whole. . . . Intimate, fragmented, self-analytical, open, emotion-ally volatile, the sequence meets the needs of modern sensibility even when the poet aspires to tragic or epic scope" (p. 9). A sequence is a "compelling process, the result of sheer, psychically powerful need on each poet's part to mobilize and give direction to otherwise scattered energies" (p. 9). As the study pro-gresses, the criteria for inclusion in the canon of sequencers seem to soften and broaden a bit, and it certainly can be said that Wilbur's work comes of sheer and psychically powerful needs of his own. It may be possible to reread volumes in the *New and Collected Poems* as some species of sequence, if Wilbur's deep kinship with the modern and postmodern sensibility needs to be established further.

5. "For W. H. Auden" first appeared in *Atlantic Monthly* 244.4 (October 1979): 98. This was six years after Auden's death.

6. See W. J. T. Mitchell, "*Ut Pictura Theoria:* Abstract Painting and the Repression of Language," *Critical Inquiry* 15.2 (Winter 1989):348–71.

7. Helen Vendler's introductory essay in her *The Harvard Book of Contem-porary Poetry* (Cambridge: Harvard, Belknap, 1985) is a fine example of how an overview of postmodern verse can be achieved, with neither an immersion in transient rivalries nor a reduction of the central problems and anxieties of this time. Vendler connects Wilbur seamlessly to his contemporaries and to a "haunted and accused" condition which, in her view, runs back at least as far as Blake:

> In what Richard Wilbur has called the "mad *instead*" of poetry, things have their meaning only in the context of the world that they there create. The world of the poem is analogous to the existential world, but not identical with it. In a famous created world of Blake's, for instance, there is a rose doomed to mortal illness by the love of a flying worm who is invisible. We do not experience such a poem by moving it piecemeal into our world, deciding what the rose "symbolizes" and what the worm "stands for." On the contrary, we must move ourselves into its ambience, into a world in which a dismayed man can converse with his beloved rose and thrust upon her, in his anguished jealousy, diagnosis and fatal prognosis in one sentence. . . .
>
> This truth—that we live in the poem's world, not it in ours—applies

not only to "symbolic" poems. One can equally well inhabit, and be haunted by, the world of 91 Revere Street where Lowell lived as a boy, a house seen through the myopic and baleful lens of the Freudian memory. Or one can live in the ignited air of Plath's "Lady Lazarus"; or in the somber bus ride from New York to Ohio in Clampitt's "Procession at Candlemas," where the poet reviews the cultural images of femaleness from Athena to Mary. A successful poem is, as Williams said, a machine made out of words. (Pp. 8–9)

The rivalries are not all ended, however, and admirers of some of Wilbur's friends and peers sometimes feel the need to fight a defensive war for their preferences. Sidney Lea's new collection, *The Burdens of Formality: Essays on the Poetry of Anthony Hecht* (Athens: University of Georgia Press, 1989), includes an introduction which expresses concerns about what Lea calls "the Buckaroo School" of contemporary verse, which suspects Hecht's "civic poetry" of

archaism, of insufficient "honesty" or "authenticity," these virtues for that school's academicians residing in unadornment, personalism, directness, what have you? (The litany is familiar, I think.) I do not suggest that there are no splendid practitioners of such preachment, but to many of their partisans it is scarcely imaginable that a man could have seen combat against the Nazis, for example, and not subsequently rendered the experience as "confessionally" or "nakedly" as possible. (P. xii)

Paradoxes of this sort have been observed from time to time in the book at hand. Lea's volume eventually pursues the critic's best strategy, to encourage patient, compassionate reading of poetry one is moved by, rather than persist in disparaging other camps.

8. Letter, n.d. (Spring 1959?) in the Robert Lowell Papers, Houghton Library, Harvard University.

9. Douglas Messerli has brought together a number of these poets in a collection called *"Language" Poetries: An Anthology* (New York: New Directions, 1987). Messerli's introduction offers this explanation of the movement:

The poets in this anthology have all foregrounded language itself as the project of their writing. For these poets, language is not something that *explains* or *translates* experience, but is the source of experience. Language is perception, thought itself; and in that context the poems of these writers do not function as "frames" of experience or brief narrative summaries of ideas and emotions as they do for many current poets. Communication . . . is seen not as a "two-way wire with its transom (read: ideology)," but as "a sounding of language from the inside, in which the dwelling is already/always given." What I call "portmanteau poetry"— poetry that, revealing its message to the reader, is used up and closed until the reader again seeks such feelings or knowledge—such poetry is rejected in favor of the production of a living document of the author's engagement with the reader and the world through language as the agent of their shared thinking. (Pp. 2–3)

238

10. From James's "The One and the Many":

Hold a tumbler of water a little above your eyes and look up through the water at its surface—or better still look similarly through the flat wall of an aquarium. You will then see an extraordinarily brilliant reflected image . . . situated on the opposite side of the vessel. No candle-ray, under these circumstances gets beyond the water's surface: every ray is totally reflected back into the depths again. Now let the water represent the world of sensible facts, and let the air above it represent the world of abstract ideas. Both worlds are real, of course, and interact; but they interact only at their boundary, and the *locus* of everything that lives, and happens to us, so far as full experience goes, is the water. We are like fishes swimming in the sea of sense, bounded above by the superior element, but unable to breathe it pure or penetrate it. We get our oxygen from it, however, we touch it incessantly . . . and every time we touch it, we are reflected back into the water with our course re-determined and re-energized.

This is a fair approximation of Wilbur's own understanding of our ontological condition—an understanding from which he can waver in an entirely human way. From *Pragmatism* (Cambridge, Mass.: Harvard University Press, 1975) 63–64.

11. However, it seems a reasonable bet that Wilbur has in mind a dry-brush sketch called simply "Milk Cans," painted in 1961. According to Wanda Corn in *The Art of Andrew Wyeth* (Greenwich, Conn.: New York Graphic Society, 1973) the painting measures 13¼″ × 20¾″, and is now reported to be in a private collection.

12. The peculiar good humor of scientist-essayists, in a time when poetic discourse, supposedly traumatized by the scientific revolutions of this century has seemed so unhappy, is a large-scale anomaly of our time worth sustained discussion by itself. The composure and cautious hope among these scientists, a temper which sometimes resembles Richard Wilbur's, can be sampled by a look at some of the following works: *The Invisible Pyramid,* by Loren Eiseley (New York: Scribner's, 1970); *Flanagan's Version,* by Dennis Flanagan (New York: Knopf, 1988); *The Lives of a Cell,* by Lewis Thomas (New York: Viking, 1974), or virtually any of the overviews written by Carl Sagan, Rene Dubos, or Jacob Bronowski. For some brief speculations on this possibly major split in the literary morale, with the scientists going one way and the poets and humanists another, see my essay, "The Tragic Scientists," in *Elizabethan and Modern Studies,* ed. J. P. Vander Motten (Ghent: R.U.G., 1985), pp. 173–80.

13. Wilbur describes this conversation in his introduction to Alan Gussow's *A Sense of Place: The Artist and the American Land* (San Francisco: Friends of the Earth, 1972); the essay is reprinted in *Responses;* the quoted material appears on p. 153.

14. Some critics seem at the moment to be concerned with maintaining the academic-ideological purity of Ashbery, which seems odd, considering how recently the critical community rejoiced in the swings in mood, form, and

thinking among poets like Rich, Lowell, and Berryman. Charles Altieri's essay "John Ashbery and the Challenge of Postmodernism in the Visual Arts," *Critical Inquiry* 14.4 (Summer 1988): 805–30, seems insistent on Ashbery's fidelity, year after year, to aesthetics and epistemological principles to be found in important painters of the seventies and eighties:

> We shall see that Ashbery's *A Wave* is not the conservative retreat from his more whimsical and enigmatic ways which many readers see. Instead the volume takes as its basic challenge the need to establish a model of speech able to create values within the duplicitious folds of [Jasper] Johnsian intentionality. (P. 815)

In describing what he sees as a primary weakness in the postmodern sensibility, however, Altieri seems to be making room (probably without meaning to) for a reappraisal of Richard Wilbur, who may have the sort of completeness which Altieri finds generally lacking on the art and poetry scene:

> Once we begin to spell out his [Ashbery's] particular way of coming to terms with contemporaneity, I think we shall find ourselves increasingly uncomfortable with both of those dominant models for postmodernism—the first for its excessive metaphysics that lacks a plausible psychology or ethics for bourgeois life, and the second for its fantasies of revolution that leads [*sic*] it to prize what Hal Foster calls oppositional political gestures over those that try to make art a way of learning to accommodate to social conditions that are not likely to change in any significant qualitative ways. (P. 806)

15. For example, Richard Kostalanetz's *The Old Poetries and the New* (Ann Arbor: University of Michigan Press, 1981) offers such a chart of "Characteristics of American Poetry in 1945, and Subsequent Reactions to the Predominant Style." The chart, on page 38 of that book, runs eight columns across, uses rubrics like "Associational Coherence," "Formal Diction," and "Reverent Solemnity." The chart is filled out with the names of two dozen poets; there are ten or twelve listings under each heading, seventy-five or eighty in all. Kenneth Koch seems to win the prize in this tally, appearing in six of the eight columns; Ted Berrigan scores only once. Wilbur does not appear anywhere, either as a "predominant style" or as a "subsequent reaction." Kostalanetz has been witty as a poet in his own right, yet the humor of this table seems to be unintended.

Robert Pinsky's thoughtful study *The Situation of Poetry* (Princeton: Princeton University Press, 1976) makes no mention of Wilbur; his absence is a more serious fault in Bruce Bawer's *The Middle Generation,* subtitled *The Lives and Poetry of Delmore Schwartz, Randall Jarrell, John Berryman, and Robert Lowell* (New York: Archon Books, 1986), which cuts Wilbur out of his own circle of colleagues and friends, apparently because he does not "fit." Psychologically he may not: three of these four committed suicide; the last, also dead now, had notorious bouts of madness. But as a poet he does—if we can get beyond the idea that notorious spiritual pain is the admission price to a "generation" of poets. Sometimes being left out is an advantage: Robert Peters's *The Great*

American Poetry Bake-Off (Metuchen, N.J.: Scarecrow, 1979) includes no discussion of Wilbur, but satirizes the work of nearly everybody else.

The Norton Anthology of American Literature, the nation's top seller in the undergraduate survey courses, offers something of a cultural determinist explanation of Wilbur and what has come since his appearance. The two general choices this summary seems to allow for artists in the postwar world are to swallow one's traditional education whole (as Wilbur is alleged to have done), or to join the "children of Midas," reacting fiercely against that "training":

> A young writer . . . trained to read intricate traditional lyrics, did not expect to encounter much, if any, contemporary verse in the classroom. The student had to seek out modern poems in the literary quarterlies or come upon them through chance recommendations of informed friends and teachers. And whether a beginning poet fell, in this private, accidental way, under the influence of Eliot's ironic elegies or Stevens's high rhapsodies or William Carlos Williams's homemade documentaries, he was prepared to think of a poem as something "other" than the poet himself, objective, free from the quirks of the personal.
>
> . . . Avoiding the first person, poets would find an object, a landscape, or an observed encounter which epitomized and clarified their feelings. A poem was the product of retrospection, a gesture of composure following the initial shock or stimulus which provided the occasion for writing. Often composed in intricate stanzas and skillfully rhymed, such a poem deployed its mastery of verse form as one sign of a civilized mind's power to explore, tame, and distill raw experience. . . .
> It was a time of renewed travel in Europe; there were Fulbright fellowships for American students to study abroad, prizes for writers who wanted to travel and write in Europe. Wilbur and others wrote poems about European art and artifacts and landscapes.

David Kalstone, *The Norton Anthology of American Literature,* ed. Nina Baym et al., 2nd ed. (New York: W. W. Norton, 1985), 2: 2249.

While the influential *Harvard Guide to Contemporary American Writing* likewise attempts to settle the first rank/second rank issue with dispatch, it does countenance the possibility that a long career passed in the perfection of a particular voice might result in an achievement which could alter the chart:

> Four poets of this generation who have not felt Shapiro's impetus to cast off their former selves but rather have developed by processes of ripening are Richard Wilbur, Howard Nemerov, William Meredith, and Elizabeth Bishop. Not for them Roethke's descent into the primordial id, or the attempts to navigate such troughs and crests as swamped Schwartz and Jarrell. The poets of their generation who dominate the second half of this period were of course Robert Lowell and John Berryman; compared to them, with their intensities and stylistic veerings, these poets seem to operate at lower keys, treating more restricted ranges of feeling from the security of an aesthetic grounded upon assumptions Lowell and Berry-

man felt they had to abandon. . . . Yet the poets named above have not been swayed by fashion, and each in his own way has helped to temper the prevailing romanticism with the virtues of discipline, restraint, and poise.

Perhaps the "of course" in the above paragraph has a defensive edge to it. Daniel Hoffman, ed., *Harvard Guide to Contemporary American Writing* (Cambridge: Harvard, Belknap, 1979), p. 473.

16. On page 9 of Jonathan Holden's *Style and Authenticity in Postmodern Poetry* (Columbia: University of Missouri Press, 1986), Wilbur is referred to as "graceful, late-modernist, domestic"; Wilbur is later a voice like a "literary expert, a specialist" (p. 31) and an "elite specialist" four pages later. In that way Holden can maneuver, as others have, around the difficult question of Wilbur's importance in postwar American literature.

Bibliography

J. W. C. Hagstrom and John Lancaster are nearing completion of a thorough bibliography of Wilbur's work. Five useful bibliographies have been published to date of works by and about Richard Wilbur; three of these are quite old. John P. Field's *Richard Wilbur: A Bibliographical Checklist* (Kent, Ohio: Kent State University Press, 1971) was exhaustive at the time of its publication, and nearly so was Marcia B. Dinneen's "Richard Wilbur: A Bibliography of Secondary Sources," *Bulletin of Bibliography* 37 (Jan.–Mar. 1980): 16–22. Dinneen has recently published an expansion of this resource: "Richard Wilbur: An Annotated Bibliography of Secondary Sources, Continued," *Bulletin of Bibliography* 47 (June 1990): 143–50. Frances Bixler's essay, "Richard Wilbur: A Review of the Research and Criticism," forthcoming in the series *Resources for American Literary Study,* promises to be an exhaustive evaluation of the criticism through 1989. The "Selected Bibliography" in Donald Hill's 1967 volume *Richard Wilbur* (q.v.) lists Wilbur's volumes through 1964, and reviews of volumes up through "Advice to a Prophet." Hill also offers pithy commentary about critical reception through 1965. My own bibliographical essay, "Richard Wilbur" in *Contemporary Authors: Bibliographical Series: American Poets,* ed. Ronald Baughman (Detroit: Bruccoli Clark, 1986), includes some discussion of the criticism through 1985, and evaluations of several published interviews with Wilbur.

WORKS BY RICHARD WILBUR

Collections of poetry

The Beautiful Changes and Other Poems. New York: Reynal & Hitchcock, 1947.
Ceremony and Other Poems. New York: Harcourt, Brace, 1950.
Things of This World, Poems by Richard Wilbur. New York: Harcourt, Brace, 1956.
Poems 1943–56. London: Faber and Faber, 1957.
Advice to a Prophet and Other Poems. New York: Harcourt, Brace and World, 1961. London: Faber and Faber, 1962.
The Poems of Richard Wilbur. New York: Harcourt, Brace and World, 1963.
Walking to Sleep, New Poems and Translations. New York: Harcourt, Brace and World, 1969. London: Faber and Faber, 1971.

The Mind-Reader. New York: Harcourt Brace Jovanovich, 1976.
New and Collected Poems. New York: Harcourt Brace Jovanovich, 1988.

Chapbooks of poetry and limited editions

A Bestiary. Compiled by Richard Wilbur, with illustrations by Alexander
  Calder. New York: Spiral Press for Pantheon, 1955. Mostly translations
  by Wilbur and other hands but also some original poems, including
  "Beasts," which appeared subsequently in *Things of This World.*
Digging for China: A Poem. Garden City, N.Y.: Doubleday and Company,
  1970.
Seed Leaves. Boston: David R. Godine, 1974.
Seven Poems. Omaha: Abattoir Editions, 1981.
Advice from the Muse. Illustrations by Timothy Engelland. Deerfield, Mass. and
  Dublin, Ireland: The Deerfield Press / The Gallery Press, 1981. Signed,
  limited edition of a poem which also appears in *New Poems* (1987).
Pedestrian Flight: Twenty-One Clerihews for the Telephone. N.p.: Palaemon Press,
  1981. Signed, limited edition, illustrated by Wilbur, of four-line comic
  poems for Stuart Wright's answering machine.
Elizabeth Bishop: A Memorial Tribute. New York: Albondocani Press, 1982. A
  fourteen-page edition of a speech which Wilbur originally delivered to the
  American Academy of Arts and Letters on 7 December 1979.
Lying and Other Poems. Omaha: The Cummington Press, 1987.
A Wall in the Woods: Cummington. Sea Cliff Press, 1989. Single poem in a two-
  page pamphlet.

Other works, poetic and imaginative

"A Game of Catch." *New Yorker,* 18 July 1953, pp. 74–76. Reprinted in
  American Accent, ed. Elizabeth Abell. New York: Ballantine, 1954. Re-
  printed in *Prize Stories 1954: The O. Henry Awards,* ed. Paul Engle and
  Hansford Martin. New York: Doubleday, 1954. Reprinted in *Stories from
  "The New Yorker," 1950–1960.* New York: Simon and Schuster, 1960. This
  is Wilbur's only widely published short story.
Candide: A Comic Operetta Based on Voltaire's Satire. Lyrics by Richard Wilbur;
  book by Lillian Hellman; score by Leonard Bernstein; additional lyrics by
  John Latouche and Dorothy Parker. New York: Random House, 1957.
Loudmouse. Illustrated by Don Almquist. New York: Crowell-Collier; London: Collier-Macmillan, 1963. A comic children's story, possibly reflexive, about a well-meaning mouse blessed and cursed with a great, loud
  voice.
Opposites. New York: Harcourt Brace Jovanovich, 1973. Though these are
  children's poems, some of them are paradoxical in ways that will appeal to
  grown-ups and intrigue people interested in Wilbur's complex view of
  the world.

Translations

Molière. *The Misanthrope.* New York: Harcourt, Brace, 1955; London: Faber
  and Faber, 1958. With an introduction by Wilbur.

―――. *Tartuffe*. New York: Harcourt, Brace and World, 1963; London: Faber and Faber, 1964. With an introduction by Wilbur.

―――. *The Misanthrope and Tartuffe*. New York: Harcourt, Brace and World, 1965. With additional note by Wilbur.

―――. *The School for Wives*. New York: Harcourt Brace Jovanovich, 1971. With an introduction by Wilbur.

―――. *The Learned Ladies*. New York: Dramatists' Play Service, 1977; New York: Harcourt Brace Jovanovich, 1978. With an introduction by Wilbur.

Jean Racine. *Andromache*. New York: Harcourt Brace Jovanovich, 1982. With an introduction by Wilbur.

The Whale and Other Uncollected Translations. Brockport, N.Y.: Boa Editions, 1982. With an introduction by Wilbur.

Jean Racine, *Phaedra: A Tragedy in Five Acts*. 1677. San Diego: Harcourt Brace Jovanovich, 1986. With an introduction by Wilbur; drawings by Igor Tulipanov.

Edited books

Modern American and Modern British Poetry. Ed. Louis Untermeyer, in consultation with Karl Shapiro and Wilbur. New York: Harcourt, Brace and Co., 1955. Revised ed., 1959.

Poe, Edgar Allan. *Poe: Complete Poems*. Ed. with an introduction by Wilbur. New York: Dell, 1959.

Shakespeare, William. *Poems*. Ed. Wilbur and Alfred Harbage, with an introduction by Wilbur. Baltimore: Penguin, 1966. Revised and republished as *Shakespeare: The Narrative Poems and Poems of Doubtful Authenticity*. Baltimore: Penguin, 1974.

Poe, Edgar Allan. *Poe: The Narrative of Arthur Gordon Pym*. Ed. with an introduction by Wilbur. Boston: David R. Godine, 1973.

Bynner, Witter. *Selected Poems*. Ed. with an introduction by Wilbur. New York: Farrar, Straus and Giroux, 1978.

Essays

"The Genie in the Bottle." *Mid-Century American Poets*. Ed. John Ciardi. New York: Twayne, 1950. 1–15. This early essay has been overtaxed by readers who would characterize Wilbur as a diehard, "rear-guard" champion of traditional aesthetic values. His *Hudson Review* essay, "Poetry's Debt to Poetry" (reprinted in *Responses*) does a better job of describing directions he has actually taken and how his sentiments have matured.

"Poetry and the Landscape." *The New Landscape in Art and Science*. Ed. Gyorgy Kepes. Chicago: Paul Theobald, 1956. 86–90. A good short essay in a forgotten collection, with some provocative comments on the primordial centers of language and poetry.

"The House of Poe." *Anniversary Lectures 1959*. Washington, D.C.: Library of Congress, 1959. Essentially about Poe's fiction, this allegorical reading changed the course of Poe criticism; it provides insights into Wilbur's own experiments with similar metaphors.

Commentary on three critiques of "Love Calls Us to the Things of This

World" and "On Robert Lowell's Skunk Hour." *The Contemporary Poet as Artist and Critic: Eight Symposia*. Ed. Anthony Ostroff. Boston: Little, Brown, 1964.

Responses, Prose Pieces: 1953–1976. New York: Harcourt Brace Jovanovich, 1976. Selected by Wilbur, this collection brings together many of his best commentaries and reviews, including some hard-to-find pieces originally written for small publications. The place to begin in exploring Wilbur's prose discussions of the act of poetry and his relationship to Poe, Shakespeare, Whitman, Housman, Frost, Bishop, Lowell, W. C. Williams, Yeats, and others.

"The Poetry of Witter Bynner." *American Poetry Review* 6 (Nov.–Dec. 1977): 3–8.

"Elizabeth Bishop." *Ploughshares* 6. 2 (1980): 10–14.

Richard Eberhart: A Celebration. Ed. Sidney Lea, Jay Parini, M. Robin Barone. Hanover, N.H.: Kenyon Hill, 1980. Three-page tribute, with some biographical information.

"On Robert Francis's " 'Sheep.' " *Field* 25 (Fall 1981): 28–30.

"Poe and the Art of Suggestion." *University of Mississippi Studies in English* 3 (1982): 1–13. More commentary about Poe, focusing here on the place of passion in poetry.

Stanislaw Baranczak, William Barrett, Cynthia Ozick, Richard Wilbur, and Hortense Calisher. "The Writer's Role: Responses to Hortense Calisher." *New Criterion* 1. 6 (Feb. 1983): 31–40.

Richard Wilbur and Ludmila Marjanska. "Zbytkowny Niedostatek." *Dialog* (Warsaw) 26 (Nov. 1981): 80–86.

"A Word from Cummington." In *Under Open Sky: Poets on William Cullen Bryant*. Ed. Norbert Krapf. New York: Fordham University Press, 1986. 29–32. Wilbur comments on his neighbor's poem "To a Waterfowl."

"Ash Wednesday." *Yale Review* 78. 2 (Winter 1989): 215–17. Brief appreciation of Eliot's poem as an "enactment of continual struggle."

"The Persistence of Riddles." *Yale Review* 78. 3 (Spring 1989): 333–51.

Recordings

Poems. Spoken Arts, 1959.
Richard Wilbur Reading His Own Poems. Caedmon, n.d.

Interviews

William Butts's new edition, *Conversations with Richard Wilbur* (Jackson: University Press of Mississippi, 1990), brings together many of the best, most substantive interviews with Wilbur published to date. If Butts's book is not available, some of the following interviews can be found in good libraries:

Bogan, Christopher, and Carl Kaplan. "Interview with Richard Wilbur." *Amherst Student Review*, 16 Mar. 1975, pp. 4–5, 13–14.

Curry, David. "An Interview with Richard Wilbur." *Trinity Review* 17 (Dec. 1962): 21–32.

Dillon, David. "The Image and the Object: An Interview with Richard Wilbur." *Southwest Review* 58 (Summer 1973): 240–51.

Frank, Robert, and Stephen Mitchell. "Richard Wilbur: An Interview." *Amherst Literary Magazine* 10 (Summer 1964): 54–72.

Graham, John. "Richard Wilbur." *Craft So Hard to Learn: Conversations with Poets and Novelists about the Teaching of Writing*. Ed. George Garrett. New York: Morrow, 1972. 41–45.

———. "Richard Wilbur." *The Writer's Voice: Conversations with Contemporary Writers*. Ed. George Garrett. New York: Morrow, 1973. 75–91.

Honig, Edwin. "Conversations with Translators, II: Octavio Paz and Richard Wilbur." *Modern Language Notes* 91 (Oct. 1976): 1084–98. Reprinted in Honig, *The Poet's Other Voice: Conversations on Literary Translation*. Amherst: University of Massachusetts Press, 1985.

Hutton, Joan. "Richard Wilbur Talking to Joan Hutton," *Transatlantic Review* 29 (Summer 1968): 58–67.

"An Interview with Richard Wilbur." *Crazy Horse*, no. 15 (Fall 1974): 37–44.

Packard, William, ed. *The Craft of Poetry: Interviews from the New York Quarterly*. New York: Doubleday, 1974. 177–94.

Pate, Willard. "Interview of Richard Wilbur." *South Carolina Review* 3 (Nov. 1970): 5–23.

Stitt, Peter, Ellessa Clay High, and Helen McCloy Ellison. "The Art of Poetry: Richard Wilbur." *Paris Review*, no. 72 (Winter 1977): 68–105.

SECONDARY SOURCES

Works about Richard Wilbur

Barksdale, Richard K. "Trends in Contemporary Poetry." *Phylon Quarterly* 19 (Winter 1958): 408–16.

Bly, Robert. "American Poetry: On the Way to the Hermetic." *Books Abroad* 46 (Winter 1972): 17–24.

———. "The First Ten Issues of *kayak*." *kayak* 12 (1967): 45–49.

Bosquet, Alain. "Preface" and "Richard Wilbur." *Trente-Cinq Jeunes Poètes Américains*. Ed. Bosquet. Paris: Gallimard, 1960. 9–37, 345–52.

Boyers, Robert. "On Richard Wilbur." *Salmagundi*, no. 12 (1970): 76–82.

———. "Richard Wilbur." In his *Contemporary Poetry*. London: St. James Press, 1975. 1676–79.

Breslin, James E. "The New Rear Guard." In his *From Modern to Contemporary*. Chicago: University of Chicago Press, 1984. 23–52.

Cambon, Glauco. *Recent American Poetry*. University of Minnesota Pamphlets on American Writers, no. 16. Minneapolis: University of Minnesota Press, 1962. 8–16, 42.

Cargill, Oscar. "Poetry Since the Deluge." *English Journal* 43 (Feb. 1954): 57–64.

Clough, Wilson O. "Poe's 'The City in the Sea' Revisited." In *Essays in American Literature in Honor of Jay B. Hubbell*. Ed. Clarence Ghodes. Durham, N.C.: Duke University Press, 1967. 77–89.

Cooke, Michael G. "Book Reviews." *Georgia Review* 31 (Fall 1977): 718–29. Review essay on *The Mind-Reader*.

Crowder, Richard. "Richard Wilbur and France." *Rives* (Paris) 25 (Spring 1964): 2–8.

Cummins, Paul F. *Richard Wilbur*. Grand Rapids, Mich.: Eerdmans, 1971.

———. "Richard Wilbur's 'Ballade for the Duke of Orleans.'" *Concerning Poetry* 1 (Fall 1968): 42–45.

———. "'Walking to Sleep,' by Richard Wilbur." *Concerning Poetry* 3 (Spring 1970): 72–76.

Daiches, David. "The Anglo-American Difference: Two Views." In *The Anchor Review* 1. Ed. Melvin J. Lasky. Garden City, N.Y.: Doubleday, 1955. 219–33.

Deutsch, Babette. *Poetry in Our Time*. Garden City, N.Y.: Doubleday/Anchor, 1963. 284, 347–48.

Eberhart, Richard. "On Richard Wilbur's 'Love Calls Us to the Things of This World.'" In *The Contemporary Artist as Poet and Critic: Eight Symposia*. 4–5. *See* Ostroff.

Faverty, Frederic Everett. "The Poetry of Richard Wilbur." *Tri-Quarterly* 2 (Fall 1959): 26–30. Reprinted in *Poets in Progress*. Ed. Edward Hungerford. Evanston, Ill.: Northwestern University Press, 1967.

Fiedler, Leslie A. "A Kind of Solution: The Situation of Poetry Now." *Kenyon Review* 26 (Winter 1964): 54–79.

Fraser, G. S. "Some Younger American Poets, Art and Reality." *Commentary* 23 (May 1957): 454–62.

Freed, Walter. "Richard Wilbur." In *Critical Survey of Poetry*. Ed. Frank Magill. Englewood Cliffs, N.J.: Salem Press, 1982. 3091–100.

Fussell, Paul, Jr. *Poetic Meter and Poetic Form*. New York: Random House, 1965. 78–79, 89, 103.

Garrett, George. "Against the Grain: Poets Writing Today." In *American Poetry*. Ed. Irvin Ehrenpreis. Stratford-upon-Avon Studies 7. London: Arnold, and New York: St. Martin's, 1965. 221–39.

———. "'Grace Is Most of It': A Conversation with David Slavitt." *Georgia Review* 26 (Winter 1972): 455–68.

Greene, George. "Four Campus Poets." *Thought* 35 (Summer 1960): 223–46.

Gregory, Horace. "The Poetry of Suburbia." *Partisan Review* 23 (Fall 1956): 545–53.

Hall, Donald. "The New Poetry: Notes on the Past Fifteen Years in America." In *New World Writing: Seventh Mentor Selection*. New York: New American Library, 1955. 231–47.

Hamilton, Ian. "A Talent of the Shallows." *Times Literary Supplement*, 15–21 Sept. 1989, 999–1000.

Harris, Peter. "Forty Years of Richard Wilbur: The Loving Work of an Equilibrist." *Virginia Quarterly Review* 66 (Summer 1990): 412–25. Friendly review of *New and Collected Poems*.

Heyen, William. "On Richard Wilbur." *Southern Review*, n.s. 9 (Summer 1973): 617–34.

Hill, Donald L. *Richard Wilbur*. New York: Twayne, 1967.

Holmes, John. "Surroundings and Illuminations." In *A Celebration of Poets*. Ed. Don Cameron Allen. Baltimore: Johns Hopkins University Press, 1967. 108–30.

———. "A View of Three Poets." *Partisan Review* 18 (Nov.–Dec. 1951): 691–700. Reprinted in his *Poetry and the Age*. New York: Vintage, 1953. Collected in excerpted form in Salinger.

James, Clive. "As a Matter of Tact. *New Statesman,* 17 June, 1977, 815–16.

———. "When the Gloves are Off." *Review* (London) 26 (Summer 1971): 35–44.

Jerome, Judson. *Poetry: Premeditated Art*. Boston: Houghton Mifflin, 1968. 168–69, 179–83, 348–49.

Johnson, Kenneth. "Virtues in Style, Defect in Content: The Poetry of Richard Wilbur." In *The Fifties: Fiction, Poetry, Drama*, ed. Warren French. De-Land, Fla.: Everett/Edwards, 1970. 209–16.

Kinzie, Mary. "The Cheshire Smile: On Richard Wilbur." *American Poetry Review* 6 (May–June 1977): 17–20.

Langbaum, Robert. "The New Nature Poetry." *American Scholar* 28 (Summer 1959): 323–40.

Leibowitz, Herbert. Review of *The Mind-Reader*. *New York Times Book Review,* 13 June 1976, 10.

Leithauser, Brad. "Reconsideration: Richard Wilbur—America's Master of Formal Verse." *New Republic,* 24 Mar. 1982, 28–31. Revised and collected as "Richard Wilbur at Sixty" in Salinger.

Livey, Virginia. "The World of Objects in Richard Wilbur's Poetry." *Publications of the Arkansas Philological Association* 7 (Spring 1981): 41–51.

McClatchy, J. D. "Dialect of the Tribe." *Poetry* 130 (Apr. 1977), 44–45.

McConnell, Frank. "Reconsideration: The Poetry of Richard Wilbur." *New Republic,* 29 July 1978, 37–39.

McGuinness, Arthur E. "A Question of Consciousness: Richard Wilbur's *Things of This World*." *Arizona Quarterly* 23 (Winter 1967): 313–26.

Mack, Perry. "Richard Wilbur's Three Treatments of Disintegrative and Metamorphic Change." *Innisfree* 3 (1976): 37–44.

Mattfield, Mary S. "Some Poems of Richard Wilbur." *Ball State University Forum* 11 (Summer 1970): 10–24.

Miller, Stephen. "Poetry of Richard Wilbur." *Spirit* 37, 3 (1970): 30–35.

Monteiro, George. "Redemption Through Nature: A Recurring Theme in Thoreau, Frost, and Richard Wilbur." *American Quarterly* 20 (Winter 1968): 795–809.

Myers, John A., Jr. "Death in the Suburbs." *English Journal* 52 (May 1963): 377–79.

Nejgebauer, Aleksandar. "Poetry 1945–1960: Self versus Culture." In *American Literature Since 1900*. Ed. Marcus Cunliffe. London: Barrie and Jenkins, 1975. 145–49.

Nims, John Frederick, ed. *Poetry: A Critical Supplement* 71 (Jan. 1948): 1–9.

Ostroff, Anthony, ed. *The Contemporary Poet as Artist and Critic: Eight Symposia*. Boston: Little, Brown, 1964. 1–21.

Plath, Sylvia. "Poets on Campus." *Mademoiselle* 37 (Aug. 1953), 290–91.

Reedy, Gerard, S. J. "The Senses of Richard Wilbur." *Renascence* 21 (Spring 1969): 145–50.

Reibetanz, John. "What Love Sees: Poetry and Vision in Richard Wilbur." *Modern Poetry Studies* 11. 1–2 (1982): 60–85.

Rosenthal, M. L. "Epilogue: American Continuities and Crosscurrents." In his *The New Poets: American and British Poetry Since World War II*. New York: Oxford University Press, 1967. 328–30.

———. *The Modern Poets: A Critical Introduction*. New York: Oxford University Press, 1960. 8, 248, 253–55.

Salinger, Wendy, ed. *Richard Wilbur's Creation*. Ann Arbor: University of Michigan Press, 1983. Salinger has brought together most of the interesting reviews and lengthier commentary written about Wilbur in the first three decades of his career. Essays in this volume by Randall Jarrell, Michael Benedikt, Charles Duffy, Ralph J. Mills, John B. Farrell, Charles Woodard, and Anthony Hecht should not be missed.

Sarton, May. "The School of Babylon." In *A Celebration of Poets*. Ed. Don Cameron Allen. Baltimore: Johns Hopkins University Press, 1967. 131–51.

Schulman, Grace. " 'To Shake Our Gravity Up': The Poetry of Richard Wilbur." *Nation*, 9 Oct. 1976, 344–46.

Shaw, Robert B. "Richard Wilbur's World." *Parnassus* 5. 2 (Spring/Summer 1977): 175–185.

Simon, John. "Translation or Adaptation." In *From Parnassus: Essays in Honor of Jacques Barzun*. Ed. Dora B. Weiner and W. R. Keylor. New York: Harper and Row, 1976. 147–57.

Stephanchev, Stephen. *American Poetry Since 1945*. New York: Harper and Row, 1965. 93–106.

Sutton, Walter. "Criticism and Poetry." In *The Contemporary Poet as Artist and Critic*. 174–95. *See* Ostroff.

Swenson, May. "On Richard Wilbur's 'Love Calls Us to the Things of This World.' " In *The Contemporary Poet as Artist and Critic*. 12–16. *See* Ostroff.

Taylor, Henry. "Cinematic Devices in Richard Wilbur's Poetry." *Rocky Mountain Modern Language Association Bulletin* 28 (1974): 41–48.

Thurley, Geoffrey. "Benign Diaspora: The Landscape of Richard Wilbur." In his *The American Moment: American Poetry in the Mid-Century*. New York: St. Martin's Press, 1978. 35–50.

Torgerson, Eric. "Cold War in Poetry: Notes of a Conscientious Objector." *American Poetry Review* 11 (July–Aug. 1982): 31–34.

Waggoner, Hyatt. *American Poets: From the Puritans to the Present*. Rev. ed. Baton Rouge: Louisiana State University Press, 1984. 591–600.

Weatherhead, A. K. "Richard Wilbur: Poetry of Things." *English Literary History* 35 (Dec. 1968): 606–17.

Other works cited in this study

Altieri, Charles. "John Ashbery and the Challenge of Postmodernism in the Visual Arts." *Critical Inquiry* 14. 4 (Summer 1988): 805–830.

Baur, Dom Chrysostomus, O.S.B. *John Chrysostom and His Time*. London: Sands and Co., 1959.

Bawer, Bruce. *The Middle Generation: The Lives and Poetry of Delmore Schwartz, Randall Jarrell, John Berryman, and Robert Lowell*. New York: Archon Books, 1986.

Baym, Nina, et al., eds. *The Norton Anthology of American Literature*. 2nd ed. 2 vols. New York: W. W. Norton, 1988.

Bedient, Calvin. Review of *The Mind-Reader*. *New Republic*, 5 June 1976, 21.

Bishop, Elizabeth. *The Complete Poems*. New York: Farrar, Straus, and Giroux, 1969.

Brazeau, Peter. *Parts of a World: Wallace Stevens Remembered*. New York: Random House, 1983.

Carroll, Lewis. *The Annotated Alice*. Illustrated by John Tenniel. Introduction and notes by Martin Gardner. New York: New American Library, 1960.

Corn, Wanda M. *The Art of Andrew Wyeth*. Greenwich, Conn.: New York Graphic Society, 1973.

Eiseley, Loren. *The Invisible Pyramid*. New York: Scribner, 1970.

Flanagan, Dennis. *Flanagan's Version*. New York: Alfred A. Knopf, 1988.

Frost, Robert. *Complete Poems of Robert Frost*. New York: Holt, Rinehart and Winston, 1962.

Gioia, Dana. "The Successful Career of Robert Bly." *Hudson Review* 40. 2 (1967): 207–23.

Gussow, Alan. *A Sense of Place: The Artist and the American Land*. San Francisco: Friends of the Earth, 1972.

Hamilton, Ian. *Robert Lowell: A Biography*. New York: Random House, 1982.

Hecht, Anthony. *The Hard Hours*. New York: Atheneum, 1967.

Hoffman, Daniel, ed. *The Harvard Guide to Contemporary American Writing*. Cambridge, Mass.: Harvard, Belknap, 1979.

Holden, Jonathan. *Style and Authenticity in Postmodern Poetry*. Columbia: University of Missouri Press, 1986.

Jarrell, Randall. *The Complete Poems*. New York: Farrar, Straus and Giroux, 1969.

———. *Kipling, Auden and Co*. New York: Farrar, Straus and Giroux, 1980.

———. *Poetry and the Age*. New York: Farrar, Straus and Giroux, 1971.

———. *Randall Jarrell's Letters*. Ed. Mary Jarrell. Boston: Houghton Mifflin, 1985.

James, William. *Pragmatism*. Cambridge, Mass.: Harvard University Press, 1975.

Kalstone, David. *Becoming a Poet*. Edited with a preface by Robert Hemenway. Afterword by James Merrill. New York: Farrar, Straus and Giroux, 1989.

Kenner, Hugh. *The Pound Era*. Berkeley: University of California Press, 1971.

Kostalanetz, Richard. *The Old Poetries and the New*. Ann Arbor: University of Michigan Press, 1981.

Kunitz, Stanley, ed. *Twentieth Century Authors*. First Supplement. New York: H. W. Wilson Co., 1955.

Lea, Sydney, ed. *The Burdens of Formality: Essays on the Poetry of Anthony Hecht*. Athens: University of Georgia Press, 1989.

Lowell, Robert. *Day by Day*. New York: Farrar, Straus and Giroux, 1977.

——. *Life Studies* and *For the Union Dead*. New York: Farrar, Straus and Giroux, 1964.

——. *Lord Weary's Castle*. New York: Harcourt, Brace, 1946.

——. *The Mills of the Kavanaughs*. New York: Harcourt, Brace, 1951.

——, trans. *Phaedra*. New York: Farrar, Straus, and Cudahy, 1961.

McQuade, Donald, et al., eds. *The Harper American Literature*. 2 vols. New York: Harper and Row, 1987.

Messerli, Douglas. *"Language" Poetries: An Anthology*. New York: New Directions, 1987.

Mill, John Stuart. *Autobiography and Literary Essays*. Ed. John M. Robson and Jack Stillinger. Vol. 1 of *The Collected Works of John Stuart Mill*. Toronto: University of Toronto Press, 1981.

Mitchell, W. J. T. *"Ut Pictura Theoria: Abstract Painting and the Repression of Language." Critical Inquiry* 15. 2 (Winter 1989): 348–371.

Nelson, Cary. *Our Last First Poets*. Urbana: University of Illinois Press, 1981.

Peters, Robert. *The Great American Poetry Bake-Off*. Metuchen, N.J.: Scarecrow Press, 1979.

Pinsky, Robert. *The Situation of Poetry*. Princeton: Princeton University Press, 1976.

Pound, Ezra. *The Translations of Ezra Pound*. Introduction by Hugh Kenner. London: Faber and Faber, 1970.

Reed, Christopher. "Off the Wall and onto the Couch: Sofa Art and the Avant Garde Analyzed." *Smithsonian Studies in American Art* 2. 1 (Winter 1988): 32–43.

Rosenthal, M. L., and Sally M. Gall. *The Modern Poetic Sequence*. New York: Oxford University Press, 1983.

Steiner, George. *Language and Silence*. New York: Atheneum, 1967.

Stevenson, Anne. *Bitter Fame: A Life of Sylvia Plath*. With additional material by Lucas Myers, Dido Merwin, and Richard Murphy. Boston: Houghton Mifflin, 1989.

Symons, Arthur. *The Symbolist Movement in Literature*. New York: Dutton, 1958.

Thomas, Lewis. *The Lives of a Cell*. New York: Viking, 1974.

Thompson, Lawrance, and R. H. Winnick. *Robert Frost: A Biography*. New York: Holt, Rinehart and Winston, 1982.

The Poems of Francois Villon. Trans. with an introduction and notes by Galway Kinnell. Hanover: University Press of New England, 1982.

Vendler, Helen, ed. *The Harvard Book of Contemporary American Poetry*. Cambridge, Mass.: Harvard, Belknap, 1985.

Index

Alfred, William, 40
Allen, Woody, 139
Altieri, Charles, 240–41 n.14
Ammons, A. R., 215
Arnold, Matthew, 138, 143, 165; on
  translation, 162, 164; "Dover
  Beach," 93
Ashbery, John, 83, 162, 217–18, 223
Auden, W. H., 103, 193, 211, 214

Baudelaire, Charles, 20; "Corre-
  spondances," 188–89
Bawer, Bruce, 240 n.15
Bellow, Saul, 58
Bennett, Arnold, 153
Berryman, John, 15, 27, 214
Bishop, Elizabeth, 13, 15, 27, 62–63,
  229 n.6; at Harvard, 40; "Filling
  Station," 141; "Love Lies Sleep-
  ing," 63–65; "The Monument,"
  89
Blackmur, R. P., 40.
Blake, William, 26, 59
Bly, Robert, 20, 138–39, 146, 227; as
  translator, 162
Bogan, Louise, 229 n.6
Borrow, George, 94
Bouchet, André du, 39, 40
Britten, Benjamin, 180
Bynner, Witter, 228 n.13
Byron, Lord (George Gordon), 200

Calder, Alexander, 191–92
Cambridge, Mass., postwar poetry
  scene in, 38–41

Carroll, Lewis, 110
Carruth, Hayden, 205
Chase Manhattan Bank, 121
Ciardi, John, 40, 153, 163
Coleridge, Samuel T., 208
Conrad, Joseph, 116
Cope, Wendy, 214
Copeland, Aaron, 160
Creeley, Robert, 122
Cutrone, Ronnie, 121, 232 n.1

Dante Alighieri, 17
Delacroix, Eugene, 94–95
Dickinson, Emily, 6, 9, 28, 30, 147,
  148, 198
Didion, Joan, 96
Dillard, Annie, 116
Disraeli, Benjamin, 198
Donne, John, 11
Duchamp, Marcel, 121–22

Eberhart, Richard, 40
Edwards, Jonathan, 221
Eiseley, Loren, 42, 239 n.12
Eliot, Thomas Stearns, 15, 131, 154;
  Ash Wednesday, 103; "The Love
  Song of J. Alfred Prufrock," 103
Emerson, Ralph Waldo, 109, 198
Everett, Edward, 112

Ferlinghetti, Lawrence, 142, 145;
  "One Thousand Fearful Words for
  Fidel Castro," 146
Fiedler, Leslie, 40
Field, Edward, 214

Forster, E. M., 149
Frankenburg, Lloyd, 40
Freud, Sigmund, 88
Frost, Robert, 6, 13, 28–31, 41, 84, 116, 142, 156, 158; in Cambridge after WWII, 40; public persona, 200; "Directive," 6, 9; "For Once, Then, Something," 7–8; "The Gift Outright," 158–59; "Nothing Gold Can Stay," 29–30, 31; "Putting in the Seed," 29; "Stopping by Woods on a Snowy Evening," 201; "The Woodpile," 6

Gall, Sally M., 237 n.14
Garrigue, Jean, 229 n.6
Géricault, Jean, 94–95
Ginsberg, Allen, 142, 146; *Howl,* 39, 82
Gioia, Dana, 167, 214, 234–35 n.14
Glascock (Kathryn Irene) Poetry Contest, 153
Gorey, Edward, 40
Grangerford, Emmeline, 30
Gray, Thomas, 52
Gropius, Walter, 160

Hall, Donald, 14
Hamilton, Ian, 154–55, 157
Harrison, Tony, 235 n.8
Harvard University, poets on campus after WWII, 38–40
Hecht, Anthony, 229 n.2, 238 n.7; "Behold the Lilies of the Field," 90
Herbert, George, 26
Hiawatha, 164
Holden, Jonathan, 242 n.16
Homer, 211
Homer, Winslow, 93
Hope, Anthony, 140
Hopkins, Gerard Manley, 26
Housman, A. E., 228 n.13
Howard, Richard, 162
Hugo, Richard, 138
Huizinga, Johan, 51

Inness, George, 103

James, Clive, 155
James, William, 130, 215, 239 n.10
Jarrell, Randall, 12, 27, 108, 222, 226 n.6, 232 n.9; "A Camp in the Prussian Forest," 12; "90 North," 101–2, 210–11
Jeffers, Robinson, 199
Jensen, Ejner, 231 n.1
Johnson, Lyndon, 144

Kalstone, David, 62–63, 229 n.6, 241 n.15
kayak, 138, 227 n.10, 233 n.7
Kazantzakis, Nikos, 131
Keats, John, 88
Kenner, Hugh, 234–35 n.2
Kepes, Gyorgy, 72
Kerr, Deborah, 141
Kilmartin, Terence, 163
Kinzie, Mary, 231 n.1
Kipling, Rudyard, 161
Kostalanetz, Richard, 240 n.15
Kunitz, Stanley, 38

Lattimore, Richmond, 163
Lautréamont (Isidore Ducasse), 151
Lea, Sidney, 238 n.7
Leavis, F. R., 207
Leithauser, Brad, 214
Levertov, Denise, 31, 122, 142, 217
Lewis, Wyndham, 143
Lieberman, Laurence, 222
Lindsay, Vachel, 143
Linnaeus, Carolus (Carl von Linné), 111
Lowell, Robert, 12, 34, 131, 138, 146, 155, 200, 237–38 n.3; in Cambridge with RW, 40; translation of Racine's *Phèdre* compared to RW's, 179–86; as translator, 162–63; "After the Surprising Conversions," 221; "For the Union Dead," 97; *Life Studies,* 63; *Lord Weary's Castle,* 12; *The Mills*

of the Kavanaughs, 15; *The Old Glory,* 180; "Skunk Hour," 87, 89

MacLeish, Archibald, 40, 108, 142, 231 n.9
Mademoiselle, 153
Mallarmé, Stéphane, 20, 41
Markandeya, 151
Masefield, John, 158
Melville, Herman, 98
Merrill, James, 222
Merwin, W. S., 15, 142
Messerli, Douglas, 238 n.9
Mill, John Stuart, 200, 236 n.1
Milton, John, 131, 209, 211–12
Molière (Jean Baptiste Poquelin), 170, 177. *See also* Wilbur, Richard: Translations
Monet, Claude, 93
Moore, Marianne, 153, 226 n.6

Nemerov, Howard, 145
Nerval, Gérard de, 200
Newman, Francis, 164

Oliver, Raymond, 172, 235 n.8
Olson, Charles, 145
Ovid, 33

Pascal, Blaise, 102
Pei, I. M., 160
Peters, Robert, 240–41 n.15
Phillips, Robert, 214
Pinsky, Robert, 240 n.15
Plath, Sylvia, 138, 152–57, 200
Plato, 211
Poe, Edgar Allan, 9, 65, 74, 84, 88, 118, 171; affinities of, with RW, 73; and dreams, 59; and hypnagogic state, 22; RW's editions and published discussions of, 186; RW's interest in, during WWII, 38; RW's "quarrel with," 54, 61–81; RW's study of, at Harvard, 40; "The Bells," 73; "The City in the Sea," 75; "The Coliseum," 73; "A Descent into the Maelstrom," 69; "Dreams," 74–75; *Eureka,* 129; "MS Found in a Bottle," 66, 68; "The Philosophy of Composition," 82; "The Power of Words," 72; "To Science," 101
Poetic sequence, 201, 237 n.4
Poets' Theatre, 40
Pompeii, 49
Ponge, Francis, 189
Pope, Alexander, 165
Pound, Ezra, 20, 115, 188–89, 216; as translator, 162–64, 193–94; "Mr. Nixon," 153; "The Seafarer," 181
Pritchard, William H., 205

Racine, Jean, 174. *See also* Wilbur, Richard: Translations
Rexroth, Kenneth, 40, 229 n.6
Rich, Adrienne, 83, 142, 146
Richards, I. A., 111
Riddles, 136–38
Roethke, Theodore, 27, 201, 206
Rosenthal, M. L., 237 n.4
Ruskin, John, 109, 198, 223

Schuman, William, 157
Schwartz, Delmore, 40
Sexton, Anne, 138, 201
Shakespeare, William, 58, 98
Shaw, George Bernard, 131
Shaw, Robert B., 233 n.9
Shelley, Percy Bysshe, 165
Simon, John, 172, 235 n.8
Snodgrass, W. D., 214
Snyder, Gary, 116, 122
Southey, Robert, 108, 158
Spender, Stephen, 214
Steiner, George, 233 n.1
Stevens, Wallace, 9, 15, 41, 102, 109, 113, 149; influence of, on RW's early poems, 13, 14; reading at Harvard, 39–40; "The Comedian as the Letter C," 82; "Of Mere Being," 71; *The Palm at the End of*

Stevens, Wallace (*cont.*)
the Mind, 111; "The Snow Man,"
33; "Sunday Morning," 150
Stone, Ruth, 40
Sweeney, Jack, 40
Symons, Arthur, 100

Thomas, Dylan, 128
Thoreau, Henry David, 76
Trilling, Lionel, 207

Vendler, Helen, 205, 237–38 n.7
Villon, François, 9. *See also* Wilbur,
Richard: Translations
Voznesensky, Andrei, 51

Ward, Edna, 154–57
Ward, William Hayes, 156
Warren, Robert Penn, 158
Wesleyan University, 145–46, 207
White, T. H., 191
Whitman, Walt, 133, 135–36,
231 n.3; "Crossing Brooklyn
Ferry," 160
Wilbur, Charlotte Ward, 29, 40
Wilbur, Ellen, 37
Wilbur, Richard: and academic life,
207–8, 214–15; Amherst and
WWII, 37–38; conception of, of
irony, 27; critical reception of, 20,
36, 222–23, 237–38 n.7, 240–
42 n.15; on culture, 41; on dreams
and poetry, 23; early life of, 37; on
formal verse and informality of
mind, 171–72; at Harvard, 38–40;
Judeo-Christian themes and iconography in, 98–99, 119–20, 124–
26; as nature poet, 42–43, 115–16;
as Poet Laureate, 107–8, 157–58;
relationship of, with Sylvia Plath,
153, 156; war experiences of, in
early poems, 14; work of, with
Poets' Theatre, 40
    Essays: "The Bottles Become
New, Too," 228 n.13; "The
House of Poe," 66; "Poetry and

Happiness," 41; "Poetry and the
Landscape," 43, 72; "The Persistence of Riddles," 136; "Round
About a Poem of Housman's,"
230
    Poems: "After the Last Bul-
letins," 148–49; "The Agent," 89–
93; "Alatus," 211; "All That Is,
88, 148, 149–52, 202; "Attention
Makes Infinity," 12–13; "Ballade
for the Duke of Orléans," 16–20,
58, 187; "The Beacon," 70–71,
138; "Beasts," 192; "The Beautiful
Changes," 60, 74; "Bell Speech,"
73; "Beowulf," 78–81; "Caserta
Garden," 13–14; "Castles and Distances," 103; "Children of Darkness," 76–77; A Christmas
Hymn," 122–24; "C Minor,"
147–48; "Complaint," 83; "Conjuration," 74; "Cottage Street,
1953," 152–57; "The Death of a
Toad," 152; "Digging for China,"
82, 187, 231 n.17; "Dodwells
Road," 133–36; "A Finished
Man," 202, 212–13; "A Fire-
Truck," 132, 213; "Flippancies,"
138–39; "For Dudley," 131; "For
the Etruscan Poets," 179; "For the
New Railway Station in Rome,"
73; "For the Student Strikers,"
145–46, 147; "For W. H. Auden,"
204–5, 237 n.5; "The Fourth of
July," 103, 108–13, 115; "Hamlen
Brook," 213; "A Hole in the
Floor," 231 n.17; "Icarium Mare,"
214; "In a Churchyard," 52–53,
83; "In Limbo," 20–27, 34, 204;
"In the Field," 99–102; "In the
Smoking Car," 212; "John
Chrysostom," 127–29; "The Jug-
gler," 74; "Junk," 195–96; "A Late
Aubade," 9–12; "Leaving," 201–
4; "The Lilacs," 195; "Looking
into History," 187; "Love Calls
Us to the Things of This World,"

48, 50–51, 64, 67; "Loves of the Puppets," 223–24; "Lying," 202, 208–12; "Marginalia," 67–71; "Matthew VIII, 28 ff," 124–25; "The Mechanist," 89, 213; "Merlin Enthralled," 77–78; "The Mill," 5–9, 204; "A Miltonic Sonnet for Mr. Johnson," 144–45; "The Mind-Reader," 53–56, 113–20; "1933," 132; "On Freedom's Ground," 158; "On the Marginal Way," 93–99; "Patriots' Day," 132; "Peter," 126–27; "Piazza di Spagna, Early Morning," 231 n.17; "Playboy," 90, 213; "A Postcard for Bob Bly," 138; "Potato," 213; "The Prisoner of Zenda," 140–42; "The Regatta," 43–48; "A Riddle," 137–38; "The Ride," 201–2; "Running," 131–36; "Seed Leaves," 28–31, 83; "Shad-Time," 218–22; "A Simplification," 142–43; "Speech for the Repeal of the McCarran Act," 143–44, 213; "The Star System," 139; "Still, Citizen Sparrow," 74, 77; "Stop," 31–34; "Superiorities," 125; "Teresa," 127–28, 129–30; "To Ishtar," 187–88; "Trolling for Blues," 56–59; "Two Voices in a Meadow," 122–23; "The Undead," 74–76; "Walking to Sleep," 79, 83–89, 116; "Water Walker," 103–7; "What's Good for the Soul is Good for Sales," 138–39; "Wyeth's Milk Cans," 216; "Year's End," 48–50, 52, 150

Translations and adaptations: Aldhelm riddles, 137; "An Anglo-Saxon Riddle," 190; *A Bestiary*, 191–92; Baudelaire, "Correspondances," 188; Baudelaire, "L'Invitation au Voyage," 187; "Beowulf's Death-Wound," 194–95; "Eight Riddles from Symphosius," 137; Molière, *The Learned Ladies*, 170; Molière, *The School for Husbands*, 170; Molière, *The School for Wives*, 170–71, 173; Molière, *Tartuffe*, 171, 173–74, 177; "The Pelican," 192–93; Racine, *Andromache*, 174–78; Racine, *Phaedra*," 179–86; "The Siren," 191; "Some Riddles from Symphosius," 190; Villon, "Ballade of Forgiveness," 170; Villon, "Ballade of the Ladies of Time Past," 165–69; Villon, "Quatrain," 170; Voltaire, *Candide*, 171; "The Whale," 191

Williams, W. C., 31–32, 135, 136, 147, 208, 219; relations with RW, 31, 228 nn.12, 13; and RW's "Wyeth's Milk Cans," 216; *Kora in Hell*, 33; *Paterson*, 82; "The Red Wheelbarrow," 32–33

Wordsworth, William, 7, 88, 191; "Tintern Abbey," 86

Wright, James, 138, 145

Wyeth, Andrew, 208, 216, 219; "Milk Cans," 239 n.11

Yeats, William Butler, 34, 149

(Permissions to reprint copyrighted material continued page iv)

and Collected Poems, © 1988 by Richard Wilbur: "Trolling for Blues"; excerpts from "The Ride," "Lying," "Leaving," "Icarium Mare," "Some Riddles from Symphosius," "Wyeth's Milk Cans," "Shad-Time," "All That Is," "A Finished Man," "On Freedom's Ground," and "For W. H. Auden." From *Walking to Sleep:* "Seed Leaves," © 1964, "A Riddle" and "Late Aubade," © 1969; excerpts from "The Lilacs," © 1963, "Ballade of the Ladies of Time Past," © 1964, "On the Marginal Way," © 1965, "In a Churchyard," "In the Field," and "Running," © 1968, "For Dudley," "A Miltonic Sonnet for Mr. Johnson," "The Agent," "Matthew VIII, 28ff," and "Walking to Sleep," © 1969 by Richard Wilbur.

BOA Editions, Ltd., 92 Park Ave., Brockport, N.Y. From *The Whale and Other Uncollected Translations,* © 1982 by Richard Wilbur: "An Anglo-Saxon Riddle"; selections from "Beowulf's Death-Wound," "Correspondances," and "The Siren."

Dell Publishing Company. From Introduction to *Poe: Complete Poems,* © 1959 by Dell Publishing Co.

Yale Review and Richard Wilbur. Excerpts from "Two Riddles from Aldhelm" and "The Persistence of Riddles," *Yale Review* 78, no. 3 (1989), © 1989 by Richard Wilbur.

kayak, George Hitchcock, Richard Wilbur. "Postcard for Bob Bly," *kayak* 13 (1968).

Acknowledgment is also made to the following publishers for permission to reprint additional material.

Farrar, Straus and Giroux, Inc. From *The Complete Poems: 1927–1979,* by Elizabeth Bishop, © 1979, 1983 by Alice Helen Methfessel: excerpts from "Love Lies Sleeping." From *Becoming a Poet,* by David Kalstone, © 1989 by Alice Helen Methfessel: excerpts of letter from Elizabeth Bishop to Carley Dawson.

Farrar, Straus and Giroux, Inc., and Faber and Faber. From *For the Union Dead,* by Robert Lowell, © 1960, 1964 by Robert Lowell: excerpt from "For the Union Dead." From *Phaedra* by Jean Racine, trans. Robert Lowell, © 1960, 1961 by Robert Lowell, © renewed 1989 by Harriet Lowell, Sheridan Lowell, Caroline Lowell: excerpts. From *The Complete Poems* by Randall Jarrell, © 1941 and renewed 1968 by Mrs. Randall Jarrell: excerpt from "90 North."

Houghton Mifflin Co. From *Randall Jarrell's Letters,* ed. Mary Jarrell, © 1985 by Mary Jarrell: excerpt.

University Press of New England. From *The Poems of François Villon,* trans., intro., and notes by Galway Kinnell, © 1977 by Galway Kinnell: excerpts.

Henry Holt and Co., Inc., and Jonathan Cape, Ltd. From *The Poetry of Robert Frost,* edited by Edward Connery Lathem, © 1916, 1923, 1969 by Holt, Rinehart and Winston. © 1944, 1951 by Robert Frost: "Nothing Gold Can Stay" and excerpts from "For Once, Then, Something" and "Putting in the Seed."

ACI 1721   3/5/92

PS
3545
I32165
Z78
1991

0 00 02 0535828 6
MIDDLEBURY COLLEGE